RUSHTON

AND HIS TIMES IN

AMERICAN
CANOEING

RUSHTON
AND HIS TIMES IN
AMERICAN
CANOEING

ATWOOD MANLEY
with the assistance of
PAUL F. JAMIESON

THE ADIRONDACK MUSEUM/SYRACUSE UNIVERSITY PRESS

The Library of Congress Cataloged the First Printing of This Work
as Follows:

Manley, Atwood.
   Rushton and his times in American canoeing. With the assistance
of Paul F. Jamieson. [1st ed. Syracuse] Syracuse University Press
[1968]
   xiii, 203 p. illus., plans, ports. 25 cm.
   "Published for the Adirondack Museum of the Adirondack Historical Association."

   1. Rushton, John Henry, 1843–1906.   1. Jamieson, Paul F.
11. Adirondack Museum, Blue Mountain Lake, N. Y. 111. Title.

GV783.M26   623.82′9   68–20484
Paperback   ISBN 0–8156–0141–7

To PETER

FOREWORD

ABOUT 1902, when I was visiting Atwood Manley in Canton, New York, we ran around, as boys do, seeking interesting sights and places. We found ourselves in the Rushton Boat Shop on the banks of the Grass River. There we saw J. Henry Rushton and his men briskly producing his famous canoes, skiffs, and guide-boats. I recall vividly the fascination of the fitting of the streaks and the clinching of the nails against the metal strips of the forms. I realized that I was seeing the work of master craftsmen. Later in the day, I helped steady the Manleys' Rushton skiff when the author's father, using a six-ounce fly rod, caught a fifteen-pound muskellonge which nearly swamped the small craft.

So it is not surprising that I welcome the opportunity of writing a foreword to this story of one of the world's great builders of small boats. Rushton's life furnishes the warp on which is woven an intricate and impressive tapestry-story of the first half century of sport and pleasure canoeing in America. The diversely colored yarns of the weft have been gathered from two continents by diligent research, and the weaving bears the stamp of a craftsman who found it more a labor of love than a task.

When persons ask me when I began canoeing, I explain that I started boating before I was born, for I was practically brought up in a St. Lawrence skiff in the waters of the Thousand Islands. Two skiffs and nine canoes later, I was still thinking of the modern canoe as a direct development from the Indian birchbark until I began the study of this book in manuscript. Although the Indian influence undoubtedly had direct effects in the Peterborough area of Ontario and the Old Town area of Maine, the author clearly shows that sport canoeing in the United States was an import from England through the influence of John MacGregor, who, strangely enough, had found his own inspiration while on a trip in Canada, where he observed the Indian birchbark and the Eskimo kayak. This gave rise to a hybrid boat. The English call all three types "canoes," as I learned when paddling on the Thames a few years ago. For them, the open boat with tiny decks is a "Canadian type" of canoe. As the reader will discover, it was Rushton's response to MacGregor influence that encouraged the beginning and rapid development of sport canoeing in the United States a hundred years ago. Only later did his shop in Canton feel and respond to the Peterborough and Old Town influences.

The advent of the automobile and the motorboat sounded the death knell of the St. Lawrence River skiff and the Adirondack guide-boat and almost of the canoe. For many years there was only one boat livery in the Thousand Islands. But the canoe held on, partly because it could be carried so easily on the car and stored in the garage. And then, less than a score of years ago, the canoe and the kayak returned to favor, largely as a result of the influence of another European import in the form of vigorous, outdoor-loving young men who found their way here after World War II. Those who are now fascinated by white water and the canoe slalom will find in this book the background for this present sport, but its full story will have to be told in another volume featuring the aluminum canoe, the rigid fiber-glass kayak, the folding boat, and that illegitimate hybrid, the "banana" boat.

As one's eyes rove over the present tapestry, one finds, as in the Bayeux tapestry, stories within a story. There is "the voyage of the paper canoe," over 2,000 miles from Troy, New York, to Florida in 1874. There is the heated controversy about the discovery of the headwaters of the Mississippi River, in which Rushton canoes were of course involved. One of the four made the trip to New Orleans and fame. Then, in 1885, the cruise of "the canoe *Aurora:* from the Adirondacks to the

Gulf," a five-month trip via the Mississippi River, logging 3,300 miles. The modern slalom racers who pass up the down-river races "because there is too much paddling," as one of them once said to me, should read how in the good old days canoeists used the waterways to go to annual meets, sometimes paddling several hundred miles.

The warp of the book, into which all these yarns are woven and tied together, is the story of Rushton, the man and the boat-builder. He was a mere wisp of a man who by a quirk of fate became one of the world's best and most famed builders of cedar canoes and other small craft, and whose products still command the admiration of the modern craftsman-builder. For Nessmuk, the well-known woodsman author of the seventies and eighties, Rushton constructed the smallest, the lightest, and one of the most historic canoes. As a founder of the American Canoe Association, Rushton rubbed shoulders with, and became the companion of, most of the great canoeists in those pioneering days. The amazing thing is that any one man, in the period in which he lived, could accomplish so much almost single handed. But the book is more than a biography because, in a most extraordinary way, Rushton and the canoes he built became the center of notable events in canoeing history, regional, national, and international.

Those of us who thrill to the challenge of white water and who now employ the aluminum and the fiber glass boat will find in these pages the evidence of the major influence Rushton had in the development of the modern canoe. Today's craftsmen find in the surviving Rushton craft this man's remarkable gift for sound and delicate construction. By good fortune and diligence, the author has been able to assemble and present photographs and designs of Rushton boats in generous numbers. Here in one book we have that which no other writer has heretofore brought together between two covers.

HOMER L. DODGE

January, 1968
Burlington, Vermont

ACKNOWLEDGMENTS

I WISH to thank warmly all those who gave assistance in the preparation of this book. Acknowledgments would be lengthy indeed if I were to name everyone who opened his boathouse or barn to show me a cherished Rushton canoe or shared some recollection helpful in reconstructing Rushton's life. Here I can mention only my greatest obligations.

It is regrettable that the four men whose interest, inspiration, and help during the first years of my research were chiefly responsible in making this book possible did not live to share in the joy attending its publication and reading. Therefore to the memory of Charles E. Brown, Harry Rushton, Dan Brenan, and A. Fred Saunders, the author can now only pay humble tribute and make acknowledgment.

I am indebted to the Ellsworth Museum and the Owen D. Young Library, both of St. Lawrence University, and to the head librarian, Andrew K. Peters, and the reference librarian, Josephine G. Mentley; to the library of the New York State Historical Association in Cooperstown, repository of the A. Fred Saunders American Canoe Association Historical Collection; and to the Canton Free Library and its three successive librarians of the past ten years: Phyllis Forbes Clark, Dorothy Moore, and Mary Ellsworth Manning, a granddaughter of Rushton's friend Joseph B. Ellsworth. The Canton Library now houses a small Rushton collection.

But for the Adirondack Historical Association, its president, Harold K. Hochschild, and its Adirondack Museum and library at Blue Mountain Lake, there would have been no continued research, no splendid collection of Rushton craft and other memorabilia, and therefore no book. Two successive directors of the museum, Robert Bruce Inverarity and H. J. Swinney, have held me to the task and given every assistance and encouragement.

Special recognition is due to John B. Johnson, publisher and editor of the Watertown *Daily Times,* and to members of the Rushton family not elsewhere mentioned: Mrs. Molly Rushton, widow of my friend Harry Rushton; and Evelyn M. Snyder and her sister, Gladys M. Hoff, surviving grandnieces of J. Henry Rushton. I am indebted to Maitland De Sormo, of Saranac Lake, New York, for the privilege of selecting from his collection of Seneca Ray Stoddard photographs; to Kenneth Durant, of Jamaica, Vermont, for sharing his knowledge of the Adirondack guide-boat; and to Lucien Wulsin, president of the D. H. Baldwin Company, Cincinnati, Ohio, for access to the trove of Rushton material in that company's files.

Seven readers of the manuscript gave helpful criticism and suggestions: Howard I. Chappelle, curator of transportation at the Smithsonian Institution and coauthor, with Edwin Tappan Adney, of *The Bark Canoes and Skin Boats of North America;* Selden T. Williams, of Middlebury, Connecticut, retired industrialist and former editor of *Automotive World;* Elaine Manley, Margaret Mangum, and Dorothy Church Woodhead. Homer L. Dodge and his wife, Margaret, of Burlington, Vermont, read the manuscript with thoroughness and understanding. Dr. Dodge, President Emeritus of Norwich University, physicist, and author, is a veteran of the paddle and patriarch of the American White-Water Affiliation. His critique of many pages was invaluable.

My greatest debt is to Paul F. Jamieson, his wife Ruth, and my ever-understanding wife, Alice. Dr. Jamieson, retired professor of English, writer on the Adirondacks, and the companion of many a canoe trip in my Rushton *Vayu,* agreed to edit the manuscript and became involved also in the research. Ruth and Alice, besides their services as copyholders and readers, managed personal relations with such gentle art that Paul and I never actually came to blows and survived many months of labor still as friends.

ATWOOD MANLEY

February, 1967
Canton, New York

CONTENTS

ILLUSTRATIONS

RUSHTON
AND HIS TIMES IN
AMERICAN
CANOEING

Chapter I

A PINT OF CIDER

"IF A MAN can write a better book, preach a better sermon, or make a better mouse-trap than his neighbor, though he builds his house in the woods, the world will make a beaten path to his door." In these words, copied by a member of the audience in one of Emerson's California lectures of 1871, the Yankee philosopher summed up the spirit of an age of optimism and enterprise.

The life story of J. Henry Rushton, boatbuilder of northern New York, bears out Emerson's prophecy. Rushton grew up at the edge of a great wilderness where opportunity favored the strong and healthy. He was neither. When he moved to Canton, the county seat of St. Lawrence County, in his late twenties, he was frail and in bad health. He took a job as clerk in a shoe store. During the first half of his life of sixty-two years, no one could have guessed the prominence that was to come.

Then Rushton built a boat for himself. Another man insisted on having it. Rushton made more boats. In a few short years he was building a better canoe than anyone else. The canoe was his mousetrap. First the local people, then the world made a beaten path to the door of his boat shop in the village of Canton.

Although he manufactured guide-boats, rowboats, skiffs, and other types of small watercraft, the canoe became his specialty. Among canoeists his name became a household word, his trademark familiar to sportsmen from the Atlantic to the Pacific. Craft from his shop were shipped to such distant countries as England, France, Egypt, the Philippines, and Australia. As a builder of cedar canoes especially, he was equaled by few others. His products participated in some of the most interesting events in canoeing history. The *Kleiner Fritz,* the *Sairy Gamp,* the *Aurora,* and the *Vesper* became familiar on the pages of the leading sporting journals of the time.

Events favored him, and he had the canniness to take advantage of them and the craftsman's skill to back up a growing reputation. His advice and opinions were frequently sought. He was invited to become one of that group of twenty-three "extraordinary men" who founded the American Canoe Association. His displays and products won blue ribbons and gold medals at exhibitions. Books and articles appeared about many of the voyages made with his craft. The pioneers of modern American canoeing were the personal friends, admirers, and enthusiastic advocates of the boatbuilder from the backwoods.

J. Henry Rushton was born south of the village of Edwards within the fringe of the Wilderness or South Woods, as the Adirondacks were known in St. Lawrence County a century ago. The exact location of his birthplace is unknown. Mary Winslow Harmon, a niece whose roots go back into the same soil as J. Henry's, provides a helpful clue: "Oh, Pete's folks [Peter Rushton, J. Henry's father] lived up on the Ridge. I guess that's where Uncle Henry was born and that's where he was brought up."

The Ridge, a hogback at its northern end, rises about eight miles southeast of the village of Edwards and stretches three miles along the south bank of the Oswegatchie River. Almost under its brow at the north is the hamlet of Fine, straddling the river. In those days Fine was barely more than an outpost for trappers, hunters, and lumberjacks going into the wilderness. Whether Peter Rushton lived on the Ridge, as indicated by Mrs. Harmon, or in the little cluster of homes in Fine is immaterial. A county atlas of 1865 shows that in that year "P. Rushton" was living on the south bank of the Oswegatchie near the bridge and just across from the general store in Fine. But he may well have had a place on the Ridge, amidst his family's timber holdings, twenty-two years earlier when J. Henry was born.

Peter was the son of John Rushton, or "Old John" as he was known in Edwards, the progenitor of this branch of the family in America. A wheelwright from Bolton, England, John came to this country in 1818 rather than submit to military conscription, bringing with him his wife, Ann Norris, and their first child. He and Ann had seventeen children. Peter was born in New York City in 1822 while John was plying his trade there as wheelwright. In those days land in northern New York was being sold on city street corners. Like other recent immigrants, John Rushton was apparently persuaded that Utopia lay somewhere north of the Mohawk. So he bought and with Ann and their brood set out for a place designated on the map as Edwards. By packet boat, bateau, and wagon the family finally arrived at their destination. John Rushton immediately set about clearing the land and putting up a log house on his quarter section.

Those were the days when the crack of the ax and the whine of the saw mingled with the song of the flail, the grunt of the oxen, and the clack of the shuttle; when spinning wheels were a necessity and corn meal mush was the staple diet. It was a land of virgin forest—pine, spruce, hemlock, the hardwoods—and of hard knocks. John Rushton was industrious and thrifty, as was his eldest son, Henry. Father and eldest son developed into a well-matched business team, soon becoming the leaders of the community's economy and its largest property owners. As rapidly as cash and credit permitted, Old John purchased some of the best stands of timber nearby. In time these Rushtons owned and operated the sawmill, the gristmill, the general store, and the wood-working plant. About 1860 Henry erected "the most costly public house of the kind in the county," the Rushton House at Edwards.

Still imbued with his early English upbringing, Old John believed that the eldest son should succeed to the father's worldly goods. Therefore, as Old John prospered, Henry became his chief concern.

"How did Uncle Henry build the hotel, how did he come by all of those mills, the store, the timber lands, and that hotel?

Why, it was Grandpa's money that did it. Grandpa remained English from the tip of his toes to the top of his head. By his upbringing the old rule of succession still remained the unwritten law." In these words Mrs. Harmon explained why Peter Rushton did not fare so well as his elder brother. When Old John died in 1869, Peter received the smallest portion among the surviving children. James became the managing operator of the mills, second in line to Henry, and other sons and sons-in-law were drawn into the family enterprises. It was different with Peter. He and his young wife, Martha Glines, found life on or near the Ridge much more to his liking. There he could look after some of Old John's and Henry's timber holdings and lumbering jobs. He worked in sawmills near Fine and elsewhere in the county. The forest was just a step from the back door, with fine hunting and fishing, a way of life that Peter Rushton found congenial. Later in life he became a cabinet-maker.

On October 9, 1843, Martha gave birth to a son. When Peter first looked down at the tiny baby, he is said to have stroked the stubble on his chin and remarked: "Why, that there baby hain't no bigger'n a pint of cider, if that." Therewith, it is said, he repaired to the shed and, taking his fishing rod from its pegs, struck off into the woods to ponder in solitude why he and Martha had been treated so scrimpingly in their first-born.

The baby was so small, Mary Harmon remarks, that he had to be carried around on a pillow for months. Much of his early life was a struggle for mere existence.

This first-born was named John Henry after his grandfather and eldest uncle. In time the family abridged the name to J. Henry. So it remained. The headstone in Fairview Cemetery in Canton reads simply "J. Henry Rushton."

In 1864, the year when J. Henry reached his majority, he went to town to cast his first ballot—for Lincoln, of course. Stopping at his Uncle Henry's store, he weighed himself on the set of platform scales. The balance bar leveled off at exactly ninety-eight pounds. He stood just a hair over five feet at that time and never grew a fraction taller. He was short and skinny and was nagged by a dry cough. Chronic ailments plagued him. His mother died when he was nine, leaving him and his sister, Martha. Peter Rushton then married Jane Philpot, who gave birth to four more sons and two more daughters.

J. Henry and his four half-brothers acquired their father's love of the woods, of fishing, hunting, and camping. They grew up in close association with the wildlife of forest and stream.

J. Henry attended school in the District Four schoolhouse at South Edwards. His teacher, Cornelius Carter, was no run-of-the-mill district schoolmaster. Tall, lathy, raw boned, Con Carter, as his friends called him, had a scholarly turn and became the rustic Socrates of Edwards township and the southwestern corner of St. Lawrence County generally. Like most rural teachers he boarded around. Besides teaching the boys and girls of District Four, he cruised timber, read law, and fished and hunted in the nearby forests. There were more log than frame houses when Carter came there in 1850, more deer than people. The forest was all about, and he loved it.

Carter took a liking to his tiny pupil, J. Henry Rushton, who was quick at bookwork and had an inquiring mind. More than a teacher-pupil relationship developed. A mutual love of the woods united them. When Carter cruised timber lands between terms, the boy often tagged along. He was handy and learned fast. An enduring friendship developed. From Con Carter and from his own father, Rushton picked up a knowledge of woodcraft at an early age.

After a self-directed course in law reading, Carter turned from teaching to a practice of law in Edwards. In time he was elected the town's representative on the County Board of Supervisors, serving ten years in that capacity. He became an able trial lawyer and was appointed the county's deputy district attorney.

At the peak of his public career Carter suddenly turned deaf. He began withdrawing from office, from his legal work, and pretty much from society. At increasingly longer periods between spring thaws and fall frosts he retired to his favorite fishing and hunting retreat on the Inlet, or east branch of the Oswegatchie River, near the head of Cranberry Lake in wilderness country. A place on the Inlet is still known as Carter's Landing, and old woodsmen remember the site of Carter's camp on the Plains. There he lived alone, roving the bush, making friends with wildlife, pondering, writing poems, hunting and fishing, and guiding occasional parties of sportsmen and former friends. He was a man who had lived in two worlds, and he became a mediator between them, gently inducting the tenderfoot into the ways of the wilderness. His sportsman friends were warm admirers. One of them, L. C. Smith, the Syracuse typewriter manufacturer, published in pamphlet form with illustrations a collection of Carter's poems. Thus Carter had his day of fame as "the Adirondack poet," one of several to receive that title from time to time.

"He was one of the most remarkable men I ever knew," recalls Floyd Rasbeck, of Canton, son of a Cranberry Lake guide of the old school. "Con Carter was a scholar. He had the most beautiful handwriting I ever saw and kept a wonderful diary, always written in the third person, such as 'Mr. Carter went down to the spring this morning and found it covered with half an inch of ice.' He was a great woodsman, one of the best."

There is no yardstick by which to measure the influence this teacher, scholar, lawyer, adviser, and fellow woodsman exerted upon young Rushton, but it is probable that Rushton owed much to him.

Possibly it was through Carter that Rushton first met two lifelong friends. Frequently drawn to Canton in connection with his public service or profession, Carter became acquainted with two young woods-loving merchants there, Joseph Barnes Ellsworth, the shoe man, and Milton D. Packard, the drygoods man. Carter named his two sons "Ellsworth" and "Milton" after these Canton friends. Ellsworth and Packard are known to have made fishing trips with Carter in the Cranberry Lake region as early as 1862. Sooner or later, it seems likely, they would have met the young Rushton there in company with Carter. According to Rushton's obituary in the *St. Lawrence Plaindealer* of Canton, "it was somewhere near Cranberry Lake that Rushton met J. B. Ellsworth and M. D. Packard."

This foursome made an unusual combination. A span of nearly forty years separated Carter, the eldest, and Rushton, the youngest. But age was inconsequential. A common interest bound the four in lasting friendship, as an item in the *Plaindealer* of August 2, 1877, indicates: "M. D. Packard, J. B. Ellsworth and J. H. Rushton of this village started for the woods Wednesday morning, August 1st, expecting to take in Supervisor Carter, of Edwards, on the way."

Ellsworth and Packard were town characters. Self-educated, they were well read on world affairs. Both were positive minded, outspoken, and unendingly critical of each other. Ellsworth was a Democrat, Packard a Republican who was twice elected town supervisor and twice county treasurer. The two never agreed on political issues or much of anything else. Their verbal feuds were pungent, often vitriolic, and of great delight to their friends. But they were lifelong cronies, hunting, fishing, and camping together in a comradeship cemented by controversy and abuse. They once became so heatedly involved in a dispute about the Seminole Indians that they went to Florida to investigate and settle that issue. They failed to resolve it and the debate ran on. Ellsworth was married, Packard single, keeping bachelor quarters over his drygoods store. Ellsworth, after the death of his wife, set up housekeeping in rooms above his store and at mealtimes joined Packard in the old frame American House of Canton, where the latter sat at the same corner table for fifty-six years. Their altercations were the joy of drummers and other hotel guests. Of the two, Ellsworth became the closer friend of Rushton.

In 1869, when Rushton was twenty-six, after several years of working in lumber mills and teaching in district schools of St. Lawrence County, he accepted Ellsworth's offer to locate in Canton as a clerk in the Ellsworth Boot and Shoe Store.

Rushton's start in Canton was not auspicious. Not long after he had begun clerking in the store, the core of Canton's business district, the north side of its Main Street, was leveled by two successive, devastating fires: the lower half on August 14, 1869, and the upper half on August 7, 1870. Ellsworth's business was burned out twice in fifty-one weeks, first in its original location and then upstreet where he had taken over half of Packard's store at Packard's insistence.

To combat the first fire, the village had only the old-fashioned bucket brigades. It had no water supply other than private wells and the Grass River flowing under the wooden bridge at the foot of the street. By 1870, through the initiative of Pierre Remington, father of the artist Frederic Remington, the village had organized its new St. Lawrence Fire Department and purchased a "machine," that is, a crude hand-drawn hand-pumper. The water supply was still the river. Of the second great fire the *Plaindealer,* in its abbreviated fire-format (its plant having been reduced to ashes twice), lamented that although the Fire Department arrived on the scene promptly with its machine, "there was an insufficient length of hose to reach the flames."

Following the second fire, Ellsworth took cramped quarters in a temporary shedlike structure hastily erected along one end of the village common, an improvised shopping center known as Park Row. Business was at low ebb. It is probable that under these circumstances he needed no clerk and could not afford to pay one. At any rate, Rushton's clerkship in the shoe store ended in mutual understanding and good will after the second fire.

Meanwhile, after making one or two other abortive attempts at clerking behind local counters, Rushton spent the winter of 1872–73 in Morley, a hamlet five miles from Canton. Lodging in Leonard's Hotel, he worked in Tom Leonard's small shop building clotheshorses. In summer Tom Leonard ranged the western slopes of the Adirondacks guiding. Winters he spent back in Morley either doing small carpentry jobs or building rowboats and guide-boats. Like many guides of that time, he was a jack-of-all-trades.

In 1873, as the spring thaws set in, Rushton became increasingly concerned over his health, his dry hacking cough and the realization that either he must get the upper hand of this ailment or it might lead to trouble.

Probably he had read a little green-bound book (Ellsworth's personal copy inscribed with name and the date 1869 is today in the St. Lawrence University library) and discussed it, as everyone else was doing in those days, with his friends. The book was *Adventures in the Wilderness, or Camp-life in the Adirondacks* by the minister of the Park Street Congregational Church of Boston, the Reverend William Henry Harrison Murray. "Adirondack" Murray, as he was quickly dubbed after the appearance of his book in 1869, is often credited with starting a stampede of tourists and health-seekers into the Adirondacks. In 1870 the Canton *Plaindealer* informed its readers that "the number of Murray's Fools from the south and east who are entering the Wilderness is not so great as last season, but by no means small." Among the many virtues of the region that Murray extolled was the curative quality of the aroma rising from its forests, especially at night. Exposure to the balm of balsam, spruce, and pine on a camping trip of a few weeks or months had resulted, he claimed, in cures for sufferers from consumption, as tuberculosis was then called. He cited one remarkable instance and hinted at another in his own family. This claim prompted several reputed incurables to take a desperate last chance. People who should never have left their sickbed exposed themselves to the rough life of the woods. A few died and others returned home in worse condition from exposure and overexertion. They called Murray a liar.

By 1873 it was clear that the balsamic air of the Adirondacks was no sure cure for "consumption." On the other hand, there was enough testimony of cures or partial cures in the woods to sustain a lively controversy. In 1874 a lung specialist, Dr. Alfred Loomis, encouraged Edward L. Trudeau to stay all winter in the woods after Trudeau had found some relief from his suffering in the summer. Rushton's health was not so bad as that of sufferers who had collapsed on the carries of

Adirondack waterways. Perhaps there was something in Murray's claims after all. It would do no harm to try. Life in the woods was congenial to him anyway, and if it could help him get rid of the cough, so much the better.

First he must equip himself with a boat. From Tom Leonard he received the loan of a boat pattern, and from this he was sure he could design the type of craft he needed. He returned to Canton, and in an empty barn opposite the home of his friend Ellsworth, on State Street, he went to work. Annie Ellsworth Poste used to recall how, as a young woman, she had sat on the family porch that summer and watched her father's former shoe clerk hard at work in the barn across the street.

The traditional story in Canton is that before J. Henry had completed this boat Milton Packard arranged to buy it. Ellsworth, when he learned what his feuding friend had done, ordered Rushton to build him a boat too, "but a damned sight better one." And this was the way Rushton's career as boatbuilder started.

According to one version of this local tradition, the first boat was a canoe. Rushton, however, did not begin building canoes till three years later. His first boat was probably a light rowboat of a type built in Tom Leonard's shop in Morley, perhaps a small St. Lawrence skiff or an Adirondack guide-boat. The building of this boat was the turning point in the life of the thirty-year old Rushton. Thereafter he never stopped building boats until his death in 1906.

Chapter II

BLAZING THE PATH

CHANCE projected Rushton into his career at an opportune time. Until the middle of the nineteenth century few Americans had discovered the value of play. Outdoor sports were little practiced except for hunting and fishing, which could be justified as life-sustaining, and horse racing. The word "vacation" had not entered popular speech. By the 1850's, however, the idea of vacationing at a spa, seashore, forest, or mountain retreat, had begun to attract city dwellers. The tired intellectual and the overworked businessman sought refreshment in the out-of-door life which all Americans had lived in pioneer days. Symbolic of the times was the 1858 camping trip, taken in the Adirondacks by ten gentlemen of the Boston area, among them, Emerson, Lowell, Agassiz, John Holmes, and William J. Stillman. The following year, this same group formed the Adirondack Club, bought a large tract of land, and built a lodge on Ampersand Pond. But the Civil War soon put an end to the Adirondack Club of Boston. Vacations were suspended for the duration.

After the war an uninterrupted expansion of the outdoor movement took place. Spectator and participant sports shared popularity, and the vacation became part of the American way of life. It led eventually to the founding of state and national parks.

The year 1869, when Rushton moved to Canton as a shoe clerk, was a great year in the annals of sport. It was the year when the Cincinnati Red Stockings played the first professional baseball game; when Princeton trounced Rutgers, twenty-five men to a side, in America's first intercollegiate football match; when a Harvard crew in a paper scull engaged an Oxford crew on the river Thames in the first international rowing race—and lost. All along the American seaboard, trim sloops were under construction; sailing had become a favorite coastal pastime. On a humbler scale the velocipede craze reached its height in the summer of 1869. In that same year a small group of boating enthusiasts in New York City had taken up a sport already popular in England and France—canoeing.

Under English influence, the New York Canoe Club introduced canoe racing in 1871, and this new sport began to draw comment by editors of sporting columns in newspapers and magazines. The craft that in pioneer days had been an indispensable means of transportation in America now returned to the country as a medium of sport, not only for racing but also excursions in coastal and inland waterways.

In 1873, the year Rushton began building boats, a new sporting journal, *Forest and Stream,* with Charles Hallock as editor and publisher, appeared on the stands. It was the leading journal in its field for the rest of Rushton's lifetime and a helpful medium in publicizing his craft.

Rushton's rise as a boatbuilder was slow at first. For one thing, Canton, though close to the vacation areas of the Thousand Islands and the Adirondacks, was far removed from the large urban centers where sporting pursuits were gaining many followers. For another, Rushton continued for several years as a one-man operator. And finally, it was three years before he turned to canoe building, the specialty in which he was eventually to excel.

Working without assistants and learning his craft slowly by trial and error, Rushton turned out a limited number of boats in the years 1873–75. Apparently he built mainly for the local market and advertised only in the Canton paper. "J. H. Rushton," runs a classified advertisement in the *Plaindealer* of July 16, 1874, "has two cedar skiffs, 14 and 17 feet long, weighing 65 and 125 pounds, which he will sell cheap for cash. . . . Inquire at Ellsworth's Boot and Shoe Store." His operations were as yet on such a small scale that he had no salesroom of his own and relied on his former employer for an outlet.

In 1874 Rushton had a display at the St. Lawrence County Fair in Canton. His craft took "first premium," a fact he turned to advantage in his advertising. Early in his career he showed a knack for marketing his boats not only through exhibits and direct advertising but also through the more sophisticated device of drawing favorable comment in the columns of newspapers and sporting journals.

Herbert Sprague was another boatbuilder of the county, working in Parishville, only twenty-five miles from Canton. Sprague was building small boats four years before Rushton's debut, and survived Rushton by twenty years, practicing his craft almost to the end. Sprague, however, never became a widely known builder. Though a skilled craftsman, he seems to have lacked two assets that Rushton had on his side: responsiveness to opportunity and a knack for promotion.

By 1875 Rushton had moved from the State Street barn to Jackson's Blacksmith Shop. Later he occupied space in the old "Engine House" and then procured quarters in Champlin's Wagon Shop, all on Water Street (now Riverside Drive) in Canton.

Two items of 1875 in the *Plaindealer* show progress. He was now ready to offer boats up to the limit of the local market. He had also learned how to build a light boat of durable materials, the kind sportsmen were demanding for ease in carrying over portages. The following is an advertisement of August 29, 1875:

> Boats! Boats! Boats! Pine and cedar pleasure and hunting boats, of from 28 to 55 pounds weight, on hand and made to order on short notice. Took first premium at St. Lawrence County fair in 1874. . . . Shop over E. D. Jackson & Son's blacksmith shop, Water St., Canton, N.Y.
>
> J. Henry Rushton
Boat Builder

The second item appeared in the local-mention column on August 2: "J. H. Rushton has sold a light cedar boat shipped to Lawrence, Kansas." This marks the beginning of a wider market that crossed state and finally national boundaries.

Apparently the earliest mention of a Rushton-built boat in a periodical of national circulation appeared in the March 2, 1876, issue of *Forest and Stream* in an article narrating the events of a hunting and fishing trip to Cranberry Lake in September, 1875. The pseudonymous writer approached the lake from the west up the Oswegatchie River, carrying around the rapids. He describes his craft as one of "Rushton's sporting boats" weighing just twenty-nine pounds. He does not say how or where he procured it.

The year 1876 was one of change and progress. The boatbuilder of Canton now built his first canoes and, with his aptitude for seizing opportunity, made a successful bid for a national reputation.

On March 23, 1876, the *Plaindealer* announced that Rushton would send one of his "light oak-ribbed cedar craft" to the Philadelphia Centennial. Actually, as a later item disclosed, he sent two cedar craft for display. Just where his boats were shown, amidst the hodgepodge on the grounds at Fairmount Park, remains hidden in the mass of unindexed, uncataloged data now stored in remote corners of the Philadelphia Public Library. The flood of exhibits that poured onto the Centennial grounds had quickly overflowed all prepared space in the exposition buildings. Annexes had been hurriedly erected, soon filled, and also overflowed. Finally even tents had been restored to. In describing the Centennial from the sportsman's point of view, *Forest and Stream* made much of its own Hunters' Camp at a site bordering the Schuylkill. A typical woodsman's open camp or lean-to was set amidst foliage resembling a sylvan retreat. On the shore small boats of various kinds were drawn up. It is very possible that this was where Rushton displayed his two craft. An exhibit of this kind could hardly fail to draw the attention of the new clan of canoeists attending the fair.

Up to this time Rushton, by his own later statement, had not engaged in the making of canoes. Soon, however, the canoe would become his better mousetrap, and canoeists would be beating a path to his door.

The full details of how Rushton built his first canoes are lacking, but the main circumstances can be reconstructed. In an article entitled "Origin of Some Canoes" in the *American Canoeist* for November, 1883, Rushton states: "The writer's first attempt at canoe building was in 1876, when he built, to dimensions given, the hulls of two canoes. They were 13 x 30 with full floor 'tumble-home' [greatest width at water line, with resulting flat bottom] and about the same sheer as the Nautilus [a British canoe model]. They were decked with canvas by the purchaser and cruised to Philadelphia, via the Delaware and other streams."

Two items in *Forest and Stream* during the summer of 1876 make possible an identification of the buyer of these canoe hulls. The first appeared in the issue of June 15:

Still Another Portable Boat. — Portable boats multiply. We have received from J.H. Rushton, boat builder of Canton, St. Lawrence County, New York, whose advertisement we print, photographs of a boat built by him for parties in Louisville, Ky. It is built on the same general plan as his other styles of boat, but is lighter in weight, and cheaper. Its dimensions are as follows: length over all, thirteen feet; width amidship on top, twenty-eight inches, at bottom of top streak, thirty inches; depth amidship, eleven inches, at ends, twenty-one inches; weight, without seats, thirty-five pounds. Boat to be decked over with canvas. Copper fastened, and without seats or any fixings, it ought to bring $50 in order to pay. Such a boat as this, we think, would be much sought for by all living on or near lakes or streams. They are built on a keel—a piece of oak 1 x 1⅝ inches, rabbeted to receive the siding, which is of cedar, three-sixteenths to one-fourth inch thick. The stems are oak or elm, bent; ribs, oak or elm, three-sixteenths to one-fourth inch thick, and one-half to five-eighths inch wide, made oval, and are put in the boat one and a half inches apart. Three heavier ones are put in where the rowlocks come. Being lapstreak, eight to ten boards on a side, and ribbed so closely, makes them very strong for their weight, which is less than any other boat of like capacity, unless it be a birch canoe; and being very flat on the bottom are very steady and have great carrying capacity, and will run in very shallow water. They are well turned at the ends, both being alike, have considerable sheer, which gives them a trim, jaunty appearance on the water, and at the same time enables them to live in very rough water for boats so small and light.

In supplying the editor with this material, Rushton must have felt that he had turned a corner in his craftsmanship; that he had made progress in developing a light portable boat durable enough to stand rough usage and yet inexpensive by current standards. The second item, in the issue of August 31, names the Louisville canoeist who made the cruise of New York and Pennsylvania streams in 1876:

The Louisville *Commercial* is now publishing an interesting account of a canoe voyage lately accomplished by its manager, Mr. A. H. Siegfried, and a friend. Their little craft was first launched in the Canisteo River at Hornellsville [Hornell], this state, and thence floated down the Chemung River to the Delaware.

Boat, builder, and buyer are thus linked. Thanks to A. H. Siegfried, Rushton made his start as a builder of canoes, joining others in pioneering in America the modern pastime of canoeing.

The "portable boat" referred to in *Forest and Stream* of June 15, 1876, was in fact a canoe. And the specifications described in the article were followed by Rushton in making the two hulls, his first attempt at canoe building. These he shipped to Siegfried in Louisville. Siegfried and his fellow sportsman, James M. Barnes, a confectionery salesman, then decked the hulls with canvas and set forth on the "canoe voyage" mentioned in the August 31, 1876, issue of *Forest and Stream*. They entrained at Louisville with their two completed canoes as baggage. At Hornell, New York, they began the voyage afloat by the Canisteo, Chemung, Delaware, and Schuylkill rivers, with a lengthy portage by rail, to the same Philadelphia Centennial where Rushton boats of a different type were on exhibit. The conjunction of the exhibit and the voyage made a dramatic introduction for Rushton on the national scene, though the full impact would have been felt only by readers of the Louisville *Commercial*.

A. H. Siegfried was business manager of that paper. He contributed to it an account of his voyage and of the Rushton craft it was made in. In an installment dated from "Hornells-ville" August 2, 1876, and published in the Louisville *Com-mercial* on August 12, he writes as a member of the new clan of canoe enthusiasts in this country. No apology is needed for quoting at length from this knowledgeable amateur, alert to what was going on in canoeing circles during his time. He re-fers to the revival of interest in the canoe:

Of late years canoe traveling and canoe clubs have engaged the at-tention of the best business and professional men in London and other great English towns, and have secured a hold upon the same classes in New York and other Eastern cities in our country. Pioneered by "Rob Roy" MacGregor and Baden-Powell, of London, the latter city has a canoe club of three hundred members, while New York has a club of half that number.

In a discussion of the "canoeist's outfit," Siegfried goes on to consider the canoe itself as the essential feature:

Upon this, much careful study and experiment have been ex-pended. The boat required must meet many and peculiar demands. It must be light and portable, yet strong and seaworthy; it must be of the smallest dimensions possible to good paddling and sailing quali-ties, yet roomy enough to serve as a vehicle and a home in one; it must reject every superfluous ounce of weight, yet supply the many quali-ties of a miniature yacht.

THE ROB ROY MODEL

is a boat of oak or cedar, fourteen feet long, twenty-six inches wide, about nine and one-half inches deep, and, as are all canoes, pointed at both ends, with much sheer and a very slight curvature. In a canoe of this sort, weighing about seventy pounds, MacGregor has been cruising hundreds and thousands of miles, on both continents, for years. The

BADEN-POWELL MODEL

is of the same length, but twenty-eight inches wide and ten and one-half inches deep. This has been very generally adopted as the stand-ard model, the weight averaging, with all fittings, from seventy to eighty pounds. These boats, however, seemed to us too heavy and to draw too much water for our Western and Southern streams, while the weight seemed too great for ready portability. To obviate these difficulties, one of our dual club devised a boat thirteen feet long, eleven inches deep, thirty inches wide at a point four inches below the gunwale, twenty-eight inches wide at the gunwale, and twenty-one inches deep at stem and stern. The problem then was to build this model so as to secure minimum [*sic*] lightness. Different methods of construction were considered, but the peculiar and splendid ideas as to hull building of

MR. J. H. RUSHTON,

of Canton, N.Y., were finally adopted, and the model already described was laid before him. With a most refreshing willingness to hear the suggestions of amateurs, Mr. Rushton considered the plan, approved it, and in less than one month turned out two canoe hulls of rare grace and beauty, weighing less than thirty-five pounds, and which, in actual, frequent and severe trial, have proven themselves strong, swift, seaworthy, and comfortable both for traveling and sleeping in. The hulls are built of white cedar, on a light rake-keel, lapstreak, with ribs one-fourth of an inch thick by five-eighths of an inch wide, placed one and one-half inches apart, making a boat so light that a child can handle it, but so strong as to resist choppy waves that have made our huge Jeffersonville ferries rock and roll, and have driven smaller steam craft to the shore. For the uses of the canoeist we believe Mr. Rushton's plan only needs to be known to secure universal adoption.

That this letter may be of practical use to boating men, and especially to the canoe fraternity, we particularize yet more fully. These hulls alone, painted, or finished in oil and shellac, can be had for about $50; finished completely, with paddle, mast, sail, cordage, decks, &c., they will cost from $75 to $80, while complete canoes of other and no better construction cost from $120 to $175. Our little Louisville club bought the two hulls and supplied its own rigging and outfit— a course we commend to all canoeists of mechanical skill. We decked our canoes with good canvas, supported on light hickory carlings, each four and a half feet from stem and stern, with a curvature which raises the deck midships fifteen inches from the floor, and supported on light basswood ridge poles running forward and aft, and serving the additional purpose of braces for mast and backboard. These carlings are four feet apart midships, and support on each side sloping deckboards with a light coaming, leaving a manhole as cabin-hatch four feet long by eighteen inches wide.

Thus Siegfried blazed a path to the door of Rushton's shop in faraway Canton, a path soon to be trodden by canoeists and buyers of other types of pleasure boats from every part of the country. In Siegfried's estimate Rushton's two cedar hulls surpassed the models that British sportsmen had spent years in developing. The letter offers no answer to the tantalizing question of how Siegfried had discovered Rushton, then only three years launched in boatbuilding and selling in a mostly local market. But it does indicate one major reason for Rushton's success as a craftsman—his readiness to listen to the needs of sportsmen and to adopt their suggestions when practicable.

Light and portable, yet strong and seaworthy; of the smallest dimensions possible to good paddling and sailing, yet a miniature yacht—were these not impossibly contradictory demands? Another builder might have said so. Rushton was willing to try.

Evidence is lacking to show whether Siegfried furnished Rushton with detailed drawings and specifications. Presumably not. Several years later, in connection with another canoe built on Siegfried's order, Rushton asserted: "We are indebted to Mr. Siegfried, as to other canoeists, for many kind suggestions—but no plans—that have aided us in perfecting our work."

In dealing with a sophisticated amateur like Siegfried, he was ready to turn his craft into a cooperative venture between builder and customer. He was not lacking in craftsman's pride, but his satisfaction in a finished product was subordinate to his aim of making better boats. He had learned from his own early experience that there is no end to experiment and learning. His youth along the Oswegatchie and his countless sorties into the wilds of Cranberry Lake country after venison and trout had provided him with much native intuition and know-how in handling log dugouts, bark canoes, skiffs, and guide-boats. But there was no quick and easy way to turn this woodsman's intuition into a satisfactory finished product. In an article contributed to the first issue of the *American Canoeist* in 1882 and entitled "How I Came to Be a Canoe Builder," he recalls the stumbling, trial-and-error progress which taught him the value of experiment:

Many years ago I paddled my first canoe. It was a dugout, water-soaked and heavy. I was a boy—a small boy. Didn't we have a time of it. Round and round that canoe would go, but never straight ahead. In order to get ashore we had to steer for the middle of the pond.

Just how or when I mastered the art of using the single blade I can not tell; but certainly before I had arrived at manhood I would vacate the stern seat for no one. Many a time, both by day and night, I have occupied it when the least ripple or noise of boat or paddle would send the wary deer flying through the forest with a shrill whistle that said very plainly, "Good-bye, old man! Salt pork for breakfast at your camp tomorrow! Ha! Ha!"

Well, dugouts are heavy. They can't be carried from stream to stream, from lake to pond; and often, just when and where you wanted one, there it was not. Sometimes Pard and I (mostly Pard) would cut down a pine tree and make one. Sometimes we would cut a spruce, and, peeling off the bark long enough for the purpose, would form *that* into a canoe, with the aid of balsam pieces for keelson, stems, and gunwales, and birch limbs for ribs. Rather a ticklish craft to venture out in when the night was so dark you could not see your hand before you, and the skipper could not swim. The joints of such a boat are apt to be rather loose, even after a liberal application of spruce gum, melted in the frying pan.

Necessity is said to be the mother of invention. After a time I said to myself, "Why not build a cedar boat, so light that I can carry it from place to place?" Well, why not? I tried it. It was light; but part your hair in the middle, and, you fellow in the bow, mind that you shoot straight ahead, else over you go.

Well, try again! I did. Result, a better model; but far from satisfactory. Again and again, and I have a pretty fair boat, weighing thirty-nine pounds, that will carry four men and is steady.

Some one wants to buy it,—must have it. Well, take it then. Thirty dollars pays for it. And I build another for myself. Oh, no! Another man wants that; and another; and yet one more.

Then the skipper scratched his head; and this was the idea he dug out.

Why not build boats? You have got to earn your bread and butter some way. So at it I went.

Precisely what Siegfried meant by his reference to Rushton's "peculiar and splendid ideas as to hull building" is hard to say. His admiration for Rushton's work may have been that of any amateur of that time on first acquaintance with the products of a craft native to the Adirondack region and already highly advanced by 1876. For a quarter century or more, Adirondack guides had spent the long winters trying to perfect a light, durable rowboat for transporting the sportsman and tourist through country where travel was still mostly restricted to waterways, and where the streams connecting lakes and ponds were sometimes navigable, sometimes not. Boat and duffle often had to be carried over rough portages. The guide was proud of his boat and willing to lavish much time and ingenuity on its construction. Some guides became master craftsmen. Today, visitors to the boat collection of the Adirondack Museum at Blue Mountain Lake wonder at the patience and skill of the builders.

Alongside the guide-boats on display there are Rushton cedar canoes of several models. The basic construction is similar. The narrow planks of the hull are thinned to three-sixteenths or a quarter of an inch. They are beveled and joined to one another in a smooth surface or are clinker-built, the feather-edge laps secured by innumerable copper tacks or rivets. When Rushton added canoes to the line of rowboats he had been making, he adapted to the new craft the mode of construction developed in his region by the best small-boat craftsmen in the country.

In late years Rushton came to regard his own methods as "unique." Doubtless they were, in the sense that a real craftsman develops an individual style, individual techniques in such operations as beveling, nailing, and ribbing, and preferences in materials used. The ribbing is perhaps the most original feature of Rushton construction. The ribs of the typical guide-boat of the time were carefully selected spruce roots of the natural crook desired. These were joined at the keel in pairs and spaced generally about six inches apart. The ribs of Rushton canoes, half round or oval, are in one piece of red (slippery) elm, steamed to pliability, and bent and fastened into the shell before drying. They are spaced closely, often two or two and one-half inches from center to center. Though they are light and small, their close spacing gives strength to the hull and prevents it from warping. As a canoeist, Charles E. Chase, wrote in *Harper's* (July, 1880), "Unless the ribs are very close to each other—not more than three inches apart— and snugly fitted, they will warp into most tantalizing shapes." Further details on Rushton's construction are given in the Appendixes.

Rushton's success in years to come was grounded on qualities he showed during his first four years as boatbuilder: his craftsman's skill, his alertness to opportunity, his knack for public relations, and above all his willingness to take suggestions from customers and to experiment endlessly in the search for the near-perfect boat.

Chapter III

MODERN CANOEING
BEFORE RUSHTON

CANOEING as a sport was still in its infancy in 1876. The Eskimo kayak and the Indian birchbark were in use on this continent before the first colonists arrived, and the white man quickly adopted the canoe as a means of transport in the fur trade. But the voyageurs, though they led adventurous lives, were not sportsmen.

Modern canoeing had its start about the middle of the last century, a few years before J. Henry Rushton and his boyhood pal, Pard, were making crude dugouts and spruce-bark canoes on the banks of the Oswegatchie.

The English were the first to popularize canoeing as a sport. According to an account of the founding of the Royal Canoe Club in the English journal *The Canoeist* (January, 1876), the first logged cruise in a modern canoe was made by a member of the club. This was in 1847 when Sir Henry De-Bathe cruised the Thames River in a tin canoe. About the same time John MacGregor, also a member of the London club, made his first try in a canoe of India rubber with air cells in each end. It was not till several years later, however, that Mac-Gregor introduced his Rob Roy, the first widely known canoe model of modern times. Rushton adopted this name for the canoes he made from 1876 to 1880.

John MacGregor best deserves to be called the father of modern canoeing. He was a Scottish traveler and philanthropist and a descendant of Rob Roy Macgregor, a historical character in one of Sir Walter Scott's novels. Son of General Sir Duncan MacGregor, John enjoyed many advantages. He was educated at Trinity College, Dublin, and Trinity, Cambridge, where he was an honors student. He elected law as his profession; but instead of practicing it, he pursued for the rest of his life a variety of other interests. He was an odd mixture of religious zealot, intellectual, and sportsman. In college he taught Sunday school and rowed stroke on the racing crew. In later life he was a captain in London's Scottish Rifle Volunteer Regiment, the crack shot of that outfit, and the organizer of its Volunteer Prayer Society. He was a proficient swimmer, gymnast, boxer, and oarsman. At first an advocate of the movement within the Anglican church called Muscular Christianity, he later followed his college chaplain, the Reverend Wriothesley Noels, in seceding from the Church of England and joining the Baptists. He became honorary secretary of the Protestant Defence Alliance. His religious zeal found expression in missionary activity and philanthropies on behalf of needy youth. He helped organize the Ragged School Union for destitute boys and was one of the founders of the Shoe-black Brigade.

But it was as traveler, canoeist, and writer that MacGregor made his name known in Europe and America. Of independent means, single until nearly fifty years of age, creative, and of a mechanical and scientific bent, he wrote extensively for learned journals on science and other topics, including yachting. He also traveled widely. In 1849 he visited Egypt, the Holy Land, Greece, and Italy. In 1859 he crossed the Atlantic to see what scope America had to offer for spreading the gospel. From this American trip came his first book, *Our Brothers and Our Cousins,* and also his first-known extensive participation in canoeing. He canoed on the Ottawa River in a dugout, a birchbark, and an India rubber canoe. He extended his travels as far as Kamchatka on the Bering Sea. After returning home, according to his biographer Edwin Hodder, he modeled the first of his series of Rob Roy canoes on the Eskimo kayaks he had seen on these travels.

In 1865 he turned to canoeing on a grand scale. This time the scene was the European continent. The boat he designed was suitable for long travels on the rivers, canals, and lakes of France, Switzerland, and southern Germany, using both double-bladed paddle and sails. Into the compartments of his decked *Rob Roy* he stowed a heavy stock of literature, such as copies of the New Testament and religious tracts which he himself had written and published. Thus equipped, he was ready to see Europe at a leisurely pace, rub shoulders with the common people, and at the same time do a little missionary work. This trip of 1865 is a landmark in the sport of canoeing in modern times. Subsequently MacGregor wrote and published, in 1866, his famous little book *A Thousand Miles in the Rob Roy Canoe on Twenty Rivers and Lakes of Europe.*

With this a new day dawned for MacGregor and for canoeing as a pastime. How many religious converts MacGregor won on that cruise was never recorded, but back home in England the number of his converts to canoeing were many. His book ran through many editions. He also took to the lecture platform, asking handsome fees—up to one hundred pounds—a lecture. The proceeds from his lectures and books on canoeing all went to institutions for wayward and needy boys. In 1879 he wrote in the fifteenth printing, an edition combining the narratives of two other canoe voyages with the first, that he had raised by these means ten thousand pounds, all given to various philanthropies. Canoeing served his interests well and became a dominating part of his life. Thanks to his books and lectures, it also became one of the leading pastimes in England.

In all, MacGregor designed at least five types of Rob Roys, four of them of canoe dimension, the one exception being a sailing yawl in which he cruised across the Channel and up the Seine in 1867 to attend the Paris Exhibition and regatta. Two of the canoes were used on MacGregor's other famed cruises: one in 1869, of which he wrote *With the Rob Roy on the Baltic,* and the other in 1872, resulting in *With the Rob Roy on the Jordan.* Each of these canoes was a modification of No. 1, changes being made to meet the special needs and conditions of the respective cruises.

MacGregor's Baltic cruise was largely on the streams and lakes of Sweden. For this he wanted a lighter canoe than his No. 1 *Rob Roy,* with slightly less depth and draft. For the Jor-

25

dan his canoe was to be home and kitchen, a canoe in which to live as well as to paddle. Part of its equipment was a canoe tent, one of the first ingenious devices of this kind ever contrived— if not the first. He slept in it at night, either afloat or when drawn up on some shore.

MacGregor and his Rob Roys had become world famous by the time Rushton began his first boat in the State Street barn, Canton, 1873. Starting with the two cedar hulls ordered by Siegfried and Barnes three years later, Rushton developed his own Rob Roy designs. By 1880, when his business began to boom, other canoe types had become popular, among them a British model contemporary with MacGregor's first Rob Roy. This was the Nautilus brought out by Warington Baden-Powell, an English barrister and the elder brother of Robert, Lord Baden-Powell, the founder of the Boy Scouts and Girl Guides. MacGregor and Baden-Powell were friends.

With accustomed zeal MacGregor enlisted the interest of fellow canoe enthusiasts, and therewith the Royal Canoe Club was founded in 1866, the first of all canoe clubs. The Prince of Wales (later Edward VII) not only accepted the position of honorary commodore of the RCC but met with its members and indulged in the sport. Not to be outdone by the British, the French took up the sport in Paris. Back in England, John MacGregor was elected commodore of the club and Baden-Powell one of its vice-commodores.

What MacGregor and Baden-Powell did for canoeing in England, a young New Yorker, William L. Alden, did in the United States. He succeeded in popularizing the sport along the Atlantic seaboard and west to the Mississippi and became recognized as the father of modern canoeing in this country. He was not, however, the first modern canoeist in America, nor was the New York Canoe Club, which he founded in 1871, the first group to hold canoeing regattas.

Across the Canadian border, in the province of Ontario, canoeing of the modern type had been a local sport for some time in what has become known as the Peterborough country,

in the region of Rice and Stony lakes. There, fifteen years before Alden came on the canoeing scene, some young backwoods
craftsmen began playing around with canoes. The Indians
would come out of the forest and down the Otonabee River in
their bark canoes loaded to the gunwales with the winter's
catch of furs. Log dugouts were also common.

About 1855 one of these young men, George W. R. Strickland, introduced a way of constructing the log canoe so that it
could be shaped true to any model. Other ideas about canoes
and their construction took hold. In 1857 the first Peterborough Regatta was held. Some years later, its secretary, H. F.
Strickland (George's son), wrote of this pioneer regatta in the
American Canoeist:

The only other kind used in this latter occasion besides the birch bark
was one made of canvas stretched over a light frame, and was very
creditable to its maker and paddler, John Edwards. . . . It was at the
Peterboro Regatta in 1857 that I. S. Stephenson first conceived the
idea of building basswood canoes, of which he built several in the
spring and summer of 1858, and immediately afterward establishments were started for their manufacture by English, of Peterboro,
and Gordon of Lakefield, and Herrald of Rice Lake, and their canoes
have found their way to every corner of the globe.

Stephenson later perfected and patented what became his celebrated "cedar rib and longitudinal canoe," manufactured by
the Ontario Canoe Company.

Many of the early American cedar canoes followed the
lines of Baden-Powell's Nautilus, one of the first of these, if
not the first, being William L. Alden's *Violetta.* Alden later
designed his own Shadow, a model which Rushton added to
his offerings.

William L. Alden was a talented young writer on the editorial staff of the *New York Times.* As a New Yorker he was
familiar with the waters of the Upper and Lower bays and of
Long Island Sound. In selecting a canoe, he would need one
capable of weathering the winds and waves of those nearby

waters. He studied MacGregor's Rob Roy design and Baden-Powell's Nautilus. Alden preferred the latter. It had been designed for coastal use as well as inland voyaging. It could carry canvas well and was more of a sailing canoe than a paddler. A two-master, it was heavier than the Rob Roy, and just the thing for New York's bays and the Sound.

At Williamsburg, Long Island, in the borough of Queens, an able commercial builder, James W. Everson, was producing sloops, yawls, and other yachts. Everson agreed to build Alden's canoe along Baden-Powell lines. Thus the *Violetta* came into being, Alden's first canoe.

By this time Alden had enlisted the interest of several sporting enthusiasts in the city, all eager to try their skill at canoe handling and sailing. Together, in 1871, they founded the New York Canoe Club, patterned after the Royal Canoe Club of London.

The *Aquatic Monthly* devoted its leading editorial to the New York club in March, 1873. The editorial lists the slate of officers in that year as follows: commodore, M. Roosevelt Schuyler; vice-commodore, G. Livingston Morse; rear-commodore, Montgomery Schuyler; secretary, W. L. Alden; treasurer, J. S. Mosher; corresponding secretary, J. H. Kidder; measurer, W. T. Burwell. It also describes the types of canoes used by the members:

The canoes belonging to the club are, with a single exception, of the Nautilus type, that being the only sort of cruising canoe which can carry a respectable amount of canvas without wetting the crew. The exception is M. Spark's canoe, *Rip-Rap,* which is of the Rob Roy pattern and is chiefly designed for paddling. Most of the fleet, including the *Gretchen,* the winner of the October regatta, were built by Mr. Everson, of Williamsburg. The *Rip-Rap* was imported from England, and the owner of the *Gretchen* is now having a canoe built by Messenger, the crack English builder, which will doubtless prove the finest canoe in the fleet.

The *Gretchen* was owned by Montgomery Schuyler. A fourteen-footer weighing only fifty-three pounds, she was of white cedar hull construction with Spanish cedar decking. She survived the white horses of Flushing Bay on October 21, 1871, to win the first official canoe sailing race in the United States. At the close of its 1871 season the club's roster listed sixteen canoes and as many members.

"The club has already done much," says the *Aquatic Monthly* editorial, "to popularize canoeing in this country, and as it is in constant correspondence with the leading English canoeists, it is able to bring forward whatever improvements are made abroad as well as at home in canoes and canoe-rigging."

Soon after the founding of the New York Canoe Club, other events helped to dramatize the new sport. In its September 4, 1873, issue *Forest and Stream* reported that an Indian canoe race took place the previous week at Savin Rock, near New Haven, Connecticut. This attracted "the largest concourse of people ever known in that vicinity." Four canoes were entered with "paddlers chiefly Indians from Old Town, Maine." The course was one mile in length. A total of seven hundred dollars was offered in prizes, three hundred for first place. The *Alnumbra* won the top money after finishing first, third, and second in the three heats. The *Passadumbking* turned in the fastest mile heat with 21 :55.

In 1874 a young man named Nathaniel Holmes Bishop helped popularize canoeing as a challenging sport. He was the son of a family whose enterprise converted some of the New Jersey cranberry bogs into cash. Not content with a trip to South America and a one-thousand-mile hike on foot, across Argentina and the Andes to Chile and the Pacific coast, about which he wrote a book, he now engaged in another unusual undertaking, which brought forth the book entitled *The Voyage of the Paper Canoe*.

The adventure related in the book was a cruise from Troy, New York, down the Hudson, through coastal waters, to Cedar Springs, Florida, in a fifteen-foot paper canoe. This was viewed as phenomenal. Starting first at Quebec City in a light rowboat, or skiff, young Bishop proceeded via the St. Lawrence, the Richelieu, Lake Champlain, and Lake George to Troy on the Hudson. Wearied of oar-pulling and of traveling back-end-to, he decided to substitute one of Elisha Waters' celebrated paper canoes for the heavier rowboat. Upon arriving at Troy, he delayed his cruise until Waters and Son could manufacture just such a canoe as he desired. Thus the paper canoe *Maria Theresa* came into being.

By 1874 the Waters firm was producing paper boats of many types, models, and sizes. The principle on which Elisha Waters constructed his type of craft was uncomplicated. It consisted of merely building up a hull by gluing together layers of heavy manila paper strips, one ply on another, over a boat shell placed bottom side up, until a sufficient lamination in strength and thickness to form a tough, strong hull resulted. With a minimum of wooden framework this then became a serviceable boat. Waters' paper boats were displayed at the Philadelphia Centennial in 1876, where they received favorable attention.

The cruise of the *Maria Theresa* to Florida was widely publicized and made Bishop the most popular canoeist of the day. Bishop later paddled the same canoe to the Centennial and displayed it there.

In a few short years after the founding of the New York Canoe Club, canoeing became a prominent feature of the sporting scene east of the Mississippi. A favorable climate existed for a man starting a career as canoe builder. J. Henry Rushton proceeded to learn all he could from these pioneers of modern canoeing. The recent developments in England, Canada, and the United States all influenced the boats he was now to begin building.

Chapter IV

ROB ROYS ON THE MISSISSIPPI

THE RELATIONSHIP with Siegfried, one of Rushton's most valuable contacts, continued for at least five or six years. The order for the two cedar hulls in 1876, Rushton's first canoes, was followed by others, both from Siegfried and from some of his friends. Rushton's progress as a builder resulted from just such customer relations, for canoeists were impressed by his craftsmanship and, liking what they bought, became advocates.

One contact made through Siegfried was with Lucien Wulsin, the junior partner in a recently established music store in Cincinnati, Ohio, a firm which later developed into the D. H. Baldwin Company, makers of Baldwin pianos, organs, and other musical instruments. In 1877 Wulsin went to Louisville to establish a branch store for his company. While there he met Siegfried in the offices of the Louisville *Courier-Journal,* of which Siegfried, having left the *Commercial,* was now business manager. A friendship grew up that was to mean much to Rushton in years to come. Siegfried and Wulsin discovered a mutual interest in canoeing and the outdoors. A correspondence ensued between them.

Two years later, in May, 1879, Siegfried wrote to Wulsin recommending a Rushton canoe: "Your friend Ambrose can get a good second-hand Rob Roy here cheap, say $40—from C. B. Robinson, 4th and Broadway. It was built for me in 1877 by Rushton and I used it on the Scioto and James River cruises. I sold it because it was only 8½ in. deep, and so most too close for a man of my abdomen to sleep in. It is a beauty under paddle or sail."

Thus the canoe *Kleiner Fritz* was introduced into Wulsin's life. In papers found recently in the Baldwin Company's historical files, it was identified as Siegfried's first *Kleiner Fritz,* which he used on the Scioto and the James, and which Wulsin later owned and used under the name of the *Betsy D.* The *Kleiner Fritz,* alias the *Betsy D.,* is well known in canoeing history. During its life it figured in two controversies, both of which attracted considerable attention and in both of which Rushton had something at stake.

The letter exchanges between Louisville and Cincinnati became frequent during the forepart of 1879. In March, Siegfried wrote:

LOUISVILLE, March 11, 1879

MY DEAR MR. WULSIN:

It is rather early to begin planning for summer vacations, but my canoe cruise is something I think about, before and behind, each year through.

About July 7 Mr. Barnes and myself, and probably Mr. J. H. Empson, of this city, purpose starting to Itasca Lake, the head of the Mississippi, for a cruise therefrom to St. Paul, at least, and, if time shall allow, to Davenport or St. Louis. I am to write up the trip, and Mr. Barnes is to illustrate it, for *Scribner's Monthly.* It will require not less than four and not more than five weeks, with the present intent on our part to make it six weeks, and come on down to Davenport or St. Louis.

How would you like to join us? I am advised that there are bears and deer for the gunner, and trout, black bass, muscalonge, etc. for the angler. We anticipate a delightful time. The country is almost uninhabited, save by friendly Indians, for over 600 miles of the way. The expense will be railway fares to Detroit City [Detroit Lakes], Minn.—N.P.R.R.—portage of 60 miles thence to lake—fifty cents per day while on water—(say four weeks)—and railway home from St. Paul, Davenport or St. Louis, as we may elect. . . .

What do you think about it?

Yours most truly,
A. H. SIEGFRIED

In a few weeks the Itasca trip began shaping up, and under date of May 12 Siegfried wrote at length in regard to plans. Parts of this letter follow:

MY DEAR WULSIN:

Your very welcome favor is just received, and I turn at once to answer because I need the letter I sent you in my last from some already unforgotten Frenchman at White Earth, Minn. Please return it by next mail. I want to write to the guides he names. . . .

I suggested Monday for departure because we can then reach the Lake by Saturday without time and expense of lying over Sunday, can camp on Schoolcraft's island in Itasca Lake over Sunday, and get a taste of outdoor air, with time to get things well arranged before the start. . . .

Don't take an axe. A hatchet will serve all our purposes, and a canoeist *must* strangle all tendency to multiply number and weight of impedimenta. Don't take a single unnecessary article or ounce of weight. . . .

I infer from what you say that Rushton has sent Longworth and Greenwood [members of the Cincinnati Canoe Club] those infernal double-masted canoes. Don't do it! You can never sleep in a canoe with two mast tubes, unless they are located out of all sailing reason. It's all very well in a pond before a light breeze, but a dandy sail, to amount to anything, can never be quickly handled in a high wind, and a capsize is inevitable. Unless you have "been there," you can have no idea of the row a high blow raises on small lakes and big rivers. I'd rather be in mid-ocean. Let them have their two-masters, but you'll be the man who laughs when you get to where there is *sailing*. I am going to have a jib to add to my sail in light wind—rigged from bow to masthead, adding to speed and steering, and easily handled in every emergency. You can easily do the same. If you are determined on a lunacy that has long been abandoned in practical canoeing, you can get up the spars, sail, etc., at home, for say $3 and I'll show you how if need be. Rushton is a good workman and has good ideas, but he has never seen a traveling canoe except those he has built, and so lacks in practical knowledge of canoe sails, fittings, etc. Barnes, Empson and I always get our own rigs. We know from experience in all waters and winds that the moderate sized lug sail is absolutely the best,—reinforced, at choice, by the jib. Any New York or English canoe man will tell you the same, unless he wants merely to do fancy work in moderate weather. Rushton sent me a sailing rig once and I threw it away. As Dick Deadeye says, "He means well, but he don't know" as to this practical matter. . . .

I hope you have no important business on hand for Tuesday. This letter will "bust" it, sure.— How I have spun it out!

Yours most truly,

A. H. SIEGFRIED

The expedition set out by the route planned, but failed to keep on schedule. The ruggedness of the country, a miscalculation of the guides, and other circumstances caused delay. In another planning letter Siegfried had cautioned against underestimating time and rations. "Your mem. of supplies," he wrote on May 17, "seems to be that of an expert, and will meet the case admirably, except that your estimate of ten days' rations will starve us, unless you look for heavy income from hook and gun. From Detroit [Lakes] to Aitkin, a region destitute of population save a few Indians, is about 650 miles and should be reckoned upon at not less than twenty days." But this estimate, too, fell short. The trip from Detroit Lakes to Aitkin actually took four strenuous weeks.

Though Siegfried disparaged Rushton's ability as designer of sailing rigs, he never questioned Rushton's workmanship in hull construction. This expedition to the wild headwaters of the Mississippi was a stern endurance test for those three Rob Roys, the *Kleiner Fritz,* the *Betsy D.,* and the *Hattie.* The first lap from Detroit Lakes to the Chippewa Reservation agency at White Earth was by horse-drawn "prairie schooners." The whisky-filled leader of the guides set a breakneck pace. In the wagon that carried two of the canoes the *Betsy D.* "was racked and pounded beyond all excuse," and the *Kleiner Fritz* had a hole "like that made by a six-pound cannon shot" stove in the side. By good luck the agency had a true Vermont jack-of-all-trades in its midst who repaired the damaged *Fritz* while the voyageurs watched a Chippewa Fourth of July celebration. The initial leg of the trip was a mere taste of the hardships that followed.

The sixty-mile overland trip ended at Wild Rice Lake (now Rice Lake). The party dismissed its wagoners and engaged five Indian guides for the voyage afloat, which now began. The Indians had a large birch-bark canoe of their own paddled by two of them, while the three others walked through the woods. Each voyageur paddled his own Rob Roy, stocked with his share of stores and equipment and converted into sleeping quarters at night. According to Siegfried, each had

... a Rob Roy canoe, slightly improved as to model and built upon the incomparable plan of Mr. Rushton of Canton, New York. The canoes are fourteen feet long, ten and a half inches deep and twenty-seven inches wide, decked over except a man-hole sixteen by about thirty-six inches, and weighing, with the mast and lug sail, from fifty to fifty-six pounds. The paddle is eight feet long, bladed at each end, grasped in the middle, and drives the canoe by strokes alternating on each side. The traveler sits flat upon the boat's floor, facing the bow. The canoe is not only a vehicle, but furnishes a dry and secure bed for sleeping at night, and, with its rubber apron, is a refuge from rain and storm.

From Wild Rice Lake up the Wild Rice River, the party had to battle against rocky shoals, brush, and swift currents in the narrow, crooked channel:

In the early afternoon our progress became slow and excessively wearying from the shallowing of the river and its wonderful crookedness. The current ran like a mill-race around hundreds of short turns and had its own exasperating way upon our keels. Finally, we were obliged to wade and drag the canoes after us in water varying between ankle- and waist-deep. A few hours of this wore us all out, and we called a halt and camp, utterly exhausted, with not more than twelve miles to the credit of the hard day's work. . . . Early the following morning we started, four of our party with canoes, and we on foot with Kewashawkonce [head guide]. . . . Ke, as we abbreviated him, strode into an unbroken forest, grown with dense underbrush, strewn with fallen trees at almost every step, diversified by swamps and thickets through which he beat his way by main strength, and now and then traversed by rivers—all streams are rivers there —into which he plunged with never an interrogation mark, and so on briskly, up hill and down, till, with three miles of walking, wading, climbing and struggling, we were brought to bay, tired out. Half an hour's rest and some refreshing wild strawberries prepared us for such another stage. Then an hour more of this terrible strain made us drop again for rest. Another hour, and before noon, hot and jaded, we came out upon a low bluff overhanging the river and stopped for lunch.

Toward evening the Indians, having dragged the canoes up the little river, struggled wearily into camp. The word "busted" sufficed to explain what had happened to the birchbark, but the Rob Roys were still intact. Next day the Indians made yokes for the three canoes and hoisted them on their shoulders. The party portaged through a trackless forest to the Upper Wild Rice lakes. After paddling across these, they carried again, eastward across a watershed to the infant Mississippi. "We could hardly realize that in this deep, rushing brook, not more than four or five paces wide, we saw the beginnings of that majestic current which drains half a continent." Here they parted with their Indian guides—too soon as it turned out. To their consternation they discovered that they were over two days' journey below Lake Itasca, "below a region of rapids and obstructions . . . up which no craft had ever traveled" (Schoolcraft had reached Itasca by another stream and a long portage). They chopped and tugged at windfalls across their way, waded through shoals dragging their canoes, and fought inch by inch up plunging gorges. Finally they emerged on the quiet waters of Itasca and encamped on Schoolcraft Island. Henry Rowe Schoolcraft, explorer and scholar of Indian lore, had penetrated to Lake Itasca in 1832. No white man, except a wandering fur trader named Morrison, had seen Itasca before that date. Schoolcraft's claim to be the discoverer of the source of the great river was generally recognized.

But canoeists are precisionists. Was Itasca actually the uttermost of the headwaters? After exploring the mouths of several sluggish feeder creeks, the Siegfried party pushed up the largest of these to a blockage at about two hundred yards and then tramped through thicket and forest a half mile to the source of a second body of water down on their map as Elk Lake. "To all appearances," Siegfried concludes, "these bogs and this small lake are the uttermost tributaries to Itasca Lake, and the latter, concentrating these minor streams and sending them out as one, is the true head of the Father of Waters." This confirms Schoolcraft but documents the text with a footnote.

On July 14 the party left Itasca for the circuitous downstream voyage, the Mississippi flowing north for the first sixty miles of its course as if headed for an outlet in Hudson Bay. After they had retraced the clogged upper channel, their downhill journey was easy and exciting as rapids and still-waters alternated. A chain of large lakes at the northerly arc of the Mississippi enabled the little Rob Roys to unfurl their sails. Paddling, sailing, and riding the foam in the versatile craft, the party reached Aitkin and civilization in two weeks. They covered the last one hundred and fifty miles in three days. Now a week behind schedule and weary from their labor, they decided to call it a day and entrain for Minneapolis.

Two records of this cruise have been preserved. One is a little notebook diary kept by Lucien Wulsin, the other a two-installment magazine article written by Siegfried and illustrated presumably by Barnes in the August and September, 1880, issues of *McBride's Magazine*. In the concluding paragraph Siegfried writes: "Beyond reasonable doubt, our party is the only one that ever pushed its way by boat up the entire course of the farthermost Mississippi. Beyond any question, our canoes were the first wooden boats that ever traversed those waters. . . . So we may well feel an honest pride in our Rushton-built Rob Roys and our hard knocks."

There is some quibbling in this claim. True, Schoolcraft had used Indian birchbarks, not wooden canoes. True, though on the return he had come all the way down the upper river, he had approached Itasca by a tributary of the Mississippi rather than the main channel. Siegfried makes the most of these technicalities. But he leaves Schoolcraft's glory as discoverer essentially intact, claiming only a closer definition of the great river's sources.

Two years later, however, another adventurous canoeist made a bold attempt to nudge Schoolcraft out of his niche and, ignoring the claims of Siegfried, Wulsin, Barnes, and others, to pre-empt for himself the honor of discovering the true source of the Mississippi and of affixing his name to the map. Oddly enough, this venture also involved a Rushton canoe.

Willard Glazier, soldier, author, and explorer, lived a few generations too late to be the Meriwether Lewis of his inclinations. But by virtue of a thirst for adventure, a strong ego, and a well-managed publicity campaign, he overcame in part the obstacle of being born out of his due time. He prevailed on many people to credit his claims as an explorer and wound up with thirty-five lines in *Who's Who in America.*

He was born in 1841 on a farm in the township of Fowler, St. Lawrence County, about fifteen miles west of Rushton's boyhood home. He too was a pupil of Cornelius Carter, though prior to Rushton's school days under that master and in a different district school. At fifteen Glazier turned trapper and earned seventy-five dollars to continue his schooling in the nearby village of Gouverneur. Later he enrolled in the State Normal School in Albany, but he soon ran out of funds and turned to schoolteaching. The Civil War was his main chance. He came out of it with the rank of captain after fighting in sixty engagements, being captured and escaping three times, and spending fourteen months in Confederate prisons. In December, 1865, he published this story in *The Capture, the Prison Pen, and the Escape.* The book sold over four hundred thousand copies to vie with *Uncle Tom's Cabin* as a best seller. It made Glazier independent enough to pursue a career as author and latter-day pioneer and explorer. Other books followed. But the quiet life of an author, no matter how affluent, was not enough for Glazier. In 1876 he crossed the country from Boston to San Francisco on horseback in two hundred days. He paused long enough in the principal cities to give lectures, donating the proceeds to the widows and orphans' fund of the Grand Army of the Republic. The incidents of this novel ride, including an attack by wolves and capture by Indians in Wyoming, were good for another popular book.

During this trip he conceived the idea of traveling down the Mississippi from source to mouth by canoe. In 1881, along with his brother George, Barrett Channing Paine of the St. Paul *Pioneer Press,* and native guides, he pushed his way to Lake Itasca from the east. On the hunch that Itasca was not the real source of the great river, he probed its feeding streams and discovered one which he took to be the "Infant Mississippi." It was a brook about eleven hundred feet in length that connected the lake the Siegfried party had visited—Elk Lake—with Lake Itasca. One of Glazier's Indian guides knew this smaller lake as "Pokegama." Glazier was apparently unaware that it was already down on state maps as Elk Lake. He concluded that Schoolcraft, Nicollet, and others had all failed to find it because of the baffling obscurity of the mouth of its outlet in Lake Itasca. Higher than Lake Itasca, it must be the true source. Standing on its shores, the party drank the Captain's health, and he in turn made a speech on the importance of their discovery. From this day forward, he resolved, the new lake should be known as "Lake Glazier."

The party then followed the route down the Mississippi taken two years earlier by the Siegfried party. At Aitkin they abandoned all but one of the birchbarks used thus far and acquired two modern wooden canoes shipped there to await them. One was a Rob Roy type, listed as the St. Paul model and built by the Racine Boat Company; this they dubbed the *Itasca*. The other was a Rushton and was christened the *Alice* after Glazier's daughter. "It was built," Glazier wrote in his book *Down the Great River,* "by a native of Saint Lawrence County, New York, in the neighborhood of my old home." He explained that in St. Paul on the outbound trip he had met a Mr. A. H. Siegfried who had offered him the Rushton canoe. It too was of the Rob Roy type, though by now (1881) Rushton was calling it the American Traveling Canoe. Designed to carry two persons, it was sixteen feet long and weighed about eighty pounds. It could be sailed as well as paddled, but Glazier had determined to keep his record clear by paddling all the way to the Gulf of Mexico.

From Aitkin, Glazier proceeded in the *Discovery,* the remaining birchbark; his brother in the *Alice;* and Paine in the *Itasca.* At St. Paul the *Discovery* was abandoned, Glazier took the *Alice,* and Paine continued in the *Itasca.* Meanwhile George Glazier left the expedition to serve as advance agent in arranging lecture appointments downriver. At La Crosse the *Itasca* was left behind, and the Captain and Paine continued the voyage to the Gulf in the Rushton *Alice*.

It was a triumphal progress. Many newspapers throughout the land were now hailing Glazier as the discoverer of the true source of the Mississippi. At wharves along the way the two explorers were met by welcoming groups and escorted to their hotel, often preceded by a band playing "Hail to the Chief." Large audiences assembled to hear the Captain's lecture on "Pioneers of the Mississippi," in which with conspicuous modesty he passed over his own claims. That subject he left to the able George.

The little *Alice* finally nosed into the broad expanse of the Gulf in mid November. The Captain and his friend were the first of record to travel by canoe the whole length of the Mississippi from the alleged source in Lake Glazier to the Gulf, a distance the Captain generously estimated at 3,184 miles. The trip had taken 117 days. Given to off-the-cuff superlatives, the Captain called it the longest canoe voyage on record.

"Many citizens of Port Eads," wrote the Captain's ventriloquist biographer in the five-hundred-page *Sword and Pen* published two years later when its subject was only forty-two, "had assembled in small boats at the entrance of the Gulf. . . . Cheer upon cheer rent the air as the beautiful little canoe, bearing aloft at the bow a pennant with the inscription 'Alice,' and at the stern the glorious 'Stars and Stripes,' paddled from the mouth of the river out into the wide expanse of the Gulf. Firearms were discharged, flags enthusiastically waved, and every possible demonstration made which could give vent to the excitement of the occasion."

On November 21 Glazier was the honored guest of the New Orleans Academy of Sciences. This time he consented to tell about his own discoveries on the great river. He also gave the *Alice* to his admiring hosts. Though the little craft had never seen Lake Glazier, she had carried her gallant crew from Aitkin to the Gulf, which was more than any other canoe had done. Meanwhile Brother George was arranging a return engagement in St. Louis. Going there in December, Captain Glazier presented the *Itasca* to the Missouri Historical Society, along with a speech.

There were of course repercussions. All this fanfare seemed vulgar to Siegfried, Wulsin, and Barnes. In spite of the brief meeting between the Captain and Siegfried in St. Paul, Glazier blandly ignored the account in *McBride's Magazine* of the party that had preceded him by two years to the supposed source. "Glazier is a bag of wind," Siegfried wrote indignantly to Barnes, urging that they challenge his claims in the strongest terms.

There were many other challenges. The controversy raged for the next dozen years or so, newspaper editors, geographers, and map makers taking sides. There were two issues: (1) What *is* the true source of the Mississippi? (2) Who discovered it first? Glazier wrote two books to vindicate his claims. The first, *Down the Great River* (1887), is the entertaining story of the trip to the headwaters, the discovery of Lake Glazier, and the canoe voyage downstream to the Gulf. The narrative is followed by an appendix of endorsements and newspaper clippings slanted in favor of the Captain.

As map makers showed a surprising willingness to affix "Lake Glazier" to the maps of Minnesota, the protests became louder. The Minnesota Historical Society and the international congress of geographical societies in Berne denounced the attempt to change the geography of the state of Minnesota.

In 1891 Glazier organized a second trip to the headwaters, leading a party of fifteen which he hoped would confirm his findings. This resulted in a second and even longer book, more than five hundred pages, entitled *The Headwaters of the Mississippi* and published by Rand McNally and Company in Chicago. Needless to say, the Captain's chosen companions were all but unanimous in confirming his claims. The geography in that region is confusing to laymen.

Meanwhile, in 1889, the legislature of Minnesota passed an act making "Elk Lake" the official name of the so-called "Lake Glazier." And the State Historical Society sent a commission of surveyors and others to the headwaters to make an exhaustive study on the ground and produce a definitive report. The survey was carried out at intervals over the years 1888 to 1891. As reports from the field trickled in, the legislature and the Governor were so much impressed by the Itasca Basin that they decided to make it a state park. In 1891 the Governor appointed one of the prominent figures in the survey, J. V. Brower, first commissioner of Itasca State Park. Brower, representing both the park commission and the State Historical Society, wrote *The Mississippi River and Its Source*. Both this and Glazier's *Headwaters* were published in the same year, 1893. Brower's book brushes off Glazier's claims in a chapter called "The Glazier Fiasco." It is illustrated with detailed survey maps of the whole Itasca basin and reproduces in full the report of the survey commission. Its relevant findings, simplified, are (1) that other parties, including Siegfried's, had visited Elk Lake before Glazier, as surviving maps prove; (2) that Elk Lake and its outlet are not the true source of the Mississippi; (3) that Itasca is the Central Reservoir at the lowest depression; (4) that the feeder stream at the extreme southwestern tip of Lake Itasca, partially explored by Nicollet in 1836 and called by him the "Infant Mississippi," is in fact the largest and longest of the affluents; (5) that it draws its waters from the Greater Ultimate Reservoir, which is "the true and actual" source of the Mississippi River. Beyond are only the clouds.

Glazier did not concede. In data he supplied for the 1903–1905 edition of *Who's Who in America* is his claim to the discovery of the true source of the Mississippi, "now known as Lake Glazier." This feat, he felt, was the crowning event of his life. But he was not ready to write "finis" to his career as explorer. In 1902, three years before his death at sixty-four, he explored the interior of Labrador.

However insubstantial his claims to discovery may be, Glazier accomplished two things on the Mississippi that stand to his credit. He traveled in canoe from source to mouth of the great river. And he was probably the ultimate (to use a word popular with surveyors) cause of the founding of Itasca State Park, though this was not his intention.

How does all this concern Rushton? Well, it gave him a fine letter to quote in the testimonial columns of his catalogs. Here it is:

1310 Olive Street
St. Louis, Mo.
Dec. 14, 1881

J. H. Rushton
Canton, N.Y.
Dear Sir:

When I reached Aitkin in my recent voyage of observation and exploration from the source of the Mississippi to the Gulf of Mexico, I was met as arranged by three [*sic*] canoes, one of which, your No. 93, I at once decided upon for my personal use.

If you feel a pride in your workmanship you have reason to be justly proud, and let me here say for your gratification, that the *Rushton Canoe* has been seen and admired in every city, village and hamlet from Aitkin, Minn., to Port Eads. At the conclusion of my voyage, as you may have seen through the papers, I presented the canoe to the New Orleans Academy of Sciences as a souvenir of the voyage and the discovery of the source of the Mississippi on the 22nd of July last.

Although I have never had the pleasure of meeting you personally, I find some slight satisfaction in telling you that I am a native of old St. Lawrence [County], and that I shall always feel indebted to you for the staunch little craft which carried me safely through rain storms and wind storms, eddies and whirlpools; over rapids, sand bars and snags from the head waters of the Great River to the sea.

Hoping that I may have the good fortune to meet you during my next visit to Northern New York, I am, ever truly yours,

Willard Glazier
Soldier and Author

Beyond teasing Wulsin lightly ("Isn't it true that Glazier found what your party lost?"), Rushton appears to have taken no side in the great dispute. There was no need to. Whoever discovered the true source, this much was plain: the Mississippi had discovered Rushton's Rob Roys.

Chapter V

THE GO-LIGHT
BROTHERHOOD

IN THE late seventies and early eighties canoeing grew rapidly in popularity. The major cities followed New York in organizing canoe clubs. A national association was founded. Regattas were held. Individuals carried out quixotic schemes of long-distance exploration or test against extraordinary obstacles. The brave little craft in which fur traders had roved the continent sparked once again the adventurous spirit. The frontier was rapidly being closed, but with the canoe Americans could still push into remaining primitive areas and recover something of the pioneering past.

As a boy J. Henry Rushton had roved the wilderness near his home. As a young man in frail health he had easily been persuaded to try the wilderness cure recommended by "Adirondack" Murray. But the boat he built to float his way to health under open skies was snatched up by another man, and his second boat by another. J. Henry, stranded in his boat shop, forgot about his health and made boats for other men to rove in. He understood what they wanted.

They wanted a boat not merely for work and pleasure. The rowboat serves those ends well enough. It provides fast, reliable transport. It is a steady boat to fish and hunt from. But it is not a boat for the rover. Oars with fixed fulcrums are too mechanical for his temperament. He likes the free swing of the paddle and its challenge to his skill. Above all, he likes to face forward. No explorer cares to back into new country. The posture of a quest is breast forward.

J. Henry understood these latter-day voyageurs as did no other builder of his time. He made them boats fit to launch a dream in. His reward was a living and a good deal more. It was pride of craftsmanship. It was the special kind of gratitude reserved for those who aid in the realization of schemes beyond the scope of the day's work and play. He was craftsman to men's dreams of escape and fulfillment.

For a few years after 1876 canoes continued to be incidental to Rushton's main business. His "portable sporting and pleasure boats"—that is, his rowboats—came first. They were given priority in his first catalogs, probably because they were in greater demand than canoes in the local market. But as his reputation grew through the nation, there was a change in the nature of his business and in his own interests. Canoes gradually became his best-selling line, and canoeists captured his imagination. In his catalog of 1882 he addressed himself especially to "the hundreds of enthusiastic canoeists . . . whose sails have caught the breeze on hundreds of the lakes, bays and rivers with which OUR COUNTRY to a greater extent than any other is blest." Shop bound, he followed the exploits of his patrons with fascination and reported them in his catalogs. The brief testimonials about his "sporting and pleasure boats" were increasingly supplemented by page-long letters from his canoeist patrons and accounts of their voyages.

By the early 1880's his main challenge was the canoe. As builder he had the pleasurable duty, he said in his catalog of 1882, "of providing the canoeist with a suitable craft wherewith to explore the many devious and beautiful water courses intersecting our broad land. . . . The 'copy' in our writing book when we were a boy, 'many men of many minds,' applies with considerable force to *many men* intent upon the purchase of a canoe. So long as that remains a fact, it will be impossible— even if it were desirable—to have any one model, any one mode of construction or any one builder please all. It depends very much upon the individual canoeist as well as the waters upon which he will use his canoe as to what model will suit him best." And he added, by way of dedication: "We think we quote from an esteemed contemporary . . . when we say, 'The keel of the *perfect* canoe has not yet been laid.' We intend to approach perfection as near as possible aided by several years of study, observation of all the principal models both on shore and in friendly contest with each other, the advice and comments by letter and in person of hundreds of prominent canoeists and the assistance of an able corps of skilled and experienced workmen."

The last phrase implies a considerable advance in Rushton's fortunes since the building of his first canoes in 1876. The Canton *Plaindealer* documents the main steps in his progress. On May 31, 1877, it announced: "J. H. Rushton has recently issued a circular giving excellent descriptions with illustrations of his Portable Sporting Boats and Canoes." On November 15 of the same year it carried this notice: "J. H. Rushton, the manufacturer of the best light cedar boats in the country, is erecting a new building on Water Street, near the stone blacksmith shop, to accommodate the increasing demand of his business."

The "circular," the first of Rushton's catalogs, was a modest eight-page, accordion-type folder. Three sizes of open canoes are described, thirteen, thirteen and a half, and fourteen feet long, weighing from thirty-five to forty pounds and priced at forty dollars. His Rob Roys, decked in a "mode original with myself," stepping two masts, are offered at seventy to eighty dollars and advertised as "the fastest canoe afloat." Though keeping the name Rob Roy, he points out that the design is a composite one, incorporating lines of the Baden-Powell Nautilus and the Alden Shadow. A Lyman rowing gear, allowing the oarsmen to face forward, is offered for ten dollars extra.

The new building, like the first catalog, was modest, resembling the village horse barn of those days: a single-gabled, small frame structure with double, swinging front doors. Still standing in 1967 as the northern wing of a furniture store, this building is now occupied by Murphy's Appliance Sales.

In 1878, according to the *Plaindealer,* Rushton received an inquiry about his boats from Venezuela. On April 3, 1879, further evidence of an expanding business appeared:

J. H. Rushton is gaining a reputation as a builder of portable sporting boats and canoes for hunting, fishing, trapping and pleasure rowing that is equaled by but few in this country. His trade is constantly increasing and is a good evidence of what may be done by skill, perseverance and a liberal supply of printers' ink. Mr. Rushton has just got out at this office a 24-page pamphlet which he will send to his patrons in all sections of the country. He has just completed a miniature boat that he will send to the firm in New York which represents him there. It is to be placed on exhibition at Henry C. Squires', No. 1 Cortland Street.

Two weeks later the *Plaindealer* announced: "Rushton has received so many orders for boats that he has been compelled to engage another man to help him."

The workman Rushton selected in 1878 as his first assistant was Nelson Brown, a tall, skinny, cadaverous fellow who had first been hired to work in the Champlin wagon shop in Canton. Brown's father was a veteran wheelwright in the village of Russell, twelve miles south of Canton. Nelson had learned the trade as an apprentice to his father. The association he formed with Rushton in the spring of 1878 lasted till the closing of the Boat Shop with the exception of one brief interlude when he worked for a boatbuilder in Massachusetts. Brown became the most highly skilled of all J. Henry's assistants, the most trusted and faithful. For many years he was foreman of the shop. He was there when J. Henry died in 1906 and stayed on in advancing age until the key was finally turned in the shop's door. In later years, still residing in Canton, he frequently repaired and restored Rushton canoes. No single man contributed more to establishing Rushton's reputation as builder than did this modest, quiet master craftsman.

Since an increasing number of Rushton's customers wanted boats for traveling and exploring, as well as hunting, fishing, and pleasure boating, the Boat Shop was under pressure to build canoes of the utmost lightness consistent with staunchness, or even to yield degrees of the latter in favor of the former. In his catalog of 1877 Rushton remarked: "Years of study and labor have enabled me to put every pound where it will do the most good and leave out all useless weight." Other builders of course made the same claim. But constant experiment was soon to yield striking results in his shop.

In 1880 and the three following years Rushton was again lucky in forming an association with a highly vocal canoeist who was as generous in praise as he was demanding. The man in question was George Washington Sears, a spokesman for the go-light school of exploring canoeists. Through him Rushton became known as a builder of phenomenally light canoes.

Sears, or Nessmuk as he was better known under his pen name, was a shoemaker of Wellesboro, Pennsylvania, by trade and a woodsman by preference. Throughout life his impelling urge was to visit places far removed from the beaten path, in forest and jungle wilds, often alone. During his last decade, the 1880's, while fighting a losing battle against frail health, he published two books and contributed more than ninety articles to *Forest and Stream.* His book *Woodcraft,* published in 1884, ran through several printings before and after his death in 1890 and is still in print today. The Smithsonian Institution has referred to it as "a classic" in its field.

In 1880 Nessmuk made his first trip to the Adirondacks. Till then he knew the region only through the impassioned prose of the preacher William H. H. Murray and of the surveyor Verplanck Colvin, whose reports of his measurements to the state legislature are highly colored by his emotional attachment to the country. Colvin especially convinced Nessmuk that the Adirondack wilderness was worth seeing before one dies.

Most tourists at that time saw the interior of the region from the stern of a guide-boat. This meant hiring a guide at $2.50 or $3.00 a day and rations for a camping trip of a week or more. In the absence of roads and detailed topographical maps (not available till the turn of the century), visitors were dependent on the guide's woodcraft and familiarity with waterways. But only the well to do could afford this kind of vacation. Nessmuk couldn't. He would not have wanted a guide in any case. He was an old hand at woodcraft, convinced that he could find his way around in wild country anywhere.

Colvin's surveys would help, and he could locate the carries by watching routes the guides took or by asking. So he decided to go it alone. What he needed, considering his age and state of health, was a magic carpet. But he settled for the next best thing available, a Rushton canoe.

Nessmuk's three tours of Adirondack waterways in 1880, 1881, and 1883 were a breakthrough in tourism. He showed that even in roadless areas the services of a guide can be dispensed with, that roughing it alone is part of the fun, and that a small budget can be stretched a long way in the woods without back-breaking labor. He was the forerunner of the thousands of guideless canoeists of today who paddle and carry from Old Forge through the numbered lakes of the Fulton Chain, on to Raquette Lake, and down the Raquette River to Indian Carry, where a portage of three miles opens the Saranac drainage system for further travel. With the help of J. Henry Rushton, Nessmuk showed how to make a success of the do-it-yourself wilderness tour. And he wrote three series of letters about his Adirondack cruises for *Forest and Stream*.

The Nessmuk of 1880 is described by his biographer, Dan Brenan, as follows:

He was then fifty-nine years old, a small wisp of a man, five feet three inches tall and weighing perhaps one hundred and five pounds. He was also suffering from the first serious inroads of tuberculosis, although he did not realize it; but he did know that if he expected to journey through the Adirondack waterways without the help of a professional guide, his canoe would have to be lighter than any craft he had ever used before. That is the reason why he carefully studied the various makers' claims and finally settled on Rushton.*

Early in 1880 Nessmuk wrote Rushton that he wanted a canoe weighing less than twenty pounds. Rushton knew from his own experience all the arguments for lightness. "Here," he

* From *The Adirondack Letters of George Washington Sears, with Explanatory Notes and a Brief Biography* by Dan Brenan (Blue Mountain Lake: The Adirondack Museum, 1962).

said in his 1879 catalog, referring to the waterways of Northern New York, "a few pounds extra weight of boat tells, and the lamb at one end of the carry becomes an old sheep at the other." But had he not gone as far as he could? The same catalog offers portable boats in the smaller sizes weighing from thirty to sixty pounds—"less than any other boat of equal capacity." The thirty-pounder was a midget rowboat eleven feet long. The lightest canoe offered in 1879 was an open thirty-five pounder of thirteen feet.

Rushton may have wondered about the sanity of the man in Wellesboro. But a customer was a customer, and this one seemed to know what he wanted. He should be permitted—after due warning—to drown himself as and where he apparently preferred. Rushton went to work to produce the seemingly impossible—a cedar lapstreak canoe weighing less than twenty pounds and with a carrying capacity of one hundred and fifty pounds or more.

The result was the *Wood Drake,* or *Nessmuk No. 1* as it was later called, the first of five incomparably light canoes that the Boat Shop turned out for Nessmuk during the next five years.

"She's all my fancy painted her, she's lovely, she is light," Nessmuk wrote of the *Wood Drake* from the Moose River in a letter to *Forest and Stream* dated July 21, 1880. "She waltzes on the waves by day and rests with me at night. . . . Perhaps she is the lightest cedar-built canoe in the United States, or anywhere else. Her stems and keel are oak, her ribs red elm, her gunwale spruce, and six pairs of strips [cedar], three-sixteenths of an inch thick, with copper fastenings from stem to stem, leave her weight, when sandpapered ready for the paint, fifteen pounds, nine and one-half ounces. The paint adds about two pounds. She is ten feet long, twenty-six inch beam, with eight inches rise at center; and, propelled by a light double paddle, with a one-fool power in the middle, gets over the water like a scared loon." Nessmuk was still pleased with his craft at the end of the voyage. It "came out tight and staunch" and was taken by rail back to Pennsylvania to be used on the rocky feeder streams of the upper Susquehanna.

A Dickens fan, Nessmuk named his second Rushton lightweight *Susan Nipper,* after the devoted servant in *Dombey and Son.* Though of slightly wider beam than *Nessmuk No. 1,* it was lighter by nearly two pounds. Its finish was oil and shellac instead of paint. The Adirondack cruise of 1881 was dogged by bad weather and the skipper's bad health. But Nessmuk was well content with the *Nipper.* "For a light, comfortable cruising canoe, under paddle," he wrote, "her model cannot be improved."

Rushton offered "Nessmuk Canoes" (Nos. 75, 161, 162) in his 1881 and 1882 catalogs as "probably the *lightest* ones ever made for actual use." Quoting an endorsement from Nessmuk, he added: "I do not publish this statement to persuade any one that they had better buy an *eighteen pound* canoe, for very few men would like one so small, but rather to show that if *such* a boat without being *strengthened by seats, thwarts or braces* will carry 150 pounds safely on our Adirondack lakes and rivers and come out *right and tight* after a 550 mile cruise, the purchaser of the larger sizes has nothing to fear for their strength or seaworthiness." What Rushton hoped to gain from the wide publicity that Nessmuk's *Forest and Stream* articles were bringing him as builder was public confidence in his products and a stimulation in the sales of his standard models. He continued to have misgivings about the usefulness of the extremely light canoe, and the demand for it surprised him. Late in the year 1883 he wrote to Nessmuk in a letter quoted in *Woodcraft:* "I thought when I built the Nessmuk, no one else would ever want one. But I now build about a dozen of them a year. Great big men, ladies, and two, aye, three schoolboys ride in them. It is wonderful how few pounds of cedar, rightly modeled and properly put together, it takes to float a man." The Nessmuk models he refers to weighed sixteen to eighteen pounds. In 1883 he built a still lighter canoe for the little woodsman of Wellesboro.

With health somewhat improved, Nessmuk met his third Rushton canoe at Boonville for another summer's cruise on Adirondack waters. The *Sairy Gamp* (so lettered on the hull and spelled in *Forest and Stream* and *Woodcraft,* though "Sairey" is the nickname for Sarah Gamp in Dickens) was hopefully christened for the tippling nurse in *Martin Chuzzlewit* who took no water.

The *Sairy Gamp* was a phenomenon in lightweight canoe construction. Nine feet long with a beam of twenty-six inches and a rise at center of six inches, she weighed just ten and a half pounds. As the guide who gave Nessmuk a hand on a thirteen-mile carry from the Moose River to Old Forge wonderingly remarked, "It don't weigh more'n a stovepipe hat."

"The lightest canoe ever built of cedar," her skipper boasted, and took the opportunity to expand on his go-light theme. "We, the 'outers,' who go to the blessed woods for rest and recreation, are prone to handicap our pleasures in the matter of overweight; guns, rods, duffle, boats, etc. We take a deal of stuff to the woods, only to wish we had left it at home, and end our trips by leaving dead loads of impedimenta in deserted camps. . . . I hope at no distant day to meet independent canoeists, with canoes weighing twenty pounds or less, at every turn in the wilderness, and with no more duffle than is absolutely necessary." His own load, consisting of two days' rations, extra clothing, equipment for camping out, and canoe, came to about twenty-six pounds.

Nessmuk found the *Sairy* stauncher and steadier than he had been led to expect. "Her maker had warned me he would not warrant her for an hour," he wrote in *Forest and Stream* (August 9, 1883). " 'She may go to pieces like an eggshell,' he said. He had tested her with his own weight (110 pounds), and she closed in at gunwales an inch or more. He advised bracing her, and he thought with me and my duffle aboard she would only be two or two and a half inches out of water at center. 'He builded better than he knew.' She does not close in perceptibly at gunwales, and she has full five inches rise above water when on a cruise, with her skipper and light cargo stowed."

After that summer's cruise Nessmuk took the *Sairy Gamp* home with him and sat her on a shelf to admire. Then he returned her to her maker with a letter which Rushton shrewdly forwarded to the editor of *Forest and Stream*. It reads in part: "To-day I send you back the *Sairy Gamp*. She is of no further use to me. There is not a lake in Tioga County, and I am not going to rattle her over the stones of Pine Creek. She has astonished me; she will be more of a surprise to you. . . . She don't go to pieces worth a cent. . . . I send her back as tight and staunch as the day I took her at Boonville. . . . I once said in *Forest and Stream* I was trying to find out how light a canoe it took to drown a man. I never shall know. The *Sairy Gamp* has only ducked me once in a six weeks' cruise, and that by my own carelessness."

One of the most celebrated canoes in American canoeing annals, the *Sairy Gamp* has had an after-history. Nessmuk's Adirondack letters in *Forest and Stream* in 1883 boosted her into fame. She even acquired a legend. Fred Mather, sportsman, writer, and fish expert attached to Colvin's survey, tells the story that after the 1883 Adirondack cruise Nessmuk paddled the *Sairy* down the Hudson, camping all the way. When he reached New York City, he beached the *Sairy* and, looking around for a place to camp, found Central Park. He had pitched his tent there and was just preparing to cook his supper when a park policeman interfered. The old woodsman, says Mather, spent the night in a cell at police station. If this adventure had actually occurred, it would undoubtedly have resulted in another series of letters to *Forest and Stream* signed "Nessmuk." But the little craft deserves her legend.

Rushton sent the *Sairy Gamp* to New York for exhibit in the *Forest and Stream* office. In 1884 she was also displayed in an industrial exposition at New Orleans. At the Chicago World's Fair in 1893 she was shown in the *Forest and Stream* booth. Before or after that date (Fred Mather says before) she was acquired by the Smithsonian Institution in Washington. In 1918 W. Starling Burgess had her on loan in his airplane manufacturing plant; his purpose was to use her as a model for a lifeboat light enough to be carried on U.S. Navy planes during World War I. Except for this interlude, she has been on exhibit at the Smithsonian until recently. In 1965 she found her way back to the country of her triumph, on loan to the Adirondack Museum at Blue Mountain Lake. Still taut and lovely, she is the smallest of the boats on display in the Callahan Memorial Boat Building there. She seems not to rest on props but to hover, like a magic carpet ready to do the bidding of any lightweight skipper who knows her charm.

Nessmuk ordered two more canoes from Rushton. Late in 1883 or early the next year he ordered the *Bucktail,* largest of the five. Writing about the time of this order, he explained his reasons in *Woodcraft:* "Many years ago, I became convinced that we were all, as canoeists, carrying and paddling just twice as much wood as was at all needful, and . . . I advanced the opinion in *Forest and Stream* that ten pounds of well made cedar ought to carry one hundred pounds of man. The past season [1883] has more than proved it; but, as I may be a little exceptional, I leave myself out of the question, and have ordered my next canoe on lines and dimensions that, in my judgment, will be found nearly perfect for the average canoeist of 150 to 160 pounds. She will be much stronger than either of my other canoes." Like the others, the *Bucktail* was clinker-built, of white cedar, and of similar dimensions, except for greater depth. The ribs were spaced only an inch apart for strength. The weight was about twenty-three pounds.

In 1885 Nessmuk decided to try Florida for his health, which had regressed, and for recreation. Captain Samuel D. Kendall, who contributed to *Forest and Stream* under the pen name of "Tarpon," invited him to Tarpon Springs to be a guest in the Captain's houseboat until other quarters were available. Nessmuk took the *Bucktail* with him for cruising in coastal waters. While there, he ordered a fifth and last Rushton canoe, the lightest of all. Delivered to him in May, 1885, and christened in honor of its maker, the *Rushton-Fairbanks,* with a length of eight and a half feet and a beam of twenty-three inches, weighed nine pounds, fifteen ounces with an oil and shellac finish. Nessmuk considered it ideal for the Florida coast, especially after he had decked it. His adventures in the canoe prompted a new series of letters in *Forest and Stream, The Bucktail in Florida,* telling about the "little Rushton" as he nicknamed it. This canoe, according to a statement in a later Rushton catalog, remained in service in gulf coastal waters for at least two years.

Nessmuk's publicity value to Rushton is incalculable. The old woodsman was read from coast to coast in the pages of *Forrest and Stream* and in his little book *Woodcraft.* Chapter Nine of the latter, "Canoeing," is largely a puff for Rushton's canoes. Nessmuk had begun making his own canoes twenty years earlier, he says. But at forty-five to fifty pounds his best had been too heavy and awkward for him to carry. So he began interviewing by letter the many skilled boatbuilders in the country and studying their catalogs. "There was a wide margin of choice. You could have lapstreak, smooth skin, paper, veneer, or canvas. What I wanted was light weight and good model. I liked the Peterboro canoes, . . . also the veneered Racines; but neither of them talked of a 20-pound canoe. The 'Osgood folding canvas' did. But I had some knowledge of canvas boats. I knew they could make her down to twenty pounds. How much would she weigh after being in the water a week, and how would she behave when swamped in the middle of a lake, were questions to be asked, for I always get swamped. One builder of cedar canoes thought he could make me the boat I wanted, inside of twenty pounds, clinker-built, and at my own risk. . . . I sent him the order."

Thus Rushton became known as the champion builder of the go-light brotherhood. He helped to democratize the sport by supplying inexpensive canoes so light that the traveler could handle them easily on the carries without the services of a guide.

Chapter VI

LAKE GEORGE CANOE
CONGRESS

BY THE FALL of 1880 few canoeists in North
America who read the journals and talked to their fellows
could have been ignorant of Rushton and his canoes. If J.
Henry had been the master strategist of a publicity campaign
—doubtless he did give a gentle push here and there—he could
hardly have improved on the results. Siegfried's two articles in
McBride's Magazine in August and September featured three
Rushton Rob Roys in exploration of the headwaters of the
Mississippi. Numerous puffs in *Forest and Stream* throughout
1880 strongly hinted that Rushton was a favorite builder with
the canoeing editor of that journal. Rushton himself contributed a short article, "Hints on Canoe Building," to the February 12 issue. And from August to November *Forest and
Stream* was running Nessmuk's first series of Adirondack letters with their lyrical praise of the *Wood Drake* and its
builder. Just prior to the unveiling of that canoe, another canoeist, Charles E. Chase, commodore of the Jersey City Canoe
Club, singled Rushton out for praise in the July issue of *Harper's Monthly*. In an article entitled "The Cruising Canoe and
Its Outfit," Chase remarked: "American as well as English
builders, however, too often sacrifice lightness to strength—a
grievous fault, the canoeist finds, after he has tugged the heavy
craft over a few portages. The canoes built by Rushton (Canton, New York) are models in this respect, their average
weight being about fifty-five pounds, and that without sacrifice of the essential element—strength." This comment apparently refers to the fourteen-foot Rob Roy cruising canoe offered in Rushton's catalogs to 1880. As we have seen, Rushton

was soon, in the five craft made for Nessmuk, to outclass his own earlier performance in lightweight canoes.

Another event contributed toward making the year 1880 a turning point in Rushton's career. This was the founding of the American Canoe Association, along with the part that Rushton took in it.

LAKE GEORGE CANOE CONGRESS

In the forepart of the year Rushton received in the mail an invitation, headed "The National Canoe Congress," to canoeists in America to attend a congress on Lake George, New York, for the purpose of organizing a national association. The object was to bring existing and future canoe clubs and canoeists into closer relations under a single parent burgee. The congress was to meet on August 3–6.

Nathaniel Holmes Bishop, author of *The Voyage of the Paper Canoe,* was the moving spirit in this undertaking. In fact, he drafted "The First Call," as the invitation has ever since been termed, set it in type, and "kicked it off" on the small foot-treadle printing press in the attic of his Lake George cottage. It was issued over the names of fifteen of the country's foremost canoeists besides Bishop, who put himself down as "Secretary pro tem." How many copies Bishop ran off on his press, or to whom they were mailed, is not known. Canoeists in Canada as well as the United States were invited.

As Rushton read "The First Call," he must have sensed that here was a chance to meet some of the men whose names by now stood first among the clan of canoeists and to make known the high quality of his canoes. It would be up to him to make the most of the opportunity.

Bishop, who was a good advance press agent, included in one dispatch to the city papers the announcement that Rushton would be present with several of his fine canoes. Rushton followed this up by offering one of his canoes as prize in an open race.

Plans for the congress were worked out in some detail during the spring and early summer and announced in the weekly issues of *Forest and Stream.* According to the May 13 issue, a

Rushton canoe was to be offered as prize to the winner of a paddling race; the boat was already on display at Higginbotham's store in Jersey City. "Rushton's race" (issue of June 10) was scheduled for the afternoon of August 5. Rev. Charles Cressy (issue of July 15), who had won a regatta race on Lake George in the preceding year in a homemade canoe, had just finished making two new ones and would cruise them, in company with a Judge Rand, from Lisbon, New Hampshire, to Lake George by a complicated chain of waterways. Camping grounds for the congress (issue of July 22) were offered by the owners of the Crosbyside and Fort George hotels at the head of the lake, about a mile east of Caldwell, as the village of Lake George was then named. All events, then, would take place in the vicinity of Caldwell and Crosbyside at the head of the lake. The same issue announced that certain Canadian canoeists would cruise to the meeting by Lake Ontario, the St. Lawrence and Richelieu rivers, and Lake Champlain. Mr. Shedd, of Springfield, Massachusetts, would be present with a newly developed model of the Racine Boat Company of Racine, Wisconsin.

The encampment took place as scheduled on grounds adjacent to the Crosbyside Hotel. The first day, August 3, was largely devoted to hammering out a framework for the organization, electing officers, and appointing some committees. The name "National Canoe Association" had been proposed. But with canoeists present from both sides of the border and with a Canadian winning two of the regatta races, it was not surprising that the name eventually selected should have been the "American Canoe Association."

The charter members consisted of a group of "twenty-three extraordinary men," only six of whom had been signers of "The First Call." A. H. Siegfried and J. M. Barnes were among the missing. Lucien Wulsin, however, was present and brought with him the *Betsy D.* He was accompanied by his friend and fellow canoeist of the Cincinnati Canoe Club, Judge Nicholas Longworth. The twenty-three organizing members were:

William L. Alden, New York City
Nathaniel H. Bishop, Lake George, New York
Arthur Brentano, New York City
Rev. C. A. Cressy, Lisbon, New Hampshire
W. W. Cooke, Jr., Whitehall, New York
W. D. Frothingham, Albany, New York
C. F. Gardiner, New York City
E. A. Greenough, Whitehall, New York
F. S. Hubbard, Longwood, Massachusetts
L. E. James, Rochester, New York
Adolph Loewenthal, New York City
Hon. Nicholas Longworth, Cincinnati, Ohio
J. Morris Meredith, Boston, Massachusetts
George N. Messiter, New York City
Dr. Charles A. Neidé, Slingerlands, New York
Rev. George L. Neidé, Jr., Slingerlands, New York
H. H. Palmer, New York City
Frederic Read, New York City
J. H. Rushton, Canton, New York
William P. Stephens, Rahway, New Jersey
Edgar Swain, New York City
Rev. Charles A. Temple, Schenectady, New York
Lucien Wulsin, Cincinnati, Ohio

The following officers were elected:

Commodore, William L. Alden
Vice-Commodore, Hon. Nicholas Longworth
Rear-Commodore, Robert D. Wynkoop (elected *in absentia*), Jersey City, New Jersey
Secretary, N. H. Bishop
Treasurer, J. Morris Meredith

Three of the founders of the ACA were Episcopal clergymen, including George L. Neidé. His brother, Charles A. Neidé, was a dentist, who within a year succeeded Bishop as secretary and Meredith as treasurer when those offices were combined. Charles Neidé was one of the most popular members of the association—tall, handsome, and athletic. During the Civil War he had been an officer with the Army of the Potomac, with a command in the secret service division. He

59

probably did more canoe exploring of the streams along the Atlantic seaboard than any other canoeist of his time. In 1885 he published a book on one of his adventures, *The Canoe Aurora*. He and Rushton eventually became close friends and then business associates.

The name Brentano hardly needs an introduction. This member of the family of bookstore and book-publishing fame was the nephew of the founder of Brentano's in New York City. Arthur soon became manager of that store, expanding and enlarging it to its dominant position. From 1882 Brantano's published the *American Canoeist,* official organ of the ACA.

Nicholas Longworth was a judge of the Ohio State Supreme Court in the early 1880's and was urged to accept the nomination for governor of the state. He declined. His son, Hon. Nicholas Longworth, became the majority leader of the House of Representatives in Washington and was married in the Gold Room of the White House to Alice Roosevelt, daughter of President Theodore Roosevelt. Judge Longworth resigned from the bench in 1883 and resumed private practice of the law until his death in 1890. A man of varied interests and abilities, he was the author of several books, an experimental chemist, a woodcarver, and a mechanic. He designed and built canoes as well as sailed them to victory in the regattas on Lake George.

William L. Alden, the first commodore of the ACA and the leading founder of the New York Canoe Club, was a journalist and diplomat. He wrote leaders for several New York City papers and in 1880 was on the editorial staff of the *New York Times*. In 1885 he left the country to become United States consul general at Rome, and thereafter he lived abroad, in Rome, Paris, and London. He was the author of many books and articles, including several on canoeing. He was a humorist and a good-humored storyteller, a popular figure around the campfire at the Lake George encampments. His popularity with at least one of the other officers, however, seems to have

J. Henry Rushton (1843–1906)

This photograph, taken sometime between 1902 and 1904, gives little evidence of Rushton's frailty and poor health when he first arrived as a young man in Canton, New York.

Leah P. and J. Henry Rushton

Rushton and his bride posed for this c.1883 photograph, shortly after their marriage. A school teacher by profession, Mrs. Rushton soon took an active interest in community affairs.

Joseph B. Ellsworth

Shoe merchant and outdoor enthusiast, Ellsworth offered Rushton his first employment in Canton, in 1869, as a clerk in his store. The two men became close friends, and Ellsworth, along with Milton D. Packard and Cornelius Carter, accompanied Rushton on many a camping and canoe outing. Ellsworth was confidant, critic, and companion of Rushton for over 30 years.

Willard Glazier

Civil War captain, writer, and explorer, Glazier navigated the Mississippi from its source to its mouth. He used a Rushton canoe, *Alice,* and the controversy attending his generally discounted claim of having discovered the true source of the Mississippi augmented the sale of Rushton's canoes.

George Washington Sears (Nessmuk)

Partly through the influence of Nessmuk, an active and articulate woodsman, Rushton was persuaded to build his phenomenally light canoes. Of *Nessmuk No. 1*, which Rushton built for him, Sears said, "She's all my fancy painted her, she's lovely, she is light." The interest in canoes aroused by Nessmuk's prolific writing, notably in *Forest and Stream,* was helpful to Rushton at the time when his canoe business was just becoming commercially viable. (Courtesy Mrs. Marie Sears Bodine)

Lucien Wulsin I (1845–1912)

Wulsin was D. H. Baldwin's original partner in the music company of which Lucien Wulsin Jr. (III) is now the head. Upon his introduction to canoeing, he became a fast friend of Rushton, through a continuous correspondence that ran from 1879 (the date of this photograph and the Wulsin, Siegfried, and Barnes Lake Itasca expedition), through 1880 (when Wulsin became a charter member of the ACA), to about 1904. (Courtesy Lucien Wulsin Jr.)

William P. Stephens

One of the 23 original founders of the American Canoe Association, Stephens, also a boat builder, was Rushton's chief commercial rival. Both men became active in Association affairs, and while they were not always in full agreement, they maintained a friendly and cooperative relationship over many years. (Courtesy Lucien Wulsin Jr.)

Nathaniel Holmes Bishop

Bishop, author of *The Voyage of the Paper Canoe* (1878), was the moving spirit in the formation of the American Canoe Association (ACA). It was he who invited canoeists from all over the United States and Canada to meet at Lake George, in August, 1880, where formal rules were adopted and officers elected for the organization. (Courtesy New York State Historical Association)

William L. Alden and *Shadow*

Alden, unanimously elected the first commodore of the American Canoe Association in 1880, had already been active in establishing the New York Canoe Club, in 1871. Like many other canoeing *aficionados* of his time, Alden was a man of affairs. A well-known *New York Times* journalist and editorial writer, and author on canoes and canoeing, he was to become American consul to Rome.

Earliest Known Photo of the Boat Shop

Rushton is standing at the right of the elm tree in the middle foreground. His father, Peter, with beard, is shown standing to the left of the doorway. Nelson Brown stands to the right of the doorway, with Judd Rushton appearing at the extreme right, under the tree.

Rushton and *Stella Maris*

This canoe is the first of Rushton's Stella Maris models. In design, she is a successful compromise between Rushton's American Traveling Canoe and the Shadow models. *Stella Maris* was designed in 1882, at the request of Rev. Clarence E. Woodman, the canoeing Jesuit priest of St. Paul's church, New York City. (Courtesy Mrs. Evelyn M. Snyder)

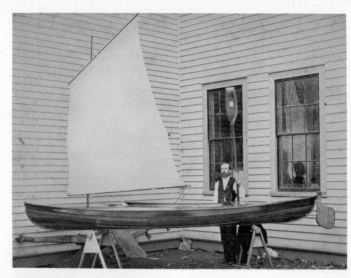

Nelson Brown

Brown was the leading craftsman at the Boat Shop from 1878 to 1916, and for many years its foreman. In this photograph, taken c.1908, he shapes a paddle. Rushton himself owed more to this man for his success as a quality builder than to any other.

A War Canoe

Built to special order, this 17-man war canoe is on its way to a customer in England. Usually, the canoes were carried down the stairs and out the front or side door; this model was so large that a hole had to be cut in the side of the Boat Shop and planking set up, in order to slide it down to ground level. The canoe was then horse-drawn to a port and shipped by water to England.

Rushton and His Workmen (c.1904)

The Rushton shop employed between 20 and 30 men, depending upon the level of demand for the canoes and his other boats. Rushton stands at the extreme left foreground; his son Harry stands at the rear, second from the left. Nelson Brown sits fourth from the left; and Clarence Roundy, under contract to Rushton to build 1,000 Indian Girl canoes in the shop, stands at the extreme right.

Rushton's Saranac Laker

The hull of Rushton's famous Adirondack guide-boat is shown in construction stages. Note that the shape of the hull was obtained by using sawed ribs instead of the usual half-rounds used in canoes, skiffs, and rowboats. The temporary stripping along the exposed ends of the ribs kept the ribs in place while the side strakes of the hull were nailed to the ribs and stems; Rushton guide-boats had no gunwales. [This is photograph #1 in Appendix B.]

Work Room of the Boat Shop

At the left is the form on which the two shells (hulls) in the background were constructed, or "laid-up" as Rushton would have said. Ribbing had yet to be inserted in the finished hulls. [This is photograph #2 in Appendix B.]

Indian Girl Mold

The Rushton Indian Girl models were constructed on this mold. Note the metal strips laid across the hull; these took the place of the hand clinching irons used in the construction of other models. [This is photograph #3 in Appendix B.]

Second Floor

This entire floor served as one large work room, divided into several specialized areas. Two steps in the construction of the Indian Girl model may be observed in this photograph. First, at the left, is a partially completed hull still over the mold. Note the steel clamps holding the inwale to the mold. The second step is shown in the foreground. A hull, removed from the mold, has spreaders in place to keep the hull shape while the remaining side strakes were nailed on. [This is photograph #4 in Appendix B.]

Sanding Room

Noted for their excellent finish, Rushton canoes are pictured during final sanding. The perfectly smooth, finely sanded outer hull not only lowered resistance, but was the obvious sign of Rushton craftsmanship in every canoe he produced.

Indian Girl Hull

The view of this partially completed hull displays the superb rib construction of the Indian Girl model. Nearing completion, three small rectangular holes are evident in the bottom and the spreaders are still in place. [This is photograph #5 in Appendix B.]

Third-floor Drying Room

The drying was a time-consuming but essential step in production. All of the canvas-covered models had to go through the drying process more than once, before the final applications of filler, paint, and varnish.

Harry Rushton

Rushton's son tests the hull-strength of a finished Indian Girl canoe.

se two pen-and-ink sketches were presented by Frederic Remington, the well-known western artist, to J. Henry Rushton
use in his sales catalogs, the winter of 1885–86. Rushton manufactured toboggans (pictured in the first sketch) as a side
during the seasonal lull in his boat-building operations. The second sketch represents a sportsman paddling a Rushton
rican Traveling Canoe in the Adirondacks. Both sketches are published here for the first time, courtesy of the Canton
ic Library, which acquired them by gift from Harry and Mollie Rushton in 1959.

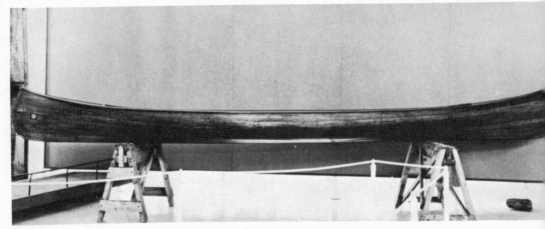

Side View of the Arkansas Traveler

The Arkansas Traveler's Interior

This model, which was not particularly stable afloat, was designed for speed enthusiasts. In 1960, Harry Rushton wrote the author as follows: "Reads like you have an Arkansas Traveler model—28″ beam and considerable dead rise instead of a comparatively flat bottom, like most of our other models. Even 60 years ago there was a slight demand for speed, and this model was so designed. Nice in the water—but if you chewed gum, you needed two sticks at a time, one in each cheek!" One of the Arkansas Traveler models is now on display in the Adirondack Museum.

The Saranac Laker, Side View

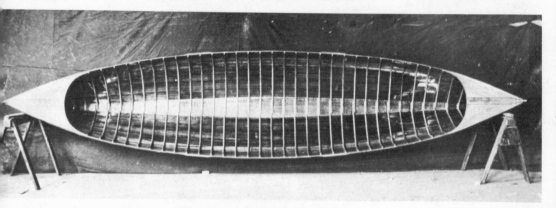

The Saranac Laker, Top View

The Saranac Laker, Rushton's Adirondack guide-boat, might be described as a semi-canoe. It was equipped to be paddled or rowed and was extremely maneuverable. At left, the prow of the hull shows Rushton's method of nailing to achieve the smoothskin construction essential to this model. The middle photograph shows his inner-hull rib construction. (Photos by Helen Durant)

The Huron

The Ugo

The Huron, a canoe with a broad, flat floor, had great carrying capacity and could be used to run shallow rapids. Rushton called it "the hunter's favorite." The Ugo (also U-G·O), one of Rushton's most popular models, was developed from his Arkansas Traveler and his Canadian models. Exceptionally stable and seaworthy, this canoe was advertised for family use.

been short lived. In a letter to Wulsin a few months after the 1880 meeting, Bishop stated that in his opinion a change in the top command would be most acceptable; he felt that there had been enough "silk-stocking" leadership. Writing to the same correspondent in 1881, he returned to this theme: "We must have an American, not an Englishman, for our next commodore, and we must have a cruiser: not a ritualist, but a broad man who will not use silk sails, twelve dollar silk stockings, or a water closet on his canoe."

Frothingham of Albany and Palmer of New York arrived at Crosbyside with two black *tin* canoes, one of them equipped with a brilliant red sail.

William P. Stephens and Rushton were the only two commercial canoe builders among the twenty-three founders and presumably the only builders to attend the congress. According to a newspaper report, canoeists were coming and going through the four days, but the serious work of putting the organization together rested with the charter members. Stephens, who began building boats about the time Rushton did, became one of the most beloved of all that company. His name will remain in the annals of canoeing and yachting.

Stephens was a frequent contributor to *Forest and Stream* over the pen name of "Jersey Blue," one of his popular canoe models, and eventually joined the editorial staff of that journal. A graduate of Rutgers, he began his career as builder with an establishment at Elizabeth, New Jersey. By 1880 he had his own boat shop at Rahway, New Jersey, and in 1881 he was the proprietor and operator of a shop at West Brighton, Staten Island. He was interested also in yachting. With his talent for writing he became the recognized dean of all reporters covering the international yacht races. He wrote books on the subject and became editor of Lloyd's Yachting Register in America.

Will Stephens had another lifelong interest, his love of grand opera. In 1946 he was given personal recognition between the acts at a performance of *Othello* when he was honored as the dean of all members of the Metropolitan Opera

Association. On that occasion Deems Taylor presented him with a platinum diamond ring. Stephens was then ninety-four and had belonged to the Metropolitan Opera Association for over sixty years.

Stephens' book *Canoe and Boat Building for Amateurs,* published by *Forest and Stream* in 1885, along with a portfolio of thirty large plates of drafting designs, was for many years a standard manual in its field. The book makes possible a comparison of his and Rushton's methods. Although both builders favored the clinker-built wooden canoe most popular in the United States at that time, their techniques differed. Stephens, for instance, used rivets; Rushton, clinched nails. Stephens specifies that he placed the ribs of his canoes five inches apart. The narrow, half-round ribs of Rushton's boats are one and a half to three inches apart, a feature that adds strength and helps to prevent warping.

Not always in full agreement, the two rival boatbuilders were nevertheless friendly and cooperative. They were appointed to serve together on a committee of three, under the chairmanship of Lucien Wulsin, to classify different types of canoes and determine time allowances and other regulations for regattas—in other words, a regatta committee. Their work required a frequent exchange of letters in ensuing months. Its immediate charge was to report on classifications for the races held at the 1880 meeting.

A definition of canoe sketched out in "The First Call" and finally incorporated in the constitution was as follows: "A canoe, in order to be placed in the association list and to be entered in races, must be a boat sharp at both ends and not more than thirty-six inches in width on deck. She may be propelled by sails or paddle, or both; but she must be capable of being efficiently propelled by a double-bladed paddle." This is broad enough to cover a variety of craft, and the task of the committee was to classify types so that canoes entered in various races would compete on fairly equal terms. This was its interim report:

Class I. Paddling canoes propelled only by paddle, as the birch bark, open Rice Lake [Ontario], etc.

Class II. Sailable paddling canoes, with paddling qualities predominant, as the Rob Roy, Ringleader [both originally English models of decked, cruising canoes], etc.

Class III. Sailing and paddling canoes, qualities equally divided, as the Shadow, No. 3 Nautilus, Jersey Blue, Clyde, etc.

Class IV. Paddleable sailing canoes, sailing qualities predominant, but adapted to cruising and capable of being paddled, as the Pearl [English model], etc.

Class V. Sailing canoes, only for sailing and not for cruising, as the No. 5 Nautilus and the No. 6 Nautilus.

Two races were held on August 4, 1880. The first, for paddles in sailing canoes, was won by Stephens. The second, for paddles in paddling canoes, was won by a Canadian named Thomas Henry Wallace, with a single-bladed paddle and an undecked canoe. Wallace, from Gores Landing, Ontario, was the champion paddler of Canada at that time, according to his grandson. Neither he nor any other Canadian is listed among the charter members, but Canadians were admitted to membership during the ensuing year. The reason for the delay may have been some initial indecision about whether to restrict membership to United States citizens. The constitution, which opened membership to all canoeists of good character, was not drafted and signed till November 1. At any rate, invitations had been issued to Canadians. The Peterborough, Ontario, canoe club sent regrets, saying that a regatta of their own prevented their coming at the time and promising attendance in 1881. One Canadian who had announced his intention of attending was late in arriving and turned around and went home after enrolling as a member.

August 5 dawned windless, but as the morning wore on without a breeze, it was decided to hold the scheduled races, substituting paddles where sails were called for. The "Rushton race," with a Rushton canoe as the winner's prize, was called at ten in the morning. This was open to all types of canoes. The course was one mile, from Crosbyside to a mark off the

Lake House and return. There were fourteen entries, the highest number to participate in any race. Again Wallace was the winner in an exciting and closely contested race. His time was eleven minutes, ten seconds. Another race, originally intended for sailing canoes only, was held in the afternoon on a course of five miles, the Cincinnati club offering a boat as prize. Cressy was the winner out of nine starters.

A dump race provided a touch of comedy. Stephens, nimbly remanning his boat after upsetting it, was the winner. One entrant lost his paddle, and Wulsin, failing to reman the *Betsy D.,* swam ashore pushing it.

Lack of wind to propel the sailing and the sailing-paddling types of canoes made the results inconclusive. This was realized in ACA circles, but the press gleefully noted that a Canadian had won the Rushton race while nonchalantly smoking his pipe and pausing to scoop up a drink of water. Up to this time Rushton had given little attention to canoes built primarily for racing. His models were all-duty cruising canoes for paddling or sailing or both. In fact, as Stephens pointed out in a letter to Wulsin dated October 20, 1880, the founding members of the ACA were comparatively new to racing, as it had never been a feature in this country "until of late." This fact, he added, made the crews very unequal, as well as the boats.

The August races in this and following years did not bring into question the value of the general-use cruising canoe that both Stephens and Rushton had been building, but they did influence Rushton's future construction. He kept his mind as well as his eyes open at the August regattas, and what he learned led to modifications in old models and the introduction of new ones, including some designed for speed.

The regatta committee carried on discussions by correspondence in ensuing months. Stephens' letters to Lucien Wulsin have been preserved, but unfortunately Rushton's have not. The following excerpts show that Wulsin had to compromise some differences between the two boatbuilders on his committee:

I enclose a letter from Mr. Rushton, with which he sent me yours of the 19th.

I think the allowance he proposes is unfair to some boats, as the long distance race showed a difference between Cressy and myself of 6 min., or about 1 min. per mile, while this rate would give me but 20 sec.

My idea would be to give in your report the results of that race, as a basis for time allowance as you suggest, leaving the matter still open until our next convention, by which time I hope we shall know more about the subject, besides which the boats then present will guide us in establishing a basis for the ensuing races.

I think such canoes as Wallace's should be a distinct class, by all means.

I do not agree with you as to sailing as I think that the Rob Roy has about reached perfection, while the Shadows etc. are yet very far from it, and notwithstanding what I saw you do in the *Betsy D.,* I think that some of our Shadows would leave any Rob Roy far astern. [Stephens was inconsistent in his attitude toward Rushton's Rob Roys. In 1882 he wrote to Wulsin: "If I am not misinformed, you are sailing a Princess this year; if so, what has reconciled you to the extra weight, size, and other disadvantages when you had a canoe that could sail with everything afloat?" The Princess was a model designed by Judge Longworth and made for members of the Cincinnati club. The answer to Stephens' question is probably the simple one that the *Betsy D.* was worn out. Up to the spring of 1882, Wulsin told Rushton, she had traveled more than 6,000 miles by rail, steamboat, and wagon, and more than 2,500 miles in her natural element under sail or paddle.] . . .

I regret that we can not reach some definite and exact conclusions, but I fear it is impossible just yet. (Rahway, N.J., October 24, 1880)

.　　.　　.　　.　　.　　.　　.　　.　　.　　.　　.

I am glad you agree with me as to the English rules as I hope to see them adopted at our next meeting with such additions as we may need. . . . Their 'second class' would include the Shadow and similar boats that we place in our third class, while their 'first class' is the same as classes four and five so that we should need in addition some limit for Rob Roys and also for paddling boats to make it complete. Mr. Rushton does not agree with me, and writes, 'This is an *American* and not an English association. It should have American and not English rules, ideas and usages.' I think this is a very narrow view, as although I have a thorough contempt for those who ape English manners, dress, etc., I believe the English know more about 'technical' canoeing than we will in some time. And I think we should profit by their experience. I expect to have soon a copy of the amended rules of the Royal Canoe Club and will send them. . . .

I think we can give in a better report by spring, as I have realized all along how very crude and incomplete our work of last summer was, and yet I think we accomplished wonders, under the circumstances. It seemed to me that there was at Lake George a tendency to look down on what some one there termed the 'technical' canoeists, as losing the principle of the sport in their racing matches, but canoeists must understand that the best racing boats are in fact the best cruising craft (of their class) and that such details as rules, etc., if formed correctly, encourage . . . cruising. We must keep in view that cruising is the prime object in canoeing, and study by suitable rules to develop a cruising boat in which we can also race if we please, and at the same time must try to shut out all racing machines. (Rahway, December 10, 1880)

The regatta committee made its report at the opening session of the ACA in 1881. At the regular annual meeting a few days later the constitution, which had been approved by a vote by mail, was formally adopted.

Lake George won general approval as the setting for the annual meetings in early years of the ACA. Longworth, who had arrived early for the 1880 meeting, wrote to Wulsin before the latter had left home, "Everything here is simply perfect. It is the ideal paradise of the canoeist." Within a few weeks after the first congress Longworth, Wulsin, and Bishop purchased the islands known as the Three Sisters, five miles from the head of the lake. On concluding the purchase, Bishop wrote rather flossily to Wulsin (August 24, 1880): "I reserve the best until last—'The Sisters' are ours—Sisters that are charming: Sisters that are lovely: Sisters that were born in purity from God's own hand. They will comfort us; they will cheer us—they will never love some one else and leave us—I see their dear forest-crowned heads rising in their glory of tender green out of the bosom of Lac St. Sacrement [the white discoverer

Father Jogues's name for Lake George]; or from the Horicon or 'Silvery Waters' of Cooper." The three owners held the islands, rechristened "Canoe Islands," for the use of the ACA and its members. There the 1881 and 1882 encampments took place.

Rushton was a regular attendant at annual meetings for many years. His dues were paid promptly down to the year of his death in 1906. His canoes often won races in later years. Both he and Stephens were much in evidence in club affairs. Rushton's son Harry (Joseph Henry) became No. 4837 on the rolls of the ACA and at the time of his death in 1963 was among the eighty-five honorary life members of fifty years or more standing. Only two of the twenty-three founding members ever qualified in this category, William P. Stephens and Arthur Brentano.

Rushton went back to Canton, as he was to do after most of the annual meetings, with a pack of new ideas. With Alden's approval, he now rechristened his Rob Roy model the "American Traveling Canoe," the name under which it appears in the 1881 and subsequent catalogs. Alden immediately ordered this model for his son and wrote Rushton on August 15, 1880, that it was "decidedly the best Rob Roy I have ever seen. Its finish is simply superb, while its model—for a canoe intended primarily for paddling—is not only better than that of any other English Rob Roy, but so far as I can judge beyond the need of improvement."

Very likely Alden, with his position on the editorial staff of the *New York Times* and as newly elected commodore of the ACA, was the writer of a full-column editorial on the 1880 congress in that newspaper on August 17. The editorial begins by commenting on the success of the meeting and its significance in canoeing annals. It goes on to particularize: "Next to the organizing of the American Canoe Association, the most valuable feature of the convention was the opportunity which it afforded for the comparison of the different models of canoes. There were present wooden canoes, canvas canoes, paper canoes, and tin canoes; canoes clinker-built and canoes smooth-built; canoes held together with rivets and canoes made of successive layers of thin veneers cemented together. There were all specimens of all the different models." Alden goes on to say that canoeists will always disagree on the question of the absolutely best type of canoe and that it is impossible to build one to serve all purposes. At Lake George it was generally conceded, he says, that the Shadows built by Everson, of Williamsburg, and the Jersey Blues built by Stephens, of Jersey City, were best in the class of sailing canoes. But the editorial reserves its highest praise for the boatbuilder of Canton. It concludes:

The peculiar pattern of the Rob Roy canoe built by Rushton of Canton, New York, and christened by him the "American Traveling Canoe," was unanimously recognized as being the most beautiful and serviceable boat of the kind to be found either in this country or in England. It has not the carrying capacity of the Shadow, nor can it carry anything like the same amount of sail; but as a paddling canoe, to be used chiefly in shallow and narrow rivers, it is without equal. Moreover, unlike the English Rob Roy, it is an excellent sea boat, and will live in any sea where a Shadow can live if it is paddled by strong and skillful arms. It cannot take the place of a sailing canoe, nor can a sailing canoe take its place, but the builder has certainly succeeded in building the strongest, lightest, most graceful, and most useful paddling canoe that has yet been devised.

J. Henry had not been idle at the canoe congress.

Chapter VII

CHANGE AND PROGRESS

THE YEARS 1880 to 1886 were a time of change, progress, and fulfillment for Rushton. They were his best years. His business prospered as the sport of canoeing drew increasing numbers of followers. Praise for his boats came from all sections of the country and from overseas. Ownership of a Rushton canoe became a status symbol among both amateurs and veterans of the sport. Rushton himself, in his late thirties and early forties, retained in the full vigor of maturity the inventiveness and adaptability of earlier years. Little was fixed or standardized in the canoe building of the eighties. Individuals, clubs, and builders engaged in a search for what they called "the perfect canoe" or the "all-around canoe." Suggestions for improvement in models poured in, and Rushton welcomed them, adopting what he found to work, carrying it a step farther—often so far in fact that he had a new model on his hands. He was too busy to stop and take pride in his work.

The effect of success on his personal life was to expand his energy. He worked harder, longer, and more fruitfully than ever before at his craft. Yet he found time for civic service in Canton. He made new friends. He fell in love, married, had two sons, and enjoyed a happy home life.

He was fortunate in that his own most vigorous and creative years coincided with the peak of enthusiasm over the sport of canoeing. Later the bicycle, the powerboat, and the motorcar diluted this enthusiasm. Moreover, as more and more rivers were harnessed for water power and lakes ringed by summer cottages or suburbs, exploration by canoe lost some of its appeal. In the eighties, however, the canoeist in America still enjoyed open horizons everywhere outside the cities. "Canoeing never flourished in any country, nor grew so fast in favor as in America," said an editorial writer in *Forest and Stream* in 1882. "The sport has seen a wonderful growth in the last two years. . . . Canoes . . . are sold to all parts of the country as fast as they can be supplied, . . . all of which is evidence of the rapid spread of a fondness for this most charming, robust and romantic method of vagabondizing with benefit of body and mind. It is probable that three canoes are turned out in America for every one set afloat in Great Britain. America is the natural home of the canoeist."

The founding of the American Canoe Association was a strong influence in promoting the sport. The original handful of twenty-three organizing members in 1880 vaulted to 172 enrollees in 1881, 224 in 1883, and over 700 by 1885. In the Lake George meet of 1881 about seventy canoes were on hand, and in 1882 one hundred and twenty-five. That year a Peterborough, Ontario, man was elected commodore, and the meet of 1883 was appropriately held in Ontario at Stony Lake. It was the largest encampment yet, with four hundred campers on hand and three hundred canoes.

In 1880 canoeing news was handled in *Forest and Stream* in a few brief notes tacked on to the yachting columns. By 1883 it was a separate department in the weekly, running to two or three columns of fine print, with editorials, news items, and contributions on canoe construction, racing, long-distance cruising, and other topics. New canoe clubs were announced at frequent intervals, several in small towns over the country as well as in the cities. Early in 1884 the founding of the St. Lawrence Canoe Club of Canton, New York, was announced and its burgee illustrated. The first officers were: commodore, J. H. Rushton; vice-commodore, M. D. Packard; secretary-treasurer, L. P. Hale; and measurer, J. W. Rushton, the builder's half-brother. There were eleven active members at the start.

The sport was by no means monopolized by club members. In December, 1882, the canoeing editor of *Forest and Stream* put in a word for the happily unorganized devotees. "Canoeing is essentially a solitary pastime, a sport for each paddler in his individual capacity; hence, clubs and organizations may not cut great figures [a reference to the popularity in the United States of the double-bladed paddle and the decked canoe with manhole in the center designed for one, though in longer models capable of carrying two]. . . . Canoe clubs are good in their way for headquarters and accommodation, but . . . organization and red tape are really foreign to the happy-go-lucky Bohemian color which is one of the chief attractions of this knockabout existence. The enthusiast with the paddle is not a racing man, but more a passionate traveler, bent upon exploring strange climes in search of nature's beauties in their purity, yet undefiled by man." This vagabond was the individualist who, along with the club members, bombarded Rushton with five thousand letters a year in the early eighties—letters full of fantasies about the "perfect canoe."

The boat business flourished. According to the Lake George *Mirror* in 1881, "The canoe manufacturers, Rushton and Stephens, have been crowded with work to fill orders received since the [American Canoe] Association was formed. Many builders have turned to this style of craft." In the same year Rushton issued a new twenty-four page illustrated catalog describing "ninety-five different patterns and sizes" of his "portable sporting boats" and canoes, the edition running to ten thousand copies. He added another agent, John Wilkinson, in Chicago. "Rushton boats," the Canton *Plaindealer* amplified, "are now known from Maine to Florida and from the Atlantic to the Pacific. Business is so heavy that Mr. Rushton keeps several hands constantly at work." On April 20 of the same year the *Plaindealer* noted that Rushton had sold forty-five boats since January 1, about half the total for the entire preceding year, and this prior to the rush orders of late spring. Most of these were canoes. "He has rented an additional work shop for the summer—the old Champlin wagon shop—and doubled his force, employing at present six workmen." He also diversified his business by taking on the agency for Winchester rifles, which he offered to barter on the local market for pine, cherry, ash, and cedar lumber.

Rushton somehow found time to act as his own secretary in these years. In closing a letter to Lucien Wulsin on March 21, 1881, he remarked, "Well, it is 9 p.m. and I have twenty-six letters yet untouched before me"—all to be answered in his beautiful Spencerian style of longhand.

Forest and Stream, in which Rushton had advertised since 1875, featured his products in a full-page article on March 17, 1881. Illustrations of his Tandem Sailing Canoe, American Traveling Canoe, Sneak Boat, Sportman's Boat, and single and double paddles accompanied the article. The writer (possibly the canoeing editor) observed: "This week we take the opportunity of discussing in full the work turned out by Mr. J. H. Rushton, of Canton, New York, whose name has become a household word among American sportsmen and canoeists alike. From small beginnings Mr. Rushton climbed the steps of the ladder to fame and competency through sheer industry, hard work and clear-headed foresight. . . . His work speaks for itself and is his recommendation wherever seen. . . . By strict selection of materials and use of much clinker fastening, as well as a plan of boat building thoroughly original, Mr. Rushton turns out a boat which has few equals in America and certainly none in Europe."

After the Lake George meet of the ACA in August, a contributor to the same periodical, William Whitlock, a prominent canoeist of New York City, offered his opinion that "of makers Rushton made much the best show, both as to finish and for good thorough work." The ACA prize for 1881 was awarded to the Rushton-built, Wulsin-owned *Annie Dell* as the best equipped canoe for cruising. Toward the end of the year (November 17) *Forest and Stream* noted that a Rushton craft would soon be floating in waters that had cradled an ancient civilization: "An American pleasure boat will be added to the motley craft on the Nile this winter. Mr. Rushton has built for Mr. August Belmont, Jr., of this city, one of his famous boats, which will be launched among the bullrushes of that famous Egyptian river. We saw the craft at the establishment of Mr. Squires before it was shipped, and it was a model of grace and beauty. We venture to say that after this no winter on the Nile will be complete without a Rushton boat."

Rushton needed larger and more centralized quarters than the scattered small shops he was using in 1881 for work and storage. On October 19, 1881, the *Plaindealer* announced that he had begun to build "a roomy building on the corner between State and Water [Riverside] streets in this village." This was soon to become known as the Rushton Boat Shop.

Rushton picked a site at the lowest point in the village deliberately. From the time of his shoe-clerking days with Ellsworth, he had never forgotten the ravages of the two village fires. In 1881 Canton was still without adequate fire protection. Its sanitary needs were also neglected and deficient. The family pump and well and outdoor privy were still necessities. Rushton now turned his attention to these matters. He was appointed chairman of a new village board authorized to install a water and sewage system throughout the "corporation." He took hold of this project with the energy and promptness typical of him.

Public sentiment had to be aroused, a large bond issue voted by the taxpayers, engineers hired to lay out the proposed systems and draw up plans and specifications, and of course the necessary contracts let. This was done in a minimum of time. For the following twenty years Rushton continued as chairman of the village's Board of Water Commissioners.

Of course, he had a personal interest at stake in bringing about such improvements, just as he had had foresight in selecting the location for his new and bigger shop. Fire was always a hazard for any woodworking establishment such as his. He also needed cheap, dependable power. So, hardly were the new water mains laid, the new ninety-foot standpipe erected, the new pumping station put on the shore of the Grass

River, than the Boat Shop was equipped with a new water motor by which to operate its machinery. Later this system was replaced by steam power, as steam was also necessary in boat construction. Interestingly, safety measures proved most effective in the plant. It never experienced a serious fire, while several other local industries fell victim to flames and some were completely destroyed.

The canoe *Annie Dell* was a product of another of those fruitful exchanges of ideas between Rushton and veteran canoeists. Such an exchange took place through correspondence with Lucien Wulsin as a new craft, evidently to be used in August at Lake George, was under order. On April 12, 1881, Rushton wrote to Wulsin: "I tried your suggestion on the siding to get full line at gunwale—won't work. In fact spoiled a canoe. The shape of the stems and siding must do it in order to stay. I think I will have to make a new form—and bend the stems different. . . . Will also try a lower deck if 10 inches is enough clear and I think it is with the 5 ft. cockpit. We will have a new canoe I guess. If successful we must name it." Always willing to learn a new trick, Rushton tried to follow the suggestions of customers whose knowledge and experience he respected. If the suggestion did not work, he tried a little experimenting of his own to achieve the desired result. Wulsin was pleased with the canoe he received that year. At the meet he and another member of the Cincinnati Canoe Club, A. E. Heighway, used this craft in the races. Manned by the latter, it won first prize in the paddling race, first class. By placing in other races too, the Cincinnati group carried off the palm that year. Rushton had offered one of his canoes as a prize in another of the races of 1881, the paddling and sailing race, which drew a large number of contestants. This prize boat may have been a twin of the *Annie Dell*. Before the meet it was described as of "modified American Traveling design," one and a half inches deeper on the bow, with a little change made in the rake of the stems and gunwale line. The announcement added: "To Mr. Lucien Wulsin, of the CCC, and the builder belong the credit for whatever improvement there is." This echoes a statement Rushton made in a letter to Wulsin: "You know I want to give you the best and most perfect canoe in every respect, if possible. I have to depend much on the opinions and experience of my friends who use the canoes."

The *Annie Dell* apparently did not result in a new model name but in an improved American Traveling Canoe. In the 1882 catalog Wulsin is quoted, "By continued experiment we have brought them [American Traveling Canoes] to the point where they will sail with anything afloat." Rushton then points out a few changes in this model "as now perfected." Its depth has been increased by adding to the curvature of the deck, thus giving more sleeping room and storage capacity for long cruises. Its sheer of three and one half inches makes it "more seaworthy."

Correspondence with other canoe enthusiasts occasionally resulted in entirely new models. The co-originator of the Stella Maris, for instance, was the young pastor of St. Paul's Church (Roman Catholic) of New York City, Rev. Clarence E. Woodman. Canoeing was among the varied interests of this churchman, who was also a lecturer on the sciences of electricity and astronomy. During the fall of 1881 he addressed letters of inquiry to Lucien Wulsin, already known as an authority from his participation in ACA meets. The following letter defers to Wulsin as an expert on design and equipment:

St. Paul's Church
59th Street and Ninth Avenue
New York, Oct. 28th, 1881

My dear Sir:

Your favor of the 26th instant is just received, and I thankfully avail myself of the permission to inquire further.

My brother and I propose to invest, respectively, in a Rushton American Traveling Canoe and a Shadow. I am not quite decided whether to order the Shadow from *Rushton,* or from *Everson*—the *soi-disant* "old original Jacobs." Can you assist me in my choice, by telling me which make you consider preferable? Your experience must have contrasted the two:—in whose favor? Rushton claims to furnish the "Lateen Rig"; is it like yours? and does he make it as well as the Mr. Ellard you recommend?

What size of Main and Dandy would your good judgement suggest

1st for A. T. Canoe (26 in. beam 14 ft. long)

2nd " Shadow " (28 " " " " ") ?

You say your Canoe is 27" beam, 14'5" long. I do not remember seeing that size on Rushton's Catalogue. What particular model is it, please.

I hope this letter won't bore you *too* much.

Very truly yours,
CLARENCE E. WOODMAN

Letters received by Rushton have not survived, except for those quoted in his catalogs. We do not know precisely what instructions or suggestions accompanied Woodman's order for a Rushton canoe. We do know, however, that a new and popular model resulted from this contact. It was the Stella Maris, or Star of the Sea, number 230 in Rushton's 1882 catalog, described in part as follows: "Some canoeists have said to us, 'If the American Traveling canoe had more sheer I should like it better.' Well, we like to please our friends, and the result of trying in this case has been the production of a most beautiful little craft with the same length and beam as the A.T., but with nearly the SHEER of the Shadow. The first of this model was built for Rev. C. E. Woodman, of New York City, who says of her, 'Perhaps there *can* be a more beautiful boat built, but I am convinced there never *has* been.' "

Woodman was not alone in his admiration of the Stella Maris. A few months after it was first offered early in the year, it became popular. Six or more of this model were at the Lake George meet of the ACA in August. A Canadian, Robert Tyson, present on that occasion, expressed his admiration of the Stella Maris and her builder in the Toronto *Mail,* as quoted in *Forest and Stream:* "This little 'star of the sea' well deserves her popularity. . . . She is very fast under paddle, and is a remarkably handsome little craft. . . . Canoeists generally owe a debt of gratitude to Mr. Rushton for the practical way in which he has worked up and developed several of the most useful and popular types of canoes, especially when, as he says, 'There is very little money in it.' There is so much fitting and special work about decked canoes that they are not nearly so profitable to build as the open rowboats."

Woodman and Wulsin were two of a kind. They were groping. They had ideas, mental images of what they thought to be the perfect canoe. So did Rushton. He might have put off their suggestions and demands and still received their orders. Instead he chose to experiment. He borrowed, he copied, he leaned heavily on the ideas of others, and then in the end he came up with something which bore the stamp of his own genius—something different and, for the purpose intended, better.

Rushton himself commented on the origin of new models in his shop in a contribution to the November, 1883, number of the *American Canoeist*. This article was prompted by an affront he had taken to an implication in that magazine that A. H. Siegfried had been the originator and designer of the original *Kleiner Fritz* and therefore of Rushton's Rob Roy model. It was an inadvertent statement by the editor, quickly modified once Rushton took up his own defense. Then, when the dispute had cooled, came the article entitled "Origin of Some Canoes," quoted here in part:

A fine canoe is never the result of chance. The designer or builder does not go to bed at night and awaken in the morning to find his craft ready for the water. Neither is his first attempt likely to be quite successful. Little by little the canoe approaches perfection....

The Rob Roy was faulty because of lack of sheer, small floor, and short manhole. The Nautilus had excessive sheer....

After a trial of these canoes [Rushton's first, ordered by A. H. Siegfried in 1876], their purchaser advised as the best model for inland work, a modification of the Rob Roy. The changes were to be greater bearings, more sheer, and longer cockpit. Other trifling changes were made, and in 1880, the canoe as thus perfected was called the American Traveling Canoe. Several of these canoes, among them the *Betsy D.* and the *Kleine* [*sic*] *Fritz,* became noted for long cruises. The former is said by her owner to have covered over 8,000 miles by rail, river, and lake. The latter served the

Racine Boat Company as a model from which their St. Paul was built, she being placed in their hands for that purpose by her owner who claimed to be her inventor (?), though all he had to do with her construction was to make the suggestions above mentioned.

Though very popular for a time, actual use for several seasons showed the weak points in her model, and time and study suggested to her builder important changes which could be made to advantage. The plans for the new canoe were yet imperfect when a correspondence was commenced with Rev. C. E. Woodman with regard to a light sailing canoe for himself. During the succeeding weeks the Post-office Department was benefited muchly, and the work on the new canoe progressed. . . .

Many changes are made in canoes to meet the wants or fancies of canoeists. Some of these are hobbies of the individual; no one else would have one like it. Others are real improvements which may be used to advantage by others.

The builder is constantly indebted to the canoeist for ideas of greater or less value. Sometimes they are just what he needs to enable him to perfect half-formed plans of his own. Again they are the germ to which he adds his own practical knowledge with good results. He also has [been] offered many plans and theories which if worked up would produce nondescripts of the worst kind.

It is doubtful whether any first-class canoe is the result of any one person's study. The builder's shop is the mill, he is the miller. The ideas of others are grists and, whatever their proportion of wheat and tares, he is expected to make good flour. This it is his study, his wish to do. It is his life work, and often it is a labor of love as he spends many a day and many a dollar in experiment.

The article is interesting evidence of Rushton's receptivity to change in the canoeing scene of the eighties. He grasped each promising new idea, suggestion, or request and adjusted himself and his business to the change. As a student of canoeing history has remarked, "Because of him, Canton became the very center of canoe-construction, the point on which both canoeist and builder focused their attention."

Early in the year 1882 the new Boat Shop was fully occupied and in production. Perhaps Rushton invited the canoeing editor of *Forest and Stream* to come to Canton and inspect the new building. At any rate, the issue of April 6 gives a description of Rushton's business and of his new quarters. "He has now built up a vast trade commanding the world for a market. The little shop has been followed by a regular 'factory' of a size and completeness which astonishes the visitor. Canton, hitherto an almost unknown inland town, has become famed across the seas as the center of one of the most thriving establishments of its kind. In fact, Rushton has become Canton." The writer adds that Rushton carried a stock of about one hundred and fifty canoes and sold them so fast in the spring that a "score of hands" could not keep up with the demand, though new labor-saving machinery had been introduced. "Canoes are now set up and finished off wholesale, in fleets at a time, though each one receives that personal care and supervision which has given to Rushton's work such an enviable reputation." The Boat Shop is described as a building three stories high, eighty by thirty feet, with two wings, each twenty-four feet long and eighteen wide. The cellar was used for seasoning timber by furnace and other processes. On the first floor lumber and other materials were received and stored. The second floor, equipped with steam boiler, was used for general work, offices, and even sleeping quarters. On the third floor boats were finished and stored. The attic was a receptacle for patterns. (Older citizens of Canton today, for whom the Boat Shop was a fascination in boyhood, remember a different arrangement of the floor space in the nineties and the first decade of the present century. Changes were doubtless made as new machines and methods were introduced.) The *Forest and Stream* writer concludes, "To Mr. Rushton's personal interest in behalf of canoeing the sport owes no little of its present popularity and the deep root it has taken with the masses of our population."

In spite of brisk business, Rushton continued to insist that there was little money in making canoes. A major reason for this was no doubt his reluctance to standardize models, his constant experimentation and introduction of new models. Linked with this feeling was his personal interest in his customers and his desire to please them by fine workmanship, good materials, and beautiful design. Then, having done all this, he sometimes offered a favorite customer a discount of up to 20 per cent on the list price. Moreover, the business was seasonal, with the bulk of orders coming in spring and summer, requiring him to build up heavy inventories in the fall and winter. In December, 1882, according to *Forest and Stream,* Rushton was working up ten thousand dollars worth of stock, representing thirty thousand dollars in finished canoes, for the spring trade. Interest on bank loans necessary to float this inventory ate into profits. "After paying all expenses," he said, "there is *not* the margin on canoes many suppose there is."

Rushton's satisfaction ran deeper than profits, however. In 1882 and 1883 occurred another of those marathon voyages in a Rushton canoe that gave drama to canoeing and prestige to the builder of a sturdy and gallant little craft.

The voyage had been planned for some time, the route carefully studied. Preparations were complete by the August meeting of the American Canoe Association in 1882. When a bystander heard of the plan to cruise from the Adirondacks to the Gulf of Mexico, he asked incredulously, "But you surely do not propose to make the trip in that little thing?" "That little thing" was the canoe *Aurora,* of the Princess model, built by Rushton expressly for this cruise. Along with her fittings, which included two lateen sails and a double-bladed paddle, she weighed eighty-five pounds. The skipper of the *Aurora* was the popular, often re-elected secretary of the ACA, Charles A. Neidé, the dentist formerly of Slingerlands, now of Schuylerville. His companion on the voyage was a retired sea dog, Captain Samuel D. Kendall, then living in St. Johnsbury, Vermont. Having served aboard nearly every type of ship afloat, Kendall had lately taken a fancy to the smallest craft of all. His canoe was the homemade *Solid Comfort,* somewhat of a misnomer as the voyage proved. Neidé had ordered a tent to fit the *Aurora.* He tells of being lulled asleep at night as his craft rocked at anchor, snugly bedded down on board under his tent, while Kendall pulled the *Solid Comfort* ashore and bivouacked.

"One glorious morning in August, 1882," Neidé writes in his book *The Canoe Aurora: From the Adirondacks to the Gulf* (1885), "at the close of the American Canoe Association meet, at the Canoe Islands, we launched our craft from the shore of lovely Lorna Island, and glided out over the shimmering surface of Lake George. The start was auspicious . . . full of happy portents for the thousands of miles before us." The voyage lasted about five months till the two canoes beached at Pensacola, Florida, in February of the following year. The route went through the southern part of Lake Champlain to Whitehall, thence through the Northern Canal (now Champlain Canal) and Hudson River to Troy; it then crossed the state by the Erie Canal and other waters to Buffalo, where began a portage of seventy miles by rail to the headwaters of the Allegheny River. They then paddled down the Allegheny, the Ohio, and the Mississippi to the Gulf. The voyage concluded with salt-water sailing eastward along the shore to Pensacola, where Neidé called it a day. Captain Kendall, reinvigorated by the old familiar element of salt water, sailed on along the Florida coast to Tarpon Springs. There he docked the *Solid Comfort* and with his wife proceeded to make his home. There too Nessmuk came by invitation to occupy a corner of the Captain's boathouse in 1885 and to write the series *With the Bucktail in Florida*.

The cruise was probably the longest recorded in the United States for any modern canoe up to that time, exceeding the mileage of Glazier's cruise down the Mississippi in 1881. Neidé's log showed 3,300 miles, Kendall's 3,800 in round figures.

One way or another, the cruise was given much publicity over a period of several years. During its course *Forest and Stream* checkpointed the voyagers, announcing, for instance, that they "were last heard from January 27 crossing from Fort Gaines to Fort Morgan, Mobile Bay." The *Aurora* became a celebrated craft in canoeing circles. In February, 1884, Neidé wrote of her in *Forest and Stream,* identifying her as Rushton-built, of the Princess model, fifteen feet long and thirty-one inches wide. She never leaked a drop, he said, except through a small hole punched through the centerboard case. Yet, he added, "My canoe had the roughest kind of usage. Heavily laden, she was portaged for seventy miles by rail and many more in a springless wagon over rough roads; was jumped over dams, tracked over the stony bed of the Allegheny River, banged against snags in the Mississippi, and dashed on the hard sand beaches of the Gulf of Mexico by the powerful force of the surf. I used her as a sleeping apartment for more than five months." Then in 1885 came Neidé's book, which had a circulation abroad as well as in this country. For the next two years *Forest and Stream* eagerly promoted it by quoting reviews (the book was published by the same company that produced the magazine). Neidé was always careful to give Rushton full credit for the *Aurora*. And with good cause. For soon after, he took the position of general sales agent for Rushton boats, an association that lasted at least a year and a half.

The Princess became one of Rushton's more popular models. Judge Longworth had designed it as a sailing rival to the Shadow, giving it fuller lines and more sheer. According to a statement in one of Rushton's catalogs, the original Princess was shipped to the builder by the Cincinnati Canoe Club, and Rushton became the official builder for that group. On March 2, he wrote to Wulsin: "Now I am going to build another [of the Princess model]. I think I can improve it." The Princess was a trim sailer with the newly invented Atwood centerboard, yet easily responsive to the paddle.

In the new canoe clubs and at the annual meets of the ACA, canoeists across America in the early 1880's were solicitously comparing the performance records of the many craft available to them, demanding improvements, and speculating on that elusive thing, the perfect canoe. Every definition of perfection was challenged by another. After many months of controversy in the pages of *Forest and Stream,* the academic mind, accustomed to waiting till the evidence and the arguments were all in and then weighing them judiciously, gave the balanced judgment. In a speech quoted in the December 6, 1883, issue, Professor Edwin Fowler, of the Knickerbocker Canoe Club of New York City, questioned the existence of any Platonic absolute. There is no more perfection in canoes than in wives, Fowler claimed; there are only convenient compromises. "An ideal canoe is a bundle of compromises, yielding something of her paddling speed to be able to sail fairly, sacrificing a portion of her sailing lines to secure reasonable lightness and sharpness, losing somewhat of her steadying weight and momentum for the sake of portability, and being less portable because she must be strong and stiff. . . . A canoe must be equally at home with wings for the breezes and with paddles for the water; yet able to move on the legs of her master over dry land."

The job of the builder was somehow to mate that bundle of compromises with those individualists who wanted in a canoe the infinite variety that never stales. Hence the new look that Rushton repeatedly gave to old models and the constant generation of new ones. A glance at his catalogs over four successive years shows what a resourceful marriage broker he was. In 1880 his circular offered, besides a line of rowboats, canoes of two kinds: first, open ones of various sizes built like his rowboats except for the fittings and a somewhat narrower beam in proportion to length; second, decked canoes of an improved Rob Roy type for paddling and sailing. Next year the circular became a catalog, and Rushton offered, besides open canoes for "hunting, fishing or trapping," the Nessmuk canoe, the Barnegat Sneak Boat (a hybrid for duck hunting), and "sailing and cruising canoes" numbers 79–95, of which the American Traveling Canoe (an improved Rob Roy) was the most popular, and a new model, the Shadow, was copied by permission from W. L. Alden's original at the Lake George meet of 1880. The catalog of 1882 retains the models of the preceding year and adds a second Nessmuk model, the Stella Maris, the Princess, the St. Lawrence (a modified Shadow with a wider beam for better sailing), and two tandem canoes (decked, sixteen feet in length, and fitted for two persons). The 1883 catalog expands the number of open canoes from thirteen to twenty-one and offers three Princess models instead of the one of the previous year; it adds also the Ellard and the Grayling. These changes reflect the ferment in canoeing circles during the early eighties.

Rushton must have read with interest Professor Fowler's statement about the canoe as a bundle of compromises. Four months later he followed it with a statement of his own in *Forest and Stream* (March 27, 1884) entitled "The All-Around Canoe." He begins by saying that the canoe articles in *Forest and Stream* have greatly interested him both because he is an old woodsman and because he is a builder of modern canoes. He gets about five thousand letters a year from canoeists, several hundred of which go into details. He continues:

What is the best all-around canoe? Is it the canoe that will suit everybody for everywhere and everything? If so, it will never be built. . . . The professional builder has not only his own ideas and experience, but those of hundreds of others, and he is constantly trying experiments either on his own account or in building to order.

In naming the best all-around canoe, there are too many things to be considered to have any one craft fill the bill. First, the boat must fit the purchaser's eye. Mind, I say his eye, not yours or mine. We must suit the mental canoeist. Second, we must fit the physical canoeist. That, you will say, is easy; a simple problem in weights and measures. True, if you take care of that other fellow, the mental man; but if you don't, it is about even chances that the mind will insist on cramming the body into a craft but half large enough, or else compel weak and untrained muscles to do the proper work of an athlete. Third, we must consider where the boat is to be used. . . .

For the canoeist of medium weight, for inland cruising, where the paddle is used as much as the sail, and where supplies may be procured easily and often, a canoe 14 ft. x 26 in. or 27 in. is the best all-around canoe. For a canoeist of heavy weight, one 14 ft. x 30 in. would be better for the same purpose. For lakes many miles in extent or the seaboard, a canoe 14 ft. x 30 in. is thought small enough, and many would prefer 15 ft. x 31 in., or even larger. If compelled to adopt one size for all men, all places and all purposes, there is no question but that the 14 ft. x 30 in. or 31 in. would be the best all-around canoe. . . .

I may say in conclusion that I build more canoes either 14 ft. x 27 in., or under, than all others. Probably because there are so many more miles of inland waters than seaboard.

Compromise is a fairly simple thing for Professor Fowler, involving only traits of the canoe; it is more complicated for the builder, who must fit into the equation the traits of the cranky canoeist.

Chapter VIII

MARRIAGE

LEAH PFLAUM, Rushton's bride, was not a local girl but came from downstate—Port Jervis. Surviving relatives have different explanations of the circumstances that brought the couple together. According to one, Rushton met Leah on one of his business trips. According to another, their friendship came about through a mutual acquaintance, a girl whom Rushton had known in Edwards and who became a teacher. When Leah came to Edwards one summer to visit this teacher-friend, J. Henry first met her.

Leah was herself a teacher. She was small, just a shade taller than J. Henry himself, and had a slender, well-proportioned figure, regular features, and dancing dark eyes.

Rushton had been a single man for forty years, and for the last ten years a man with a single purpose—building boats. Prior to that, his chief concern had been survival. Now that he had the means to marry and the right girl turned up, he did not hesitate. Apparently his Canton friends had too little time to realize what was happening. The *Plaindealer* announced that the marriage was a surprise to them. It took place early in September, 1883, in New York City, where J. Henry and Leah exchanged vows in a civil ceremony before Mayor Edson in City Hall. She was twenty-five, nearly fifteen years younger than Rushton.

Leah came to live in Canton among strangers, some of whom raised their eyes at first, especially when she accepted the church of her husband's faith. Rushton's grandfather and his Uncle Henry had been members of an Edwards group of religious liberals who established a local Universalist Society and built a church in that village. The Universalists were strong at that time in St. Lawrence County. Members of the faith pioneered the founding of the denomination's first theological school, located in Canton. By this effort St. Lawrence University came into being. The parish of the Canton church included the majority of the local businessmen. Original sin and eternal damnation had no part in the Universalist's faith. Brotherly love, the universal fatherhood of God, the universal salvation of mankind, truth, and respect for individual integrity were the essence of the doctrine. This was the faith of J. Henry and Leah. Their two boys attended the Universalist Sunday school, and they were members of the parish.

"They were such a lovely couple," Mary Winslow Harmon, a surviving niece, recalls, "so happy together. Uncle Henry was so full of fun at the table, a lively and interesting, well-informed man, always joking and telling stories. Oh, he kept those two small boys in hand, and don't you think he didn't, for he was strong on discipline. He and Leah were well matched, always interested in the same things. You see, as a young girl I lived with them in their home on Hodskin Street for a time."

Rushton built a new residence for his bride, one of the best houses in the village at that time. It was located a short block from the Boat Shop, just up Chapel Street hill and around the corner. It was a square frame house with a flat roof, unornamented except for a cupola, in a style typical of its period in Canton. There was a lattice-walled summerhouse in the side yard and a large barn in which a span of horses was kept. The house has been refaced but is still standing today. Empire furniture graced the downstairs rooms when the Rushtons owned it. Though not wealthy, they lived in comfort.

In designing the house, they planned a "sail room," over which Leah took charge. She became a proficient sailmaker. Located in a back ell of the house, this second-floor room afforded ample space for outlining the various types and patterns of lateen, Bailey rig, and leg-of-mutton sails with which to outfit Rushton skiffs and canoes. Two or three sewing machines were installed next to an outside wall. They were operated by a water-power motor. Leah hired local women to assist her.

After the canvas or muslin was washed, shrunk, and dried, the yard-wide lengths were stitched together and the sail cut out according to the patterns outlined on the floor. Then came the hemming and grommeting. During peak production the sail room hummed with action.

J. Henry Rushton was a man of strongly marked personal traits and strict principles. He was, moreover, a fearless and outspoken champion of his principles. He had grown up in an environment of hard knocks and rough living. Menfolk back on the Ridge were no strangers to the brown jug. In those days whiskey was dispensed daily as part of logging-camp and hay-field menus. Chewing tobacco and a pipe and pouch of smoking tobacco were necessities for most men. To Peter Rushton the next best thing to the bar in his son George's hotel at Pyrites was the comfort of his pipe and good company beside an old box stove. But his son J. Henry had ascetic habits. He was a total abstainer from alcohol and tobacco.

Even the smell of tobacco was repugnant to Leah. In the matter of drinking and smoking she and her husband were kindred souls. When Peter Rushton became old and a bit difficult, J. Henry adopted the practice of paying toward his support. In a letter written to "Dear Sister Eliza," wife of his half-brother George, dated December 8, 1902, he had this to say:

While I am entirely honest in wishing to provide Father with a more comfortable place than I have, I will also be honest enough to admit that it is worth something to me to be relieved of the immediate care. Certain features of this care are the same burden wherever he is. Certain others are not. . . . *I* have no place for him to loaf and smoke. You have a room set aside for this very purpose for the general public [in the Pyrites hotel]. I can stand tobacco tho' no user of it. No other member of my family can. Many a meal Leah does not eat a mouthful because of the odor and every day she is sickened by doing his room work. You are in constant contact with smokers, and while it may be unpleasant to you it probably does not strike you quite so hard. . . . At the end of each fourth week I will send you $10 or do different at any time you desire it. . . . I will say now that as a choice between having him at my house and continuing this deal I would choose the latter.

Rushton and his wife were more strongly opposed to drinking than to smoking. No doubt the problem of drink had intruded on Boat Shop morale. In those days it was one of the nightmares of most employers. Saloons lined parts of Water Street and lower Main Street in Canton. In the spring when the log drives were on, lumberjacks would storm into town on weekends, including Indians from the St. Regis Reservation and French Canadians. Canton would then vie with the Wild West. Drunks roamed the town. Fist fights were frequent. Womenfolk stayed at home until the "jacks" went back up-country for the drives.

Four Canton men decided to do something about this situation. Rushton joined two college professors and Gilbert Manley, the publisher, to organize Canton's Good Templar Society, the local instrument of a national organization contemporary with Carry Nation and her hatchet. Preaching and persuasion were its methods. The four Good Templars of Canton tried an ingenious subterfuge, something to lure the sots away from the saloons.

Thus Canton's Public Reading Room came into existence, sponsored by the Good Templars. It was located in a vacant room of the new Town Hall in the center of the business section and across the street from several dens of iniquity. It was staffed by Josephine Paige, a maiden lady who loved good books. Townsfolk contributed magazines and books, and the Reading Room opened for business. But the lure failed to work as planned. By the end of the year the Good Templars gave up, but their spouses did not. Leah Rushton, Flora Priest, and a few others were determined to keep the Reading Room even if it did not empty the saloons. Many nonalcoholics had been dropping in to enjoy its opportunities. Canton, so these dedicated wives held, needed not only the Reading Room but a regular library. They formed the Women's Library Association, moved the Reading Room upstreet to a small frame building, and founded the Canton Free Library. This long-term strategy had a modest success. Slowly, painfully, culture made inroads on the bars, though probably the decline of lumbering did more to bring this about than the rise of the library. Leah Rushton was a charter member of the Library Association and one of its most active supporters. At her death she bequeathed five hundred dollars to the library, its first bequest.

Until the year of Rushton's marriage the Boat Shop and its predecessors had been his castle. Afterward, however, his interests broadened. He put the same energy into community affairs as he had into the shop. As an old Canton resident remarks, "J. Henry Rushton was an exceedingly small man with boundless energy. He was always working under a full head of steam, under great inner pressures." "Oh, yes, I knew Mr. Rushton well," a former Canton banker informed the writer. "He was a good customer for the bank to have, a heavy borrower who always met his interest payments punctually and paid on principal. But he always seemed to have difficulty keeping up with his ideas."

A few months after his marriage, in December, 1883, he organized the St. Lawrence Canoe Club, of which he was elected first commodore. His early Canton friends, Ellsworth and Packard, were also members and officers in the club. Perhaps its ablest canoeist was William F. Kip, a powerfully built worker in the Boat Shop for over ten years and a one-time foreman. In the ACA meet of 1885, Kip, paddling the Rushton canoe *Nellie,* a Princess model, won firsts in two races. In the paddling tandem race at that meet the Canton club nearly monopolized the honors, winning first place with a canoe manned by Kip and John L. Jackson, third with another Canton pair, and dividing honors for second place with Brooklyn with a split crew. At the international meet of 1886 Kip won first place in the *Nellie* in a one-mile paddling race with four-teen starters. Rushton himself seems never to have entered competition in the ACA races.

Rushton also organized the Canton Gun Club and became its president. He proved his marksmanship by breaking more glass balls at the first meet than any other member.

In 1893, with five or six other Canton men, he organized a hunting and fishing club, the Stillwater Club, as it has been known ever since. It obtained a lease agreement for 28,000 acres of forest land on the western slope of the Adirondacks in the town of Clare, St. Lawrence County. Rushton had shortly before built a cottage on Star Lake, not far from his native town of Fine. He also took his family into the Cranberry Lake region for outings. On one such trip he trekked back into the forest with his two small sons to visit Con Carter at Carter's Camp on the Inlet, or upper Oswegatchie. But the Stillwater Club eventually became the chief woods retreat of the Rushton family. J. Henry was chairman of the committee that built the original clubhouse on the North Branch of the Grass River, two miles by trail from the clearing where the Canton-Clare road afforded access. The building was a typical Adirondack hunting and fishing club, its waters plentifully yielding trout and its woods deer. Rushton canoes and rowboats were used on the North Branch stillwater. Rushton liked to bring his whole family there, hunt till he secured a buck, and then remain till the meat was eaten on the spot. He rarely brought any of it back to Canton except as a gift for some nonhunting friend. After his death the family continued for some time to spend vacations there.

Even before the founding of the Stillwater Club, Rushton was interested in game conservation and took an active part in tightening state and county game laws. His particular interest was in bringing an end to the practice of the hounding and water-killing of white-tailed deer in the Adirondacks. In 1886 he attended hearings of a senate committee in Albany considering a proposal to prohibit the use of dogs to chase deer into lakes, where the swimming animals could easily be overtaken by hunters in boats. In the following year he wrote for *Forest and Stream* a strong protest against the cruelty of using dogs in deer hunting and against the depletion of the deer herd through this practice. In 1896 the state suspended deer hounding for five years, and then in 1901 abolished it permanently. Some hunters, however, continued to agitate for repeal of this law. In reply to one such proposal, Rushton resumed the fight in a contribution to *Forest and Stream,* February 6, 1904:

> In your last week's issue I notice that a gentleman from Essex County advocates a return to hounding. He asks that if the whole state does not want that, certain counties, among them St. Lawrence, be given such a law. Since when, I would like to ask, has the gentleman from Essex been given authority to speak for the hunters of St. Lawrence? If he will but search the records of the St. Lawrence County Board of Supervisors, he will find that they prohibited hounding (under power given them by state laws) long before the entire state became non-hounding. He will find that the first non-hounding law for the state was introduced by Gen. N. Martin Curtis, then a member of the Assembly from St. Lawrence. He did it by request of a very large majority of the hunters of St. Lawrence. A year later the law was repealed, but at our special request St. Lawrence was excepted, and we have never had a hounding law since, and we never will if we can prevent it.
>
> After St. Lawrence had a non-hounding law for a few years— the rest of the state meanwhile using hounds—we were overrun with hunters from other counties because we had deer while they had none.

This letter shows a prickliness notably absent in Rushton's business and social life but common enough among hunters. Something about this sport seems to trigger a vein of cocksureness and contention among the gentlest and most modest of men.

For the twenty-three years after his marriage and before his death, Rushton led a full life as proprietor of the Boat Shop, a man of position and influence in his community, a sportsman, and a family man with a devoted and loyal wife and sons who shared his love of the woods. A few of these years were troubled ones, with financial worries and a decline in sales of Rushton boats with rapidly growing competition. But he surmounted these troubles, and his personal life was a sub-stantially happy one.

MARRIAGE

Chapter IX

THE MOUNTING WAVE

THE rising enthusiasm over canoeing that began in the United States with the founding of the New York Canoe Club in 1871 and received fresh impetus with the founding of the American Canoe Association in 1880 reached a crest, if a precise date can be set, in the international meet at Grindstone Island in the St. Lawrence River in August, 1886, when an American canoeist won the trophy cup in competition with visitors of the Royal Canoe Club. Rushton's fortunes surged with this wave from the time when he made his first canoes in 1876 through the year 1883, and the upward cycle continued for the next three years. Rushton led the field of canoe builders in the country in prestige and production.

The canoeing editor of *Forest and Stream* explained with sly self-interest the elements of Rushton's success in the February 28, 1884, issue: "The growth of the Canton business has been commensurate with the progress of canoeing in this country.... Now his [Rushton's] annual business runs into the tens of thousands of dollars somewhere. The three points of his success, as we understand them, are: First—Charge a price for goods that will allow of first-class work. Second—Put only good material into the goods and do not scrimp on the work. Third—Advertise in *Forest and Stream*. We expect to adorn the second page of the cover with Mr. Rushton's advertisement for nine years longer." Certainly the integrity of his product counted for much. So did the paid and unpaid advertising in the leading sports magazine of the country in the last quarter of the century. Rushton's name appeared with much greater frequency than that of any other builder in the canoeing columns of *Forest and Stream* from 1877 to 1886. "You will see by

Forest and Stream," Rushton wrote to Wulsin in one of his rare self-satisfied moods, "that 'Rushton' builds canoes (and gets free advertising)."

But the Canton builder had other strings to his bow in the field of public relations. He visited canoe clubs and held informal talks with members. In January, 1884, at the Winter Camp-Fire, a meeting of canoeists in the Kit Kat Club of New York City, he answered questions on canoe construction and equipment while enjoying with others present a crate of fresh Florida oranges sent especially for this occasion from Tarpon Springs by Captain Kendall. During the same month he paid a visit to the Springfield, Massachusetts, canoe club. While in New York on the good-will tour, he inspected the *Sairy Gamp* in the offices of *Forest and Stream.* That periodical duly reported a couple of weeks later receipt of a letter from Nessmuk quoting in turn a letter from Rushton: "She [the *Sairy*] is still staunch and tight." The editor adds: "Yes, the *Sairy Gamp* is tight. We filled her half full of water the other night and launched a yacht model by gaslight."

Rushton reported a new sales record for the first half of 1884. At an early-season regatta at Newburgh-on-Hudson a large portion of the canoes were of Rushton manufacture and came in for a good share of the prizes.

During the spring and summer Rushton had his attention focused on the forthcoming ACA meet. In view of a current controversy over the relative merits of the sneakbox and the conventional canoe, Rushton announced in April that he hoped to have a new-model sneakbox, size twelve by four, ready for the August meet to give members a chance to compare it with canoes. He was planning, too, to set up a repair tent.

The ACA encampment had outgrown Canoe Islands in Lake George. The new location chosen for the meet of 1884, Delaney's Point at the foot of Grindstone Island in the heart of the Thousand Islands, was little more than sixty miles from Canton and more convenient for Rushton than the Lake George site. The Thousand Islands have proved a popular location. The ACA later purchased Sugar Island, near Grindstone, as its permanent base. Meanwhile, Canoe Islands in Lake George, birthplace of the association, were maintained for the use of members for many years. After the death of Longworth and Bishop, title was vested in Lucien Wulsin, who continued to carry the property at his expense till 1902. He then sold it, binding the new owner not to use the islands for commercial purposes and to preserve their natural beauty.

Rushton and the St. Lawrence Canoe Club were among early arrivals at the August meet. He proceeded to set up a tent fitted with a workbench and a large supply of repair material and staffed by a competent workman from the Boat Shop to make any kind of repairs on damaged canoes. This was a new and much-appreciated feature of the meet that was continued in later encampments. Rushton canoes were much in evidence, both in a special exhibit and in the fleet assembled for the races. It was reported that, of the lapstreak canoes present, Rushton's were the most numerous, including some six to eight distinct models of varying dimensions. In addition, Rushton offered for display and sale a full line of single and double paddles, oars, masts, sails, and rigging fixtures. He himself was much in evidence, serving with that other veteran ACA member and canoe designer and builder, Will Stephens, as measurer.

The contingent from Canton included several members of the St. Lawrence Canoe Club, among them J. B. Ellsworth, Ira Davis, John Jackson, and Will Kip. The women of the group, including Leah and her sister, were segregated in their own tent village on Squaw Point. Besides taking part in the races under the flag of the Canton club, Will Kip, soon to become Rushton's foreman, represented the Boat Shop along with his employer, Asa Dailey, and Judd Rushton. Son of a talented Canton family that lived around the corner from the Rushtons, young Will was a friend of Frederic Remington, the Canton born and raised artist who was just beginning to make a name for himself as a portrayer of the Old West, and who visited the Boat Shop as an interested canoeist whenever he was in town. In the 1884 meet Kip in the *Nellie* came in first in the mile paddling race but was ruled out for fouling the buoy. He won second place in the half mile. The following year he was to do better. His liveliness contributed much to the general high spirits of the Canton group.

The year 1885 was the most prosperous thus far for the Boat Shop, a result accomplished despite growing competition and a trade recession. On January 8 *Forest and Stream* commented on the growth of interest in canoeing and on Rushton's place among builders. "There are now several large establishments devoted largely or entirely to canoe building. The principal one of these, and the one best known to canoeists, is that of Mr. J. H. Rushton."

Among the evidences of this success was the catalog of 1885. The page was enlarged to make the illustrations more effective, and the length was increased to forty-eight pages. Fourteen pages were devoted to rowboats, eighteen to canoes and their fittings, and the rest to introductory material and testimonials. The American Traveling Canoe, so popular in the early eighties, was dropped from this catalog, its place taken by improved models. Added were four new cruising canoes—Mohican No. 1, Mohican No. 2, Springfield, and Daisy, the latter a light, steady "ladies' canoe"; three new open canoes; and two new Nessmuk-type go-lighters, Nessmuk No. 121 and Bucktail. In October Rushton reported sales greater by 50 per cent than in any previous year. This figure reinforces the brave statement in the spring catalog: "In the face of a general falling off in trade all over the country, our trade *has largely increased*. This is because we build better, lighter, more durable work, and, when quality and finish are considered, cheaper work than any other builder; because we are willing at any time, for a fair compensation, to build to others' ideas even if they do not agree with our own; because we attend ACA meets and local meets when we can, observing the success of this or failure of that particular thing; using the knowledge thus obtained to aid us in making our work more perfect."

Rushton now had agents in six sporting goods establishments in cities in the eastern half of the nation: Read in Boston, Squires in New York, Ellard in Cincinnati, Wilkinson in Chicago, Hinkley in St. Paul, and Phillips in New Orleans. Early in 1885 he added a general sales representative, the secretary-treasurer of the ACA, Dr. Charles A. Neidé. This name itself was an excellent endorsement for Rushton boats. Neidé's book on his marathon cruise in the Rushton-built *Aurora* went on the stands about the time this popular figure in ACA circles became Rushton's associate. "Seneca," writing in *Forest and Stream,* listed Nessmuk, Bishop, and Charles Neidé as the country's three foremost canoeists in the mid-eighties. Nessmuk replied: "Perhaps I am one of the best known canoeists. I didn't know it. And the only significance of placing me in the trio . . . is the fact that as a trio we represent the extremes in canoeing." This is a just characterization of the three: Nessmuk cruising the Adirondacks in his eight-and-a-half-foot cockleshell, the *Sairy Gamp,* Bishop rowing and paddling his paper canoe, the *Maria Theresa,* down the Atlantic Coast, and Neidé cruising over three thousand miles of inland and salt waters in his all-purpose *Aurora.*

The *Plaindealer* in 1885 referred to Neidé as Rushton's "general agent" in charge of two displays of Rushton craft in expositions in New Orleans and St. Louis. Later in the same year this rover was in Jacksonville, Florida, setting up a new Rushton agency there and managing it for a time. But he soon took to the road again. In June of the following year he was in Canton conferring with Rushton. The *Plaindealer* remarked at that time that he had visited many cities in the West as agent for Rushton boats. The connection lasted for at least a year and a half before this restless renegade from the dentist's office found some other substitute for the chair and drill.

As 1885 opened, Rushton's most popular canoes were the Princess of *Aurora* fame among larger craft and, of the smaller, the Grayling and the Ellard, both modifications of the Stella Maris. The Ellard had been designed by Rushton for George B. Ellard of the Cincinnati Canoe Club.

By the end of 1885, however, these favorites had given way to the two new Mohican models offered in the catalog of that year and named in honor of the Mohican Canoe Club of Albany. The new commodore of the ACA, General Robert S. Oliver, a member of that club, ordered for the flagship of the fleet at the August encampment a Rushton canoe of the Grayling type but somewhat larger. He named it the *Marion B.* This was the Mohican No. 2 model of Rushton's catalog. Other members of the Albany club brought to the meet Rushton boats in which they had been diligently skimming the waters of the upper Hudson for several months in an effort to make a good showing in August. One of them was a young architect of athletic build, Robert W. Gibson. He entered the meet with the *Snake,* a Rushton-built boat similar to the Ellard except for its straight sternpost. This craft had first come into notice at the Stony Lake meet of 1883, where it won the Class B sailing event. Several boats of the same type were present at the 1884 meet, and in the 1885 catalog Rushton introduced the type as the Mohican No. 1. On January 22, 1885, *Forest and Stream* ran a three-column article on the history of the *Snake,* describing it as an all-around canoe and summarizing its record. It had started in twenty regular races against other canoes, of which it had won eleven, placed second in four, and fifth in one; four races had not been finished on account of weather conditions.

The *Snake* then entered the 1885 meet with an already formidable record. Manned by one of the ablest canoeists of the time, it lived up to its reputation. It won two firsts, two seconds, one third, and one sixth. In the meet as a whole it scored 53.15 points for first place in the final record.

The scoring of an overall record was a new feature of the 1884 and 1885 meets intended to counteract the tendency of the racing events to put a premium on speed and on craft designed as racing machines, costly to build and not of much use to the owner after the day of victory. It was hoped that the record would encourage the use of less specialized and more versatile craft capable of a better than average performance in a variety of events. This hope was fully realized in the performance of the *Snake* at the 1885 meet. Gibson entered it in seven races for the record—all he was entitled to. These included the sailing class, paddling and sailing, and paddling. His final score was nineteen points ahead of the second-place winner, C. B. Vaux of the New York Canoe Club. The all-around canoe had vindicated itself against the racing machine. But it was a temporary triumph. The effect of the international trophy races of the following year was again to emphasize speed in the sailing division and to discourage the happy-go-lucky owner of the all-purpose canoe from taking part in major races. Through its racing rules and procedures the ACA, which had done much to stimulate interest in canoeing throughout the country in the early eighties, from 1886 on was one of the factors that changed the sport from a romantic and adventurous pastime to a racing-directed routine and caused a leveling-off of interest.

Meanwhile, Rushton made what he could of the *Snake's* record. In describing the model in his 1886 catalog, he refers to that record and adds: "This, we think, fairly entitles the Mohican No. 1 to be called the champion *all-around canoe*." The meet of 1885 had been an almost unqualified success from Rushton's point of view, thanks in part to the able canoeists of the Mohican Club. He was, moreover, the only canoe builder to have an exhibition at the meet that year. His repair tent won appreciation as it had the year before. Another of his boats, the *Nellie,* manned by Will Kip, starred in the paddling races in which the *Snake* had not done quite so well. In fact, the two craft had competed in one race with Kip winning a first. All in all, Rushton had reason to look forward confidently to the results of the international meet the following year.

Interest in canoeing was now at a peak in the Western world. By the end of 1886 there were nearly one hundred local canoe clubs across the United States and Canada. The ACA now had regional divisions conducting their own regattas at convenient sites. A formidable rival had grown up in the West, calling itself the Western Canoe Association. It refused an invitation to join the ACA as a Western division. The Cincinnati Canoe Club, which had been a power behind the original ACA, affiliated with the new association, which held annual meets of its own. In Great Britain interest was also running high. In the latter part of 1885 one of England's two most honored canoeists, Warington Baden-Powell, pioneer of the Nautilus model, addressed a proposal to the ACA that an international sailing canoe race be held the following summer in America. He pledged that he for one would participate and hoped that other members of the Royal Canoe Club would join him. His objectives were: first, to bring canoeists on both sides of the Atlantic into closer comradeship and thus to improve their pastime while at the same time encouraging international relations; and second, to afford an opportunity to compare and test the types of canoes being used in the two countries. Which was the better sailer, the British or the American canoe?

Officers of the ACA promptly accepted the challenge. Throughout the winter and spring months details of the forthcoming first International Sailing Canoe Cup Race were worked out. Subscriptions limited to one dollar each were solicited from the members of the ACA with which to purchase an appropriate silver-plated trophy cup to be awarded the winner of this race, the limit affording every member a chance to participate and thus creating widespread interest. It was agreed that the cup race be held in conjunction with the seventh annual meet of the ACA set for late August in the summer of 1886 at Delaney's Point, Grindstone Island. This was an appropriate location, the St. Lawrence River being the boundary between the United States and the British Dominion.

As press release followed press release and official notices went out from ACA headquarters, enthusiasm mounted. Many an American canoeist was cudgeling his brain to perfect plans for the winning sailing canoe and rig. In England, Baden-Powell with his No. 5 *Nautilus* was the favorite, and Walter

Stewart with his *Pearl* the runner-up. On both sides of the Atlantic canoeists were holding preliminary races in order to choose which and whose canoe might represent the two countries. Race No. 20 was on everybody's mind as Regatta Week at Grindstone approached.

Rushton brought out his catalog for 1886 earlier in the year than usual and expanded it to sixty pages. It emphasized the record of the *Snake* the previous year. The Springfield, the Shadow, the St. Lawrence, and the fourteen-foot Princess were dropped, but the Stella Maris, the Grayling, the Ellard, the larger Princess (15 feet by 31½ inches), and the Tandem Princess were retained. The two Mohican models first offered in 1885 were also kept, and two new Mohicans, Nos. 3 and 4, were added. *Forest and Stream* commented that the four Mohicans were the most interesting craft in the catalog and promised to become the most popular, incorporating as they did the lines of the famous *Snake*.

Early in the year Rushton received plans and specifications for a new canoe from Robert W. Gibson, skipper of the *Snake,* which had been sold to another member of the Mohican Club. The new canoe, the *Vesper,* was finished by May, in good time for spring and summer local races. The specifications of the *Vesper* were: length, 15 feet 6½ inches; beam, 30½ inches; depth, 10 inches; weight, including the Atwood centerboard, approximately eighty pounds; two mast holes, one forward and one aft of the cockpit; rudder, lung-shaped; canvas-spread capability, about seventy-five square feet; hull, clinker construction with white cedar planking and oak keelson; no ballast.

Word soon came from Albany that the *Vesper* was showing her sternpost to all other Mohican canoes. She won a sailing race over the *Snake,* manned by her new owner. She outclassed General Oliver's *Marion B.* and Phillip Wackerhagen's old *Thetis* and his new *Turtle.* She was pronounced faster than anything the Mohican Club had ever had. As the August dateline approached, the Mohicans pinned their faith on the *Ves-*

per and her able skipper. They had become convinced that there was not another canoe afloat capable of matching her. Therefore, when the time arrived for them to entrain for Clayton on the St. Lawrence, and there to continue by water to Grindstone, either on their own canoe bottoms or by steamer, these Mohicans were confident. Gibson and the *Vesper* were their champions. Victory seemed within reach. Meanwhile, a Rushton Grayling won the Gardner Challenge Cup on July 19 in the annual meet of the Western Canoe Association.

Other things besides the *Vesper* were aborning for Rushton as spring and summer brought the annual meet nearer. In early June this item made news on Canton's Main Street: "The 'strike' has reached Canton. The workmen in J. H. Rushton's boatworks 'knocked off' Monday morning, on learning that a new partner had been added to the firm since they quit work on Saturday. They struck 'for the cigars.' Rushton 'put 'em up' and all went merry as a birthday bell." The new partner was baptized Joseph Henry Rushton, Joseph in honor of Joseph Barnes Ellsworth, Henry for his father. He would soon be called Harry. He was the first of two children, both sons. The other, born two years later, was named Sidney.

During the summer the Boat Shop turned out one of the oddest productions of Rushton's fertile mind. To keep abreast of an age of change and invention, he had begun to experiment with the powerboat. On August 11 the *Plaindealer* reported: "Rushton has a full force of men hard at work upon a small steam yacht which he will take this week with him to the American Canoe Association encampment. Mr. R. has often received inquiries in regard to small steam yachts and has consequently determined to try his hand at one and if successful not to stop there."

The *Joharrie,* named in honor of Rushton's son, was not an object of beauty and grace. Though its lines were somewhat similar to those of the *Vesper,* it had a great excrescence amidships—its power plant, a Shipman engine. This device, manufactured in Rochester, New York, consisted of an upright steam boiler and a smokestack. The power was transmitted by shaft to a propeller at the stern.

The *Joharrie's* maiden voyage took place on the Grass River at Canton. Standing in the prow, dressed in a Prince Albert cutaway and a bowler hat, J. Henry was the little Napoleon of all he surveyed. Awkward as it looked, the *Joharrie* worked, after a fashion. *Forest and Stream,* in presenting some of the highlights of the 1886 meet, took note of "another new boat": "a steam launch built by Mr. Rushton. . . . She steams about all day and seems to make very good speed." The *Joharrie* was used as the turning buoy in the big cup race. One cannot help wondering how it kept from capsizing. Its top-heavy aspect seems hardly a match for the blows of the St. Lawrence.

This first venture in mechanized propulsion was not the last for the Boat Shop. The catalog of 1887 offered steam launches built to order. Drawings have come to light among old Rushton papers of a full-scale steam launch. Whether one was ever built is not known. From steam-boiler contraptions Rushton turned to electrically driven launches, a battery of wet cells providing the motive power. The catalog of 1892 listed steam, naphtha, and electric launches. Later came the internal combustion engine. After Rushton's death, his sons Harry and Sidney experimented with inboard motorboats.

Important as the *Joharrie* and other experiments with powered craft may have seemed to Rushton at the time, they remained a sideline of the Boat Shop. While the *Joharrie* chugged along the shores of Grindstone Island, the *Vesper* silently awaited her day of glory.

Chapter X

CUPS AND CONTROVERSIES

"THE bluest of deep blue skies, waters clear and pure and of the same color, in which are dropped green islets of all shapes and sizes, while far away the wooded spires merge into a softer mistier green, broken here and there by a pretty cottage, a solitary spire, or an old little lighthouse"—thus *Forest and Stream* describes the outlook from the encampment on Grindstone Island, where "again for the seventh time the members of the American Canoe Association have gathered together under the red and white flag, and for the third time their white tents shine on the sunny hillside, the white sails glisten on the blue waters, the fires burn brightly on the hilltop, and the silence that reigns unbroken for fifty weeks each year departs before the shrill signal calls of canoes and steamers, the uproarious shanty song and the merry glees." August 13-27, 1886, would long be remembered by the canoeists present. No previous meet had matched it in novelty and excitement. No previous one had caused so much controversy and division.

For months the press and sporting journals had vied in pointing up the importance of the races scheduled to follow a week of setting up camp, informal cruising, and reunion around the campfire. Attention was focused on race No. 20, the ACA Challenge Cup race in which this year for the first time British canoeists were to compete with American.

"With song, stories and pipes the evening [of the first campfire] was passed very pleasantly. Toward the end a tall figure came up out of the darkness, and for a moment was not recognized until introduced as Dr. Heighway of Cincinnati. Since last at a meet he has grown taller and more like an athlete than ever. His arrival was the signal for a grand uproar that lasted until the fire died out." With Heighway, the "Cincinnati Giant," present, the gymnastics part of the program was assured, as well as stiff competition in the races. He was director of a large gymnasium and a skilled canoeist. In 1883 he had matched his skill against the floodwaters of the Ohio to carry by a Rushton-built canoe one hundred and fifty pounds of provisions for the marooned people of Lawrenceville. He and Rushton had been friends since the meet of 1882, and he was now much in evidence at Rushton's tent on the ridge where the St. Lawrence Canoe Club was encamped. Besides his sleeping tent, Rushton as in former years had a repair tent on the point near the camp store.

Notables and novelties turned up by the hour. Baden-Powell was there with his Clyde tent of oiled muslin, complete with ventilators and windows. His canoe *Nautilus* did not arrive till the last minute. Walter Stewart, the only other representative of the Royal Canoe Club, was there with his *Pearl,* somewhat sprung in consequence of its long journey. The sloop *Ethel* put in from Oswego. Mr. Clapham was on hand with a new "double-ended cruiser," the *Red Jacket.* The *Gracie,* a big yacht, brought several Canadians from Kingston, Ontario. Neidé was present with a new canoe, but he had brought the *Aurora* for exhibit. Paul Butler, diminutive industrialist from Lowell, Massachusetts, and member of the Vesper Canoe Club, was there with his sailing canoe *Blanche,* outfitted with an ingenious new outboard deck seat, two boards the width of the boat, the lower fixed, the upper sliding in grooves and capable of being locked out to windward as an outrigger seat. Whitlock had with him the *Wraith* made from John Hyslop's design and built by Rushton.

Into camp came an odd one, the canoe *Harmony.* Her skipper was Dr. C. M. Douglas, of Lakefield, Ontario. The *Harmony* was a genuine antique. She had been built in England on the Thames River in 1864, a year before MacGregor laid the keel for his first Rob Roy. Her builder was William Biffen, of

Hammersmith, near London. Originally she was a sectional craft of three parts for benefit of crating and easy carting. Built of Spanish cedar, she was a steady paddling canoe. When she was new, Douglas had used her in England for two years. Then, on being assigned to duty in India, he shipped her to Lake Charles, near Quebec, where she reposed unused on boathouse rafters for nineteen years. Upon retiring from service, Douglas finally rescued her, converted her into a one-piece canoe, and put her in use at Lakefield. He claimed she was the first decked wooden canoe ever used in American waters. Despite her years, the *Harmony* gave a good account of herself at Grindstone in the first race of her career, pushing Johnson in his *Maggie* to a tight finish in a one-mile paddling event.

Scores of tents soon covered Delaney's Point. Pennants snapped in the breeze. A reedy smell arose from nearby pickerelweed beds. Cheer on cheer rose as arriving craft came into view. Paddles were pushed the harder, sails reefed the closer as canoe after canoe put into Eel Bay and headed shoreward. The first days brought a round of welcoming among old-timers and of making newcomers at home. Wives and daughters were encamped as usual on Squaw Point, some of them canoeists too, others there for the camping, the flirting, the gossip, the evening parties around the campfire. The common mess hall relieved them of responsibility. They hoped that this time there would not be the all-night drinking and rowdiness with which a few undesirables—outsiders of course—had marred some previous meets. Bachelors on the ridge appreciated Squaw Point. "Girling" had become a fixture of ACA meets, especially in those open Canadian-style canoes or Rushton's tandems.

Surprises and controversy and sharp-edged rivalry among both canoeists and builders marked Race Week, which began on Monday, August 23. The issues were not immediately resolved. They provoked heated and prolonged argument in the columns of *Forest and Stream* and the *American Canoeist,* the two official organs of the ACA. Type of design and construction, style of sail, skill of skipper, reputation of builder were weighed in the balance. Sides were taken. Rushton himself became involved.

The races had hardly begun before it was apparent that the two heavily ballasted British canoes, the *Nautilus* and the *Pearl,* were no match for the light, rakish American contenders. Though modern canoes on both sides of the Atlantic had evolved from MacGregor's original Rob Roy and in the early seventies were still much alike, they began to diverge soon after, partly in adaptation to the different waters in which they were sailed. Now the two British canoes had a distinctly foreign look amidst the American fleet.

Much had been written in advance of Gibson's *Vesper.* But a dark horse competitor was on hand attracting both favorable and unfavorable comments. E. H. Barney, a member of the Springfield Canoe Club and formerly a patron of Rushton, had entered his *Pecowsic,* partly of his design and built by F. Joyner. She was a racing craft in intent and design, slim and gar-like—longer than the *Vesper* and narrower in beam. She had three mast tubes, stowed five sails of different sizes, and was capable of carrying a spread of up to one hundred and five feet of canvas, though in the races at Grindstone she used but two sails of varying size with a maximum spread of seventy-five feet.

Her builder, Fletcher Joyner, was a former Adirondack guide and maker of guide-boats who about 1880 set up a boat shop in Glens Falls (he later moved to Schenectady) with his son Edgar and was soon manufacturing a varied line of rowboats and canoes. He was the builder of the canoe *Atlantis* in which S. R. Stoddard, photographer and author of a series of Adirondack guidebooks, sailed from New York harbor along the New England coast to the head of the Bay of Fundy in a three-lap journey ending in 1885. Joyner constructed his hulls with a smooth joint of the planks instead of the clinker style of Rushton boats. After studying canoes entered in races at early ACA meets, Joyner had developed a model of sailing canoe which he called the Diamond. With modifications requested by Barney, the *Pecowsic* was a Diamond. She was fast under sail but cranky. With her complicated rigging she required expert handling.

ACA canoeists quickly sized up Walter Stewart's *Pearl* as a loser. Her seams were sprung by the time she reached Grindstone, and she leaked badly. Stewart soon realized she was outclassed but sportingly carried on.

Baden-Powell's *Nautilus* (No. 5 of his designing), like the *Pearl,* carried as ballast a centerplate of fifty-six pounds and shot of one hundred pounds. The *Vesper* and the *Pecowsic* carried no ballast. By accepted British practice in coastwise sailing in usually rough waters, the English skippers slouched to the bottom of the cockpit. Gibson, Barney, Vaux, and other leading American canoeists rode the deck. Thus they could shift their weight quickly, as needed, to trim their craft and take advantage of both wind and wave. Before he left American waters, after the New York Canoe Club had staged a second series of international races, Baden-Powell had shifted from cockpit to deck, and as a result the *Nautilus* did better than at Grindstone.

The night before the Challenge Cup race an addition was made to the program. It was decided to have a second international contest between the two British canoes and the two top American contenders for the Challenge Cup. A fund was raised for a cup to award the winner of this consolation race.

Nineteen races took place on Monday and Tuesday, with sixty-one canoes participating. Since many were registered for more than one race, there was an aggregate of 358 entries. In his Rushton *Nellie,* Will Kip of the St. Lawrence Canoe Club placed first in a one-mile paddling race with fourteen starters. C. J. Bowsfield, of Bay City, Michigan, recent winner of the Gardner Challenge Cup of the Western Canoe Association, entered his all-purpose Rushton Grayling in several races and amassed the highest number of points for the meet's record. Barney in the *Pecowsic* won two three-mile sailing events, one with a restricted sail spread, the other unlimited. Gibson in the *Vesper* placed fourth in the limited, second in the unlimited. By this time the *Pecowsic* was a topside favorite to win No. 20, the Challenge Cup race. She was being heralded by her backers as the wonder canoe as Wednesday, the day of the great race, dawned.

By agreement, contesting canoes stepped two masts, each skipper free to carry as much sail as he dared. The course was seven and a half miles—five times around a one-and-a-half-mile triangle. The British canoes soon fell behind. The race was a close one between Barney and Gibson. The *Pecowsic* sailed faster on the straightaway, but lost time on each of the turns. *Vesper* finished with the best record on average of all rounds with *Pecowsic* a few seconds behind. The two British craft lagged ten minutes behind on average, *Nautilus* finishing in eighth place and *Pearl* in ninth.

As the winners of first and second places, *Vesper* and *Pecowsic* were the American contenders in the international consolation cup race next day. The course was two miles to leeward. On the home beat the two American boats outdistanced their rivals badly. *Pecowsic* finished first (1 hour, 55 minutes, 39 seconds), *Vesper* second (1:56.50), and *Nautilus* third (2:00.57). *Pearl* was forced to drop out.

The ACA races of 1886 established the superiority of American canoes over British as sailing craft, at least in inland waters. In following years the English moved toward replacing their heavily ballasted craft with canoes of light displacement equipped with many American fittings. About 1900 an English canoeist, Albert Strange, versified the outcome of the contest of 1886, in the following lines from a metrical history of modern canoeing entitled "The Passing of the Canoe":

> To the land of Yankee Doodle
> Went the heavy Rob Roy cruiser
> Full of centerplates and shot-bags,
> Balance lugs with lots of halyards,
> Stiff and slow and very stately,

Oh, so slow! The lively Yankee—
Standing-rigged and sliding-seated
Sailed around the Rob Roy cruiser,
Round the stately Rob Roy cruiser.
Left her far away to leeward,
Left her, while her British owner
(Stiff and slow and very stately)
Gazed in wide-eyed consternation
As the Yankee flyers vanished,
In the dim and misty distance.

Other issues were not so clear cut. Which was the champion craft, *Vesper* or *Pecowsic*? Two cups had been awarded to different winners in two races against British canoes. Which was the "official" international cup race? This issue was involved in a dispute between the two builders, Rushton and Joyner. Each advertised that the boat built in his shop had won the international cup race, and each failed to mention the claims of the other. In January, 1887, Joyner wrote in a vein he styled as a "big growl" to the editor of *Forest and Stream* protesting Rushton's advertisement in the same journal that *Vesper* had won the international cup race. What *Vesper* won, he asserted, was simply the ACA Challenge Cup in a race that took place every year and was hence of no great importance. The true "international cup race" was won by the *Pecowsic,* as he could prove by the handsome cup now in Mr. Barney's possession. The editor added a note softly explaining his opinion that Barney's trophy was a subscription cup in a consolation race arranged as an afterthought and, he implied, lacking the kudos of the Challenge Cup race originally planned as the main event. Rushton himself defended his claim in a letter to the editor and reaffirmed it in his catalog for 1887. In 1890, however, Joyner's ad still carried a picture of the cup *Pecowsic* had won in the "International Canoe Race" of 1886.

The dispute between the two builders was largely a quibble over words. Three other controversies were more substantial. What made the *Pecowsic* so strong a contender against the *Vesper?* Which type of canoe should racing rules encourage at the annual meets, the specialized racing craft or the all-around cruiser? Which style of hull construction is better, *Vesper's* clinker or *Pecowsic's* smoothskin?

The consensus at the meet was that *Pecowsic* was the faster craft and that *Vesper* won the Challenge Cup race by virtue of Gibson's excellent sailing, especially in rounding the buoys. But some attributed *Pecowsic's* speed to her hull construction, others to her rigging, and still others to the skill of her skipper. Gibson thought the chief factor to be her complex but highly adaptable rig.

Gibson also held that *Pecowsic* was a specialty craft not suited to all-around service. He deplored "the degeneration of a fleet of fast cruisers into a small squadron of racing machines" and hoped that the ACA would halt this trend by revising its racing rules.

Those who argued that the *Pecowsic's* speed was due mainly to her type of hull construction advocated a change from the clinker-built hull to the smoothskin. The *Vesper's* overlaying laps, they said, offered more resistance below the waterline than the *Pecowsic's* smooth surface. Perhaps, said others, but the clinker-built hull is stronger. Nessmuk estimated a gain in strength of 20 or 25 per cent. Rushton conducted a series of experiments in his shop to test the issue of speed. He made hulls by halving each plank at the edge to make a smooth surface inside and out—a "ship lap" type of construction he had used before on his sneakboxes. The results of his experiments were conflicting and inconclusive. But he anticipated a demand for smooth hulls, and in his catalog of 1887 he offered to build smoothskin at request. In later years some of his canoes, such as the Vaux and the Canadian models, were offered in smoothskin only, some in clinker, and others in either type at the buyer's request. The trend was toward smoothskin construction as the Canadian open canoe gradually replaced the decked cruiser in popularity.

Looking back on the ACA meet of 1886 fourteen years later (January 6, 1900), the canoeing editor of *Forest and*

Stream concluded that it had marked a turning point in the sport of canoeing and that its effects had been on the whole harmful. It had introduced, he pointed out, two innovations: first, "a purely racing canoe with a suit of five interchangeable standing sails" and, second, the sliding seat, which was hard to handle by anyone but an expert and prevented use of the canoe to carry duffle. "From this time on, the aim of canoeists was directed almost entirely to the construction of faster sailing canoes, regardless of general use and paddling." An era of the racing machine followed, both in England and America, and racing was for the few. "As matters are today, the sailing canoe is fit only for match racing, and such racing is dead. . . . The perfection of the sailing machine has driven out the old all-round cruising and racing canoe. Those who follow any other branch of the sport do so in the open Canadian canoe, of which thousands are in use."

Gibson and other ACA officials foresaw this outcome. Changes in the rules were proposed and made from time to time, but the emphasis on specialized racing craft persisted as general interest in racing declined. In the closing years of the century fewer craft were entered in the races, and attendance at the annual meets leveled off. Once having set up machinery that converted the canoe into a poor man's racing yacht, the ACA kept running on momentum, seeming to lack the vitality for an effective change in racing practices. The canoe is a wil-ful craft. It is not prime material for regimentation. Nor is the canoeist likely to be a prime organization man. He is happier exploring some frontier, whether a remote tributary of the Amazon or just five miles upriver from Main Street.

INTERCHAPTER

On returning from the ACA meet at Grindstone in late August, 1886, Rushton was in a relaxed mood over the success of the Vesper *and ready to indulge himself in the kind of vacation he liked best, a hunting and fishing trip in the wilderness around Cranberry Lake. We have the story in his own words as it appeared in* Forest and Stream, *March 17, 1887. It is a revealing portrait of Rushton the man; of his modesty, his humor, his love of the woods, and, at this point in his career, his serenity. The letter to the editor is signed "J. H. R., Canton, N.Y."*

W. R. Bishop, the hotel proprietor at Cranberry Lake, paid me a short visit today. That reminded me that I spent the first two weeks of last September on the inlet of Cranberry Lake and had neglected to report what I saw and heard. I left Canton September 1, reaching the foot of the lake at 2:20 P.M. Here I met Steve Ward, an old woods companion of bygone days, who, now a professional guide, was to be a helper during my outing. It was decided that we should camp near the foot of the rapids on the inlet. The sporting season had fairly closed, the last guest had departed from the hotel, and the little steamboat which plies the lake had been dismantled. This made it necessary to raise a spruce breeze. To lighten the burden, my driver and the ex-engineer of the steamboat, Will Smith, took a second boat and part of my duffle. In thirty minutes from the time we drew rein we were afloat. Darkness overtook us before we reached camp, and a toilsome hour was spent in the floodwood, which had by the falling of the water closed up the channel. At nine o'clock we were in a good open bark camp, and an hour later were tucked under our blankets.

Steve and I were afloat at dawn, hoping to get a shot at a deer, which, if successful, would enable me to send some fresh venison back home by my teamster. This was a well-arranged scheme and would have been very nice if it had succeeded. The start was rather discouraging—overcoat and mittens on and an icy seat to sit upon. Then the fog was so thick we would have been unable to penetrate it but for having a sharp-pointed boat. Half an hour of this business satisfied me that the friends at home didn't like venison anyhow, while I myself greatly preferred bacon. Breakfast over and our assistant boatmen departed, we went fishing. Faithful work until the middle of the afternoon only brought to creel a few small trout, and they were taken at odd places on the rapids. The day had been fine, but the night was too cold to think of floating, and we turned in early. The next day we went down through the floodwood, over into the Dead Creek country, and looked up the trail to Cat Mountain Pond. A glimpse of two deer taking a hurried departure out of range of the rifle gave us encouragement. Blue herons, loons and black ducks were occasionally seen and a very pleasant day was passed; scarcely less so that we had nothing to show for it on our return to camp at evening.

That night we had visitors at camp. Visitors at camp in the woods are always welcome or unwelcome. There is no halfway about it. These were two guides who had been on a little hunt on their own account. They had the meat and hides of two deer which they said they killed at daylight down on the lake. The fact that they had a dog with them, and that the dog was lame, was very suggestive of the manner in which the deer might have been killed. The venison was very good, however, and our thanks were due them for a generous piece left behind when they took their departure next morning up the river.

I had intended staying at this camp the entire trip, but by midday changed my mind, and we packed up and started up stream. First came half a mile of still water, then a hard carry past three miles of rapids. It was nine o'clock that night before we were snug in camp on the still water above. At this place, known as the Bridge on the Inlet, though the bridge has been carried away by high water and never replaced, a Mr. Steinberger [Sternburgh] was just completing a frame house intended for his own family and to accommodate a few guests. While such a stopping place will be a convenience to sportsmen belated in making camp or in bad weather, it is hardly probable it will get patronage enough to make it pay the proprietor. [Sternburgh operated the Inlet House for several years, and others after him until 1964, when the privately owned twenty-acre enclave in the midst of forest preserve land was acquired by the state.] Here we saw several friends who had just come in by road from Fine, and we read our first accounts of the Charleston earthquake.

At this particular place, and some fifty rods from where the new house is building, my nerves got quite a shaking up one night some nineteen or twenty years ago, and, as it was one of those little experiences we always remember, I will relate it. It was early in the month of May, and I had arranged with a friend to make a trip to Cat Mountain Pond, a pond at that time undiscovered by Verplanck Colvin [state surveyor] and probably unknown save to a few. There is fair fishing there for quarter-pound trout today, but twenty years ago the water fairly tasted fishy. We were to go by Foot and Walker's line from Fine, the distance being about twenty-five miles. My friend had this advantage over me—a log that I could go under he could step over; and as he had to come five miles on his road to where I lived, I thought I would pull out early and let him overtake me. I attended to my part of the program, telling my people I would stop at the inlet and wait for them if not overtaken sooner. Half an hour after I left, word came that he could not go, but in happy unconsciousness I trudged along, taking longer and more frequent rests as the hours wore away. Thus it was nearly night when I reached the inlet. In those days there was an old log cabin built against a large split rock, the rock forming one end of the shanty and the back for the fireplace. At this end the roof was left off for a little distance for the smoke to escape, and at this particular time the door was gone. As the night was cold I interwove spruce boughs the best I could to stop the wind and lay close up to the little fire I had built to keep warm. In those days we thought a blanket a useless burden.

Some time in the night I awoke. I was lying on my right side, my back to the embers. I was wide awake all at once, but did not stir. Something heavy, warm and soft was resting on my left side. What could it be? The shanty ground was infested by hedgehogs—not desirable bedfellows. The ridge was a runway for panthers and wolves, or had been in bygone days, and even then I knew that traps were set for them on either side within a mile. I thought of the stories I had read of savage animals finding people asleep and lying down beside them until they would awake. My hair "riz" a little. I thought of the story I had heard how once upon a time a fisherman had waded the middle of this same stream for a mile toward camp while a panther followed along the shore. I thought how Old Tom had, within a very few years, trapped or shot several of the var-mints within the radius of five miles from where I was. I thought of my rifle standing in the corner a few feet away and wondered how I could get it most quickly if I needed it. I won-dered what the—mischief—was on top of me. I reasoned that I must find out without disturbing my visitor, if possible, and then think what to do if I was left time to think. By turning my head a quarter way around I could see. But would not the least stir I made bring trouble, if trouble there was to come? Well, I had to risk it anyway. So far I had breathed regularly and kept perfectly still, but knew I could not continue doing so for any considerable time. I would get nervous. Slowly, an inch at a time, I turned my head.

The shout that rang through the cabin could have been heard a mile away, and I nearly died laughing to see that great big rabbit try to find the hole he came in at. I laughed myself to sleep again.

It was noon when Steve dipped his paddle in the water on

our start for the New York Camp, some dozen miles up stream. Half way up, at the Battle Ground, we stopped for luncheon. The Battle Ground is a name given to an old camp ground where two guides once settled a little difference of opinion on some subject. Unwritten history says that one got a black eye and the other got dumped into the river.

It was a beautiful day. I enjoyed very much lounging on the bow seat while Steve's strong arms wielded the paddle. We arrived at camp at 5:30. As the camp would easily accommodate twenty we had lots of house room, and after a hearty dinner and a pleasant chat turned in.

At daylight next morning, with rod and gun, we paddled up to the Plains, keeping a sharp outlook for deer. Saw none, and turning about put down the gun and took up the rod. I am no fly-fisherman, and this morning was trying to swap venison for trout. Only three or four fingerlings got the worst of the deal for the first half mile. These we dropped over and on to a sand bar on the right hand side of the stream, while on the left was some five feet of water with a gravel bottom and no particular cover. Nothing in fact to indicate a better chance for a trout than could be found every ten rods for as many miles down the stream. "Now, go slow and you'll get a good one." "How large?" "Oh, a couple of pounds, perhaps." "Think so?" "I am afraid I will not get any, then, for I doubt my hook holding a two-pounder. However, here goes," and as the line sank and was drawn toward the surface with that peculiar twist of the wrist (a novice once said to me, "I don't see how it is that you get all the trout and I none, for I watch you and wiggle my pole just as you do"), a broad gleam of gold flashed beneath it and set my heart pounding like a hammer on an anvil. A second cast and a half-pounder showed himself plainly. A third cast and—"Moses! Steve, he'd reach half across the river." "Well, why don't you catch him? I told you he was there. Cast again and a little lower down, and—is it a log I am hitched to?" Mighty lively log I found, as I struck as hard as I dared, and the fish started downward and down stream. Scien-

tific fishermen call it "giving him the butt," I believe. My
rod bent double. I could almost hold tip and butt in the same
hand. A few brief moments and he turned up stream. In a moment more I had him in sight, and the rest of the battle was
fought out on that line. The struggle was brief, not over ten
minutes, and Steve reached down into the water and slipped
thumb and finger into his gills and took him in. As he came
over the side of the boat the hook dropped out. I enclose
the hook. This was not the trout I had seen. It was a shorter
one. But I wanted no more. What if there was another big one
there, he would keep for me or some one else. We paddled back
to camp, and river weight (we had no scales) made our fish go
four to four and a half pounds. He measured 19½ inches long,
4½ deep, 2¼ through from side to side, and 11½ in girth. His
tail was 5 inches broad, and a stick 3½ inches long could be set
between his open jaws. It was the largest trout I had caught in
many years, though Steve was with a party earlier in the season
who caught two the same day of about equal size at this same
hole. Toward night we dropped down the river to Gouverneur
Camp and floated. It was cold and foggy. I got a glimpse of
eyes once for a moment only, and we drove another out of a big
cove. We soon got enough of the sport; went to camp, built a
fire, warmed up and turned in, to be awakened long after daylight by the chatter of the bluejays. Returned to our home
camp, had breakfast, cleaned the guns and paddled up to the
Plains. Leaving our boat at a chain of rocks, we walked up to
the old cabin, a mile or more. It was hot, and the drink from
the almost ice cold spring was very refreshing.

While here two hunters came for provisions from Clear
Pond, where they said they were camped and were hounding
deer into Big Deer Pond (Colvin's Lost Lake). Clear Pond is
in St. Lawrence County, Big Deer just out of it. They reported
another party at Grass Pond who were hounding into Mud
Lake. Grass Pond is in St. Lawrence and so is part of Mud
Lake. As they said our game protector (Leonard) had visited
the Grass Pond party and advised them that it was "all right"

so long as they did not put the dogs out in St. Lawrence County, I did not see as I could do more than wish that we had a protector who would give different advice.

During an hour's stay at the cabin two men on their way out of the woods came from Five Ponds, where they had left several others hounding. Five Ponds are just outside St. Lawrence County.

That night we were tired and turned in early. Our slumbers were disturbed by the quill pig who got his head into a corner of the shanty, where Steve could only make caroms on his back with a club, and I was obliged to decide the matter with the Marlin.

Next morning we decided to break camp for good and drop down to Gouverneur Camp; so we fished along down and caught small ones, enough for dinner. Here we were joined by Archie Muir, forester for this section. At night the moon shone until one o'clock, when we started out, Muir down and we up the river. The deer were well educated here, and a breaking of brush or a splash in the water around some bend was all the indication we had of game for some two miles, when, rounding a bend up at the next one and in the open water at the mouth of a cove stood a deer. It was a long shot, but the light showed him plainly, and we loaded a nice yearling buck into the boat and returned to camp. Here we loafed for a couple of days and then dropped down to the bridge again. That night we were out on the river, but a hard shower, the first for the trip, drove us to shelter. The next day the weather was colder and seemed to threaten more storm. I had planned to go down through the lake, but changed my mind, and leaving Steve to go that route alone, I hired Steinberger to carry my pack five miles to the main road, and in company with Muir started at noon. Once out to the clearings, a soft word induced honest Billy Moncrief to drive us with his big gray horse and lumber wagon to Fine Village, a distance of twelve miles, where we arrived at supper time Saturday night. How to get home thirty miles, that was now the question. The livery man thought I was his meat sure and would take me home for eight dollars. On the contrary, I spent thirty cents for a telephone message, had a pleasant ride with an old chum ten miles to Edwards, where my own team met me, and by a little past midnight I was home again. When I awoke next morning the wind was blowing a gale and the rain coming in sheets, nor do I remember a single pleasant day for the next two weeks.

INTERCHAPTER

Chapter XI

TROUBLED WATERS

RUSHTON turned forty-three soon after the ACA meet of 1886. His fortunes had taken a steadily upward course since the making of his first boat in Canton in 1873. His business had kept pace with the rise in popularity of canoeing as a sport. The next few years brought little apparent outward change in his position. Early in 1887 he had smoothskin Vespers and Bucktails on exhibit at Squires in New York. In his catalog of that year he introduced two Vesper models, taking advantage of a name widely known from Gibson's victory in the Challenge Cup race. Soon the all-purpose Vesper, clinker-built or smoothskin, outstripped all his other models of decked canoes in sales. Orders continued at a satisfactory level. In February, 1887, Rushton announced that orders were in excess of last year's; that he was busy turning out fifty canvas canoes for Squires, the first mention of his building craft of this kind in any quantity. In June of the same year *Forest and Stream* commented, "Since he first began the construction of light boats thirteen years ago, Mr. Rushton has revolutionized the boat building business, and all who have dealt with him will agree that his success is due no less to the energy and originality which he brought into his work than to his fair and honest dealing and the character of his boats."

Yet the meet of 1886 had been a challenge to Rushton's pre-eminence among canoe builders. It brought a new name to the fore in ACA circles, that of Joyner. It raised a question about the clinker-built hulls of practically all of Rushton's regular models to that date. Moreover, 1886 marked a crest in the popularity of the decked wooden cruiser adapted both to sailing and paddling and requiring materials and craftsmanship of high quality. Over the next decade the decked wooden canoe was to evolve as a specialized racer. And racing was for the few. For general use the open Canadian canoe gained steadily in favor in the United States, first with a finished wooden hull, then with a canvas-covered hull, and later still one made of aluminum or fiber glass.

Rushton had built his first boat with a view to recovering his health through an outdoor life in the woods. But ever since, he had been too busy building boats to worry about health. In 1887, however, he could no longer ignore rheumatic aches and pains and took a longer rest than usual that summer. The family removed to their cottage on Star Lake, carting the *Joharrie* there for cruises on the lake. At the end of the summer Rushton turned the launch over to one of the hotels.

Perhaps poor health made him restless. Anyway, he startled Canton in June by announcing suddenly that the Boat Shop was for sale and that he was considering moving elsewhere. This decision came as a shock to his friends, his workmen, and the whole community. Oppressive freight rates were his chief reason, he explained. Canton is one hundred and thirty miles north of the main line of the New York Central running through Syracuse and Utica. Industry located on the branch line north through Watertown to Canton and Malone or to Ogdensburg had to pay a freight differential for the privilege of isolation. Rushton also stated that he lacked adequate water nearby for testing and experimenting. The Grass River above and below Canton was clogged by the annual log drives from early spring into fall and in winter by ice. Rushton had in mind the lower Hudson near the large city markets and canoe clubs—perhaps Newburgh.

Pressure was certainly brought to bear to make Rushton change his mind. The Boat Shop was not a large employer with its approximately twenty men, but it had brought prestige to Canton. Rushton and Leah would be missed in community life. Friends must have interceded strongly. Gilbert B. Manley, editor of the *Plaindealer,* ran eulogy after eulogy of Mr.

Rushton and his boats. In the end, Rushton did not move. Instead, he built in the fall a twenty-four by fifty foot addition to the shop as storage space for lumber.

Rushton may have hoped to counter the disadvantage of Canton's remoteness and high freight rates by a determined advertising campaign. In March he announced that in 1887 alone, he would spend one thousand dollars for advertising, a large sum for such purposes by Canton standards, considering the current value of gold. The annual catalog steadily increased in size and bettered in the quality of its illustrations over the next six years. It was introduced in 1888 by the ringing statement: "We offer for your consideration a greater number and variety of boats than any other builder in the world." In the 1889 Year Book of the ACA Rushton's flamboyant ad ran, in phrases stepped down the page: "Cincinnati to Itaska, Itaska to the Gulf, Lake George to Pensacola (via Ohio and Mississippi), Rochester to Montreal—One million miles in all. To get the whole story send a nickel for our 82-page catalogue." *Forest and Stream* praised the catalog of 1892 as "far handsomer and more elaborate than anything yet."

Lest Canton once again face the threat of losing so valuable an asset, Editor Manley dealt out liberal portions of free advertising:

Mr. Rushton has sent boats to South America, to England, Scotland, France and Egypt. He has recently sent three fine sailing canoes to Paris and has a fourth nearly ready to go there. He has two going to Seattle. . . .

His canoes have traversed nearly every navigable water on the globe, some individual canoes having cruising records of 5,000 to 10,000 miles. Others have won scores of prizes. . . .

Mr. Rushton has long been noted as a builder of the finest goods in the market and therefore gets good customers and the best prices. His order book shows the names of such men as William K. Vanderbilt, Dr. Seward Webb, late Secretary of the Navy Whitney . . . President Diaz, of Mexico, and thousands of more or less note throughout this and other countries.

The Navaho

The American Beauty

Similar in design to the Indian Girl, the Navaho was built of less expensive material; it was produced to meet price competition. The American Beauty, designed by Harry Rushton after his father's death, was characterized by its sharply upturned stems, its excellent quality of construction, and its great beauty.

Rushton and Workmen Testing a Motorized Boat

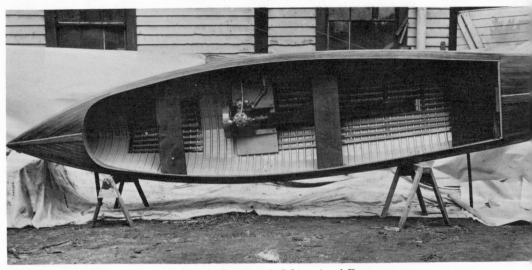

Harry Rushton's Motorized Boat

Rushton experimented with motorizing his craft, but never succeeded in developing a market for them. Shown directly above is one of the boats designed by Rushton and built by his son Harry. Although this launch ("putt-putt," as it was commonly known) became popular locally, it was never a great income producer.

Iowa
Pleasure
Rowboat

(Photo by Alfred J. Wyatt)

Testing a
Rushton Dinghy

Although they were not as attractive in line as the canoes, the pleasure boats and general purpose boats had a continuing, stable market. In the second photograph (lower left), the side of the Boat Shop may be seen.

A Rushton Sailboat

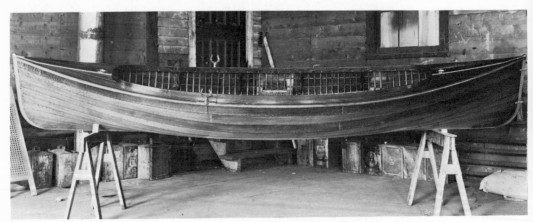

Rushton's Row-and-Sail Boat, No. 112

Rushton never hesitated to design and build any small craft. Above, W. F. Kip, Rushton's fore-man, finishes rigging the fore-and-aft (gaff) rigged mainsail of a small sloop, with the jib al-ready rigged to the mainmast. The second photograph shows a small Rushton boat equipped with a hole set in both the forward and after decks, to accommodate a mast (or masts), and a set of oarlocks as well.

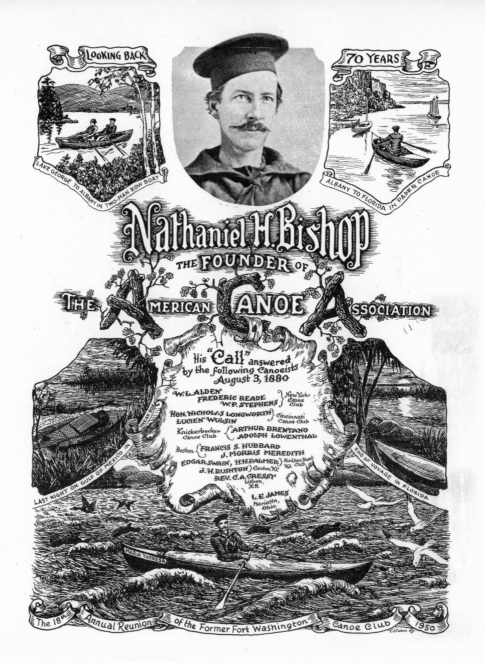

Memorial to Nathaniel H. Bishop

This pen-and-ink memorial sketch was the work of one of the latter-day ACA enthusiasts, T. J. Cornu. He prepared the sketch in 1950, of his own volition, for no official purpose. Obviously the artist did not do his homework, or he would have listed 23 canoeists who "answered the call" on August 3, 1880, instead of only 14.

The Wigwam on One of The Three Sister Islands, Lake George

In 1880, three charter members of the ACA (Nicholas Longworth and Lucien Wulsin, of Cincinnati, and Nathaniel H. Bishop, of Lake George) purchased "The Three Sister Islands" (renamed the Canoeing Islands) in Lake George, to serve as the site for annual ACA encampments. On one of the islands, they erected the Wigwam shown above, for the use of the ACA officers. Plans did not materialize, however, and two years later, the annual meet was held at Stoney Lake, Ontario, Canada. Thereafter it was held at various places in the northeastern United States, only rarely at Lake George. (Photo by S. R. Stoddard)

The American Canoe Association 1882 Meet

The three men in dark clothing, standing in the center foreground, left to right are: ACA Commodore-elect, E. B. Edwards, of Canada; ACA Commodore Nicholas Longworth, of Cincinnati; ACA Secretary-Treasurer, Dr. Charles E. Neidé. Rushton appears sitting in the extreme right foreground, his feet on the wall.

Start of the International Challenge Cup Race, 1886 ACA Meet

This photograph was taken just off Delaney's Point, Grindstone Island on the St. Lawrence River. *Vesper*, the winner, is the canoe left of the central group, its sail designation (no. 265) barely discernible. Designed by Robert H. Gibson, Albany, N.Y. architect, and built by Rushton in the Boat Shop, *Vesper* won by a hair.

Vesper,
Winner of the 1886 Cup

Vesper with a Group of ACA Members

The trophy cup can be seen on the forehatch. Grouped behind the winning canoe are Nicholas Longworth (seated directly behind the trophy), Walter Stewart, Baden-Powell's English sailing companion (seated beside the cockpit), Warrington Baden-Powell (standing directly behind Stewart), and the skipper, Robert H. Gibson (standing at left of Baden-Powell).

Warington Baden-Powell Sailing
Nautilus No. 5

The International Cup Sailing Race originated on Baden-Powell's challenge to the ACA in 1885. He assured the Americans that one or more English canoeists would come to the United States to participate in such a race, to determine which canoes and whose sailing tactics were the best.

The Rushton-St. Lawrence Canoe Club Tent at the 1886 Meet

The tent became headquarters for all of the Canton canoe enthusiasts who attended the ACA meets. Heighway, "the Cincinnati giant," because of his friendship for Rushton, attached himself to the group. From the left, standing: J. Henry Rushton, Dr. A. E. Heighway, William F. Kip; foreground: Felix Pflaum, Williston Manley, Leah P. Rushton, Fanny Dailey, John Jackson, Ira Davis, May Kip, Asa Dailey, and Judd W. Rushton.

Walter Stewart Sailing *Pearl*

A Group of ACA Members at the ACA Meet

Baden-Powell is shown dressed in white, in the middle foreground. Behind him (to the right), in the striped jersey, is his companion, Walter Stewart, skipper of *Pearl*. The second man to the left of Baden-Powell is the Springfield industrialist E. H. Barney (with sideburn whiskers), skipper of *Pecowsic*, the runner-up to *Vesper* in the Cup Race.

RUSHTON'S

PORTABLE

Sporting Boats and Canoes

—— FOR ——

Hunting, Fishing, Trapping or Pleasure Rowing.

C A N O E S,

Open or Decked, for Paddling, Rowing or Sailing.

Light Weight, Fine Models, Good Material, Moderate Prices.

J. H. RUSHTON, Manufacturer,

CANTON, St Lawrence Co., N. Y.

PLAINDEALER STEAM PRESSES, CANTON, N. Y.

The Front Cover of the First Rushton Catalog, Issued in 1877

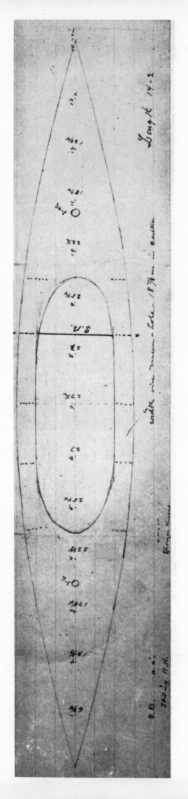
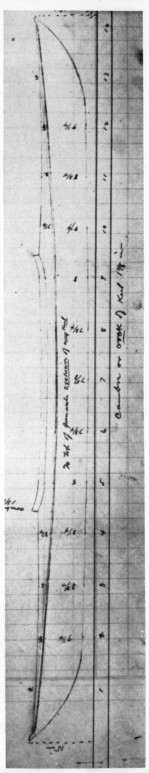

Rushton's Draftsmanship

Found in a letter to Lucien Wulsin, dated February 17, 1880, this is the only existing example of draftsmanship by J. Henry Rushton. In answer to Wulsin's request, Rushton included these scaled line drawings of his Rob Roy model cedar canoe.

Rushton's Rob Roy

The cedar canoe model was rechristened by Commodore Alden at the 1880 Charter Meeting of the ACA. On that date it became Rushton's American Traveling Canoe.

Kleiner Fritz

This Rob Roy model, made by Rushton in 1877 for A. H. Siegfried, became the property of Lucien Wulsin, who renamed it *Betsy D*. (Courtesy Lucien Wulsin Jr.)

Sairy Gamp

In 1883, *Sairy Gamp* was designated by *Forest and Stream* as "the lightest canoe ever made by man for practical purposes." Rushton made the canoe for Nessmuk's celebrated cruise through the Adirondacks. Probably the most famous canoe in history, it was in the Smithsonian Institution's collections for more than 75 years. (Courtesy the Smithsonian Institution)

Dr. Charles A. Neidé and His
Rushton-Built *Aurora*

Capt. Samuel D. Kendall and His
Homemade *Solid Comfort*

At the close of the 1882 ACA Meet, Neidé and Kendall, in these canoes, cruised from Lake George to Pensacola, Florida. The 3,300 mile trip took them to Florida via the Erie Canal; the Allegheny, the Ohio, and the Mississippi Rivers; and the Gulf Coast. This is one of the longest canoe cruises on record. (Courtesy New York Historical Association)

Diana

This Princess model was given by Lucien Wulsin Jr. to the Adirondack Museum in 1964. The 1882 ACA Yearbook lists this canoe among those participating in class races on Lake George that summer. In near-mint condition, *Diana* is one of the finest examples of Rushton's craftsmanship.

Rushton's Workshop—
Decking the Nomad

Rushton's Nomad Sailing Canoe

The Nomad, developed from the Arkansas Traveler and the Ugo, was the last and probably the most popular of Rushton's cedar sailing canoes. The workshop photograph shows the Nomad before and after decking: a good example of the high quality of Rushton's workmanship that carried through to the closing days of the Boat Shop.

Yes, business was good at the Boat Shop in the years 1887–92. If there was no longer a large annual increase in sales, there was hope that new products and increased advertising would soon put the business back on the upgrade. Rushton continued his experiments with powered craft. Small inboard steam engines were tried out, ranging from one-eighth up to two horsepower. A sister to the *Joharrie* was built. Then came the testing of electric power. In December, 1887, Rushton announced that he had lately run a Vesper canoe with a one-eighth horsepower motor and four Julien storage cells, the weight of the load being 460 pounds. The craft had a speed of four miles an hour, and Rushton hoped to better this with an improved motor and more cells. Soon after, he installed a one-half horsepower electric motor in larger hulls and advertised electric launches for sale. Yet, in spite of all this experimenting with powered craft, there is no evidence that the Boat Shop ever reached a profitable level of production in this field.

Even when ill at home or vacationing upcountry, Rushton kept close track of operations at the shop. He could well affirm that "our business has been our study; our workshop was our blackboard and the problems to be solved the greatest possible perfection of our work."

One problem he solved in an ingenious way. He wanted to determine what size air chamber a boat should have for safety. Since a dunking experiment might offend the dignity of workmen in the shop, Rushton looked around for another labor supply. Every warm summer day boys of all sizes passed the Boat Shop door on their way to a swimming hole at Princess Rock on the Grass River. They liked dunkings. With a small bribe it was simple to enlist their help. Whooping and laughing, thirty-four boys averaging sixty-eight pounds stripped down and took turns jumping into a large calibrated vat of water. Rushton found the water displacement per pound of boy and, by calculations satisfying to himself at least, arrived at the conclusion that four hundred cubic inches of air would be enough to float a person weighing one hundred pounds and

keep his head above water. The men at the shop had sport
dunking the boys; the boys too had fun. No protest was reported from parents or other authorities. Today, what would
the P.T.A., the S.P.C.C., the Labor Department, the Children's Court, et cetera, have to say about such use of small
naked bodies?

Rushton's pre-eminence among canoe builders through
1886 had rested chiefly on the high quality of his all-purpose
decked cedar canoes. He was less successful in turning out the
specialized racing craft thereafter required by the expert sail-
ors in trophy races who changed canoe models every year or so,
seeking new refinements for greater speed. Gibson re-entered
the Challenge Cup race of the ACA in 1887, his last year of
active racing, and again won the trophy, but it was with a new
canoe, the *Notus,* made by another builder. In 1888 a Rushton-
built smoothskin cruiser decked with a handsome piece of mahogany, the *Girofla No. 5,* owned by Nickerson of the Springfield Canoe Club, won much praise about camp. But it was the
Eclipse, a Ruggles-built craft owned by M. V. Brokaw, of
Brooklyn, that carried away racing honors. In an article in
Forest and Stream on the new racing craft at the ACA meet of
1890, no Rushton boat is mentioned. In 1892 the largest repre-
sentation at the meet was that of a new club, the Bulwagga of
Port Henry, New York, all with Rushton canoes and all nov-
ices. The Bulwaggas carried off first and second places in
both the novice race and the Jabberwock Trophy. But this was
a far cry from the *Vesper*'s victory in 1886.

Other men had learned how to build good canoes. Competition grew fast in the late eighties. Younger men than Rushton
set up shop, attracted by the good market and congenial work
for a craftsman's hands. When the ACA was founded in 1880,
the field of widely known quality builders was pretty well pre-
empted by Rushton, Stephens, the Racine Boat Company, and
Everson, the last the chosen builder of the New York Canoe
Club from its start in 1871. By 1890 the situation was very different. Several new builders had won reputations in canoeing

circles. F. Joyner, now located in Schenectady, was doing a thriving business. The *Notus,* trophy-winning craft in 1887, was built by Bowdish and Son of Skaneateles, New York. In the following year's meet the same builder's *If* won much attention. A formidable new rival had appeared also in Rochester—Captain George W. Ruggles. In the 1888 meet Barney, of *Pecowsic* fame, had a new craft named the *Ruggles* in honor of its designer and builder. The *Eclipse,* which won the Challenge Cup that year, was also built by Ruggles. Rushton's presence at the annual meets was no longer so conspicuous as in the past. In 1888 he shared presence with Captain Ruggles, Bowdish, and Spencer, the latter a well-known builder of Hartford, Connecticut. Stevens of Portland, Maine, was building craft designed by Paul Butler for racing experts of the Vesper Canoe Club of Lowell. Herbert Sprague, of Parishville, twenty-five miles from Canton, was still building canoes and in 1889 patented a new method of making a tight seam by laying a thin strip of treated rubber between planks. Sixty miles away was the Watertown Boat and Canoe Company. One of the fastest growing competitors in the East was located sixty-five miles away in Clayton, port of embarkation for the meets on Grindstone Island—the St. Lawrence River Skiff, Canoe and Steam Launch Company. By 1890 this maker was represented in ACA meets by fleets of canoes. In 1895 it outgrew its building in Clayton and moved to a large new factory in Ogdensburg, nineteen miles from Canton. And there were other builders. In the face of such competition Rushton canoes no longer enjoyed the lion's share of attention of former years.

It was time for strong measures. Rushton must have seen in the World's Columbian Exposition a chance to re-establish his lead. He had been successful in previous exhibits at St. Louis and New Orleans. With the *Sairy Gamp* as centerpiece of his display in the World's Industrial Exhibition in New Orleans, he had carried off a blue ribbon award and two gold medals.

The Columbian Exposition had been planned for 1892, but

the elaborate preparations were not complete until the next year, which happened to be one of financial panic. Yet as an artistic creation the Chicago Fair of the spring, summer, and fall months of 1893 was a triumph. The "White City" beside Lake Michigan was an apparition that made visitors wish it might last forever.

For months the Boat Shop prepared diligently for an eye-catching exhibit. Even the catalog for 1893 was slanted toward the fair with its title "The World's Columbian Exposition Edition." Ten fine boats were prepared for shipment to Chicago to represent the range of the Boat Shop's products: one single and one two-man cruising canoe, one racing sailer with bucket cockpit and silk sails, a racing paddler, several open canoes, a Saranac Laker or Adirondack guide-boat, and a pleasure boat. The latter, resembling one just delivered to Governor Proctor of Vermont, had a canopy top with scalloped, valanced edges. Other features of the exhibit were a miniature fleet and two manikins. Rushton assigned one of his most skilled workmen, young John Howe, to the task of turning out a set of miniature rowboats, skiffs, and canoes made to scale. Of the original thirteen made, nine have of late been found and are now in the small Rushton Collection in the Canton Library. To show how boats are portaged in wilderness country, canoes rested bottoms up on the shoulders of two life-sized figures.

To prepare the exhibit, rent space, ship the display to Chicago, and put a man in charge of it, Rushton had to borrow heavily. His credit was unquestioned, his business prospering. What could not be foreseen was the financial depression in the making. Hardly had the Exposition gates swung open in May when the panic came. America's economy was paralyzed. During the summer, with many banks failing or suspending operations, business houses closing, and failures snowballing, President Cleveland called Congress into special session to take emergency measures.

That was an unhappy summer for Rushton. Orders dried up. Even his display in the Transportation Building was not attracting as much attention as he had hoped for. A competitor, the St. Lawrence River Skiff, Canoe and Steam Launch Company, had a larger display—twenty-eight boats in all—and shared awards with Rushton. More disturbing was a turn in the public fancy. People were more interested that summer in bicycles than in boats. The crowds milled for a moment in front of the boat exhibits and then moved on to gather in large numbers before an exhibit of Columbia bicycles.

A board of international judges decreed a "medal for specific merit" to Rushton for his exhibit of "boats, canoes, oars, and paddles . . . of most excellent form and workmanship." An engraved certificate (now in the historical collection of St. Lawrence University) was sent to his home in the fall. But the esteem of a jury of peers had little influence on the fickle public that year or the next. When the certificate arrived, Rushton framed it to hang in his office. But not many customers came in to see it. Potential ones were rapturously engaged in pedaling Columbia bikes up and down the street past the Boat Shop. People with cash or credit to squander on luxuries that year of the panic bought bicycles, not boats.

Rushton became worried and short tempered. Henry W. Sudds, cashier of a bank in the neighboring village of Gouverneur, wrote Rushton's foreman, Will Kip, on October 18, 1893, when the fair was drawing to a close:

Since writing my letter I have attended the world's fair, and saw Mr. Rushton there and asked him in regard to the lumber.

He said he would not furnish it, and in fact was so disagreeable in general that if I could purchase as good articles in the boat line elsewhere I certainly would never buy another thing of him.

I see your letter has an entirely different tone so I write this so as not to make you any trouble, and if when he returns you may be able to soften his heart would be pleased to hear from you and order the stuff I want.

The depression was a setback from which recovery was slow. Harry Rushton stated before his death that the debt under which his father labored as a result of the investment in the Columbian Exposition hung like an anchor about his neck for years.

Business continued slow in 1894. In the spring Will Kip wrote to his younger brother, Benjamin, that trade was slow and that he had little confidence in Rushton's experiments in promoting small launches. Late in the year Rushton himself wrote to Ben, who was attending the Art Students' League in New York, in regard to some art work for the Boat Shop: "Now as to cost. If you can make it less than $1.50 do so, for times are awful—no trade at all." On January 8, 1895, he wrote again to Ben to acknowledge receipt of the drawings: "The balance of drawings & bill rec'd. The former are o.k. and the latter seems to be also. Today my bank a/c is in red figures but I have something almost in sight and will not leave you out in the cold many days. Thanking you also for your kindness in the matter." Before the end of the month he sent Ben a check for $2.50.

Gradually Rushton reduced his bank indebtedness. In 1898 the directors of the First National Bank were at the point of writing off the remainder, but characteristically he insisted on meeting his obligation—and in a practical manner. He proposed that the bank accept a canoe in place of cash. The bank was not in the market for canoes, but its cashier, Wriley N. Beard, was. He accepted the proposal, paid Rushton cash for half the price of the canoe, and turned the other half of the payment over to settle Rushton's small remaining note. The Columbian Exposition and the depression reduced Rushton to near-poverty for a period of five years, caused worry and occasional irritability. But he weathered hard times with less damage to morale than hundreds of thousands of other Americans, and at the turn of the century he was in the market with a popular new canoe.

Yet his business seems never to have recovered the full prosperity it enjoyed on the eve of the Columbian Exposition. The bicycle proved more than a passing fad. Rushton's Canton friends, once reliable purchasers of his boats as the ice went out in the spring, were now, young and old, riding bikes through village streets and on country roads. One of his best local customers of former years and by now a well-known artist, Frederic Remington, besported himself on a Columbia bike whenever he visited his family in Canton. Remington's poundage was mounting dangerously in those years, and there was much more man to be seen than bike. In a letter (now in the Remington Collection of St. Lawrence University) to his Yale classmate, Poultney Bigelow, then in Europe, Remington wrote: "I am riding a bike—it's great fun— Everybody in America is riding the 'bike.' It makes the grease come out of a fellow and is the greatest thing to produce a thirst for beer—besides everyone can desecrate the Sabbath on a bike and be forgiven by other U.S.A.'s who all do the same. In that respect it is like going to hell—everyone is there whom I like."

It must have pained Rushton to see this familiar burly figure in knickerbockers wheeling past the Boat Shop and to remember better days when the artist had expended surplus energy in paddling a canoe on North Country waters. But Remington was soon after to redeem himself by buying two Rushton canoes for his new camp in the Thousand Islands. A bike wasn't of much use on the five-acre island of Ingleneuk.

Family burdens were also a drain on Rushton's resources. In recalling those years of hardship, Harry Rushton later wrote:

Father had a very deep sense of family responsibilities. He set his father and step-mother up in housekeeping in a place on Water Street next to the Shop, after Peter was no longer able to get along on his farm at Crary Mills. [Later, after his wife's death, Peter lived briefly in the Hodskin Street house, then with Eliza in Pyrites.] One summer he set his youngest half-brother, Ed, up in business in a boat livery at Oneida Lake near Syracuse. It failed to pay off. His mother's sister lived with us a number of years until she went to Hannawa Falls to live with another sister. My mother's father, Nathan Pflaum, and my mother's sister lived with us a good many years, and their housekeeper as well.

The failure of Rushton's display at the Exposition to meet expectations, the financial crash of 1893, dwindling sales in the following years of depression and of the bicycle craze, and dependent relatives were harsh tests for a man who for twenty years had grown accustomed to uninterrupted success. Yet throughout this period his habits of work changed little. Harry Rushton told me that before and during his high school and college years his father was always up with the sun and off to the shop before the workmen arrived. There J. Henry would sort out the day's supply of lumber, discarding the knotty and imperfect planks. Often he would find time to rough out some of this material on the saw before the force put in an appearance. The rest of the day he was most often found in his office on the second floor in his shirt sleeves, designing and perfecting specifications on a twelve-foot drawing board. In the evening he was again often at work on business matters, posting his books or writing letters.

His chief avenue of rest and relaxation was the Stillwater Club. Many a weekend he spent there, hunting, canoeing, fishing. "He managed to set aside August each summer," said Harry Rushton, "so the entire family could go into camp at the North Branch clubhouse. As the guide, Jim O'Brien, expected Mother to do all of the cooking, Father limited this outing strictly to the immediate family." He would not overburden Leah with extra plates to fill.

Chapter XII

FROM CRUISER
TO PADDLER

CANOEING in America survived the depression of the mid-nineties; survived the competition of tennis, golf, and yachting. It survived even the bicycle craze, a deadly enemy that closed Rushton's shop down for a brief period in 1896. But in surviving, it underwent changes that old-time canoeists thought crucial and diminishing. In the seventies and the eighties canoeing had been more than a sport. It had been a way of life to men like Bishop, Kendall, Neidé, and Nessmuk. By 1900, however, it was little more than a pleasant pastime, one of many outdoor sports competing for the leisure time of the public and in no stronger position than any other to meet the rivalry of the automobile still to come.

The passing of the old order of canoeists brought a radical change in the canoe itself. It became cheaper, simpler, less adaptable to the long cruise, less challenging to the craftsman's art; more standardized in design and materials, more democratic; more the plaything of an idle hour, less the companion of a quest. The Rob Roy cruiser of MacGregor and its progeny in England and America gradually gave way to the open canoe, first of cedar, then canvas covered, and finally of aluminum. Taking a long view back, a canoeist of today, Calvin Rutstrum, has this word of regret: "The all-wood cedar canoes, more prominently used in the early part of the century, are delightful. I have warm feelings also for the wood-and-canvas models. If an aluminum violin gave you the same mellow tone as a Stradivarius, you would undoubtedly still object to an aluminum violin and take the wooden Stradivarius."

Many of those who saw the change take place also regretted

it. In the last year or two of the century Albert Strange wrote in the nostalgic meter of *Hiawatha:*

> Sadly mused the old canoeist,
> Sitting in his winter wigwam,
>
> . . . .
>
> On the changes time was making,
> In himself—and in canoeing.
> Gone—he mused—the days delightful
> When we sailed forth with paddle
> (Tiny sail and trusty paddle),
> Apron-mackintoshed and cosy,
> In our dainty Rob Roy cruiser,
> Bound for nowhere in partic'lar,
> Down the rapid, down the river,
> Out to sea—no matter whither:
> When we couldn't sail, we paddled,
> When we couldn't paddle, pushed her,
> Over bars, and over sandbanks,
> From the river to the railway,
> From the railway to the carrier,
> Over mountains—over deserts;
> Nature set no bounds to journeys
> In the dainty Rob Roy cruiser.

About the same time these lines were written the canoeing editor of *Forest and Stream* commented (May 27, 1899): "The canoe, as canoeists first knew it, has passed away, and apparently beyond recall. . . . We do regret that the old 'paddleable' or 'paddling and sailing' canoe and . . . canoe cruising as introduced by MacGregor are practically extinct in America and Great Britain."

Looking back, we now recognize the change as inevitable. The growth of population, the demand for cheaper, mass-produced articles, the decline of the crafts are factors in the change. Even more decisive in the long run would have been the scarcity of prime lumber. Already in 1904 Rushton was writing to Lucien Wulsin, his piano-manufacturing friend in Cincinnati, about West Coast lumber as an alternative to depleted supplies in the East.

But there were other, more immediate factors involved in the passing of the decked wooden cruiser. Its decline began even before the depression of the nineties and the bicycle craze. A canoeist using the pen name "Retaw" deplored as early as 1888 the effects that the emphasis on racing in ACA circles was having on the canoe and on canoeing. It was lessening interest in cruising and leading to the specialized racing craft. "When, however, its [the canoe's] future destinies passed into the keeping of an Association not unaffected by the racing mania, the danger that it would be ruined by being specialized arose. . . . To such a point has the specialization of the wooden canoe been carried that two classes have been created and are generally recognized, the cruiser and racer, whereas there should be but one class, the canoe. Worse than all, the racer is the popular craft, the spoiled child of the Association." Ten years later this trend had run its full course. Through the nineties the complaint was often raised in *Forest and Stream* that attendance at ACA meets was barely holding its own, that interest in racing was declining, that fewer canoes were entered in the races. This waning interest is reflected in the shrinking space devoted to canoeing in that journal. "It is no wonder," wrote the canoeing editor in 1897, "that there is so little interest in the trophy and unlimited sailing, as the successful canoe in this work must be a fearful and wonderful machine, comparatively costly, only to be obtained by hard work on the part of her owner, and of no use whatever except for a few days' racing at the meet." The cost and the limited use of such a racing machine in a time of business depression limited racing activities to the few.

By 1900 many local canoe clubs had been inactive for some time, and there was little designing and building of new craft. "With the exception of a few extreme racing machines, the decked canoe, the craft which gave birth to modern canoeing and made it what it once was, has disappeared," said *Forest and Stream* on January 6, 1900. Racers, it went on, were not numerous enough to make good racing, yet served to bar other types. Most cruising was done in the open canoe of Canadian style. The editor felt that a strong effort should be made to revive interest. In cooperation with ACA officials *Forest and Stream* inaugurated a new policy in its canoeing department at the beginning of 1900. Regular weekly columns on canoeing were abandoned, but in their place the journal offered expanded coverage in the first issue of each month. Canoeists across the country could subscribe to these twelve issues separately at one dollar a year, a fourth of the price of a full annual subscription. Cash prizes were offered for winning narratives about canoe cruises, a policy carried out for one year. Canoeing news was covered with a fullness not known in the journal since the eighties. There were long editorials and communications from officials of canoeing clubs. Later in the year the fruits of the contest began to appear in stories of cruises. For the historian of canoeing in America, 1900 is a well-documented year. Once a month at least the canoeing columns vied in length with those devoted to yachting. But apparently the effort failed to achieve the results hoped for. It was abandoned the next year, and thereafter coverage of the sport tapered off to brief news items and the very occasional narrative of a cruise. In the annual index "Canoeing" was no longer a heading followed by subject listings, but a single line followed by a few page numbers.

One wonders whether the factors alleged at the time were sufficient to cause the sharp decline of interest in the sport apparent in the files of *Forest and Stream* from about 1888 to 1906, the year of Rushton's death. During this period the journal was the only official organ of the ACA in unbroken publication. In 1893 it predicted, correctly it seems, that "there is a marked lack of vitality in both cruising and racing that must, sooner or later, have a bad effect on canoeing at large." The specialization and costliness of the racing canoe may largely account for the decline of interest in racing. But why was there not sufficient enthusiasm for cruising to combat a business depression and the competition of other sports over the next few years?

Perhaps the passing of the frontier in America had something to do with diminishing enthusiasm for cruising. The lure of the unknown, the zest of exploring are undercurrent notes in the narratives of canoe voyages glanced at in this biography. In the seventies and the eighties there were still unsettled, unmapped areas in the West. The stories of pioneers entering these regions circulated across the country. The spirit of the pioneers was shared by men like Siegfried and Glazier as long as there were still untraveled waterways such as the headwaters of the Mississippi and rivers in the West. The canoe then gave Easterners an opportunity to share to some extent in the adventure of westering while it was still going on. Canoeists found a deep satisfaction in penetrating little-known waters in a craft as fragile but versatile as the canoe. For this purpose the decked cruiser, which could be paddled or sailed, used for dry storage, slept in, lived in day after day—tight, maneuverable, and gallant in swift water, dainty and responsive in calm —was ideal.

The zest of pioneering in unmapped waters is evident in a letter which Rushton prized enough to dispense with all other testimonials in the catalog of 1888, and which he quoted in full. Its author, J. C. Haines, had the privilege of pushing the explorations of Lewis and Clark a little farther, to the source of the Columbia River. The letter is addressed to Rushton and is dated September 9, 1887, from Seattle:

I have just returned from a canoe trip which has lasted just one month and which has involved about 325 miles of canoeing and over 1200 of travel by rail, steamer, and on horseback. I have navigated my canoe, a *Rushton Vesper,* to the very source of the Columbia River and have planted the A.C.A. flag at its very head waters, Three Silver Springs, which pours from the mountain sides of a basin just large enough to float a canoe and from which that mighty river springs. It is in the heart of the Rocky Mountains, far up in British Columbia, 2,775 feet from the sea. I have run the Kootenay River from the first point where a canoe will float, for over 300 miles a continuous rapid, rushing through the Rockies and downhill all the way. I have seen and portaged that which few white men have ever beheld and no map makers ever located, the Great Falls of the Kootenay, and am here to tell the tale, although had it not been for the thorough and honest workmanship displayed in the building of my canoe, I should now have been sleeping at their foot. I have jumped lesser falls, overcome huge whirlpools, run roaring mountain canyons and rapids without number; and have returned with the most thorough respect for the decked canoe that man can have for any creation of man.

There were four in our party, two in a 17 x 42 open Peterboro, one in a Mohican No. 2 that you built for me, and myself in my Vesper. Before we started down the Kootenay, the Peterboro contended and we were half inclined to admit that in rough and rocky water . . . the open canoe with two men was superior to the decked with one. But a dozen miles in swift water completely changed our views.

The decked canoe will turn quicker and shorter and avoid obstacles far better than the open; and in broken water the odds in favor of the former are tremendous. With our aprons close around us, we were always dry and our boats buoyant, while the open canoe was always half full of water and narrowly escaped swamping a dozen times. The long blade of the drop rudder is far more serviceable in turning, and our lives often depended on the quickness of the turn, than the steering paddle of the stern man in the Peterboro. I was thrown against the rock as I have mentioned; the blow crushed the planking, but the ribs held and what would have swamped an ordinary boat proved only a small leak to mine. . . .

On this trip I carried the A.C.A. flag farther north than it was ever taken before, but on my coming cruise I intend taking it very much farther north than that, and all in a Rushton canoe. . . .

Haines's letter is interesting for the comparison it makes of the open Canadian type of canoe and the decked cruiser. It is also interesting as an expression of the joy of exploring uncharted waters and pitting one's resources against unknown risks. Already in 1887 Haines and his companion were crossing the border into Canada to seek such opportunities. Soon after, no man could say with conviction of any waters he explored in North America, "I was the first." With the passing of the frontier passed some of the romance of canoe cruising. Canoeing remained, as it always will be, a healthful exercise; a test of skill in white water; an excellent device for girling, as men discovered in the nineties; an agreeable way to travel and camp in state and national parks with a topographical map in hand; and for nature lovers an unmatched mode of observation, though the aluminum canoe of today is a little noisy for this purpose. These are perhaps values enough. But the passing of the frontier left canoeists with somewhat less incentive to devote time and money to perfecting the cruising canoe when in guidebook waters the simpler and cheaper paddling canoe is serviceable enough.

In Rushton's catalogs the Vesper survived for many years the waning popularity of the cruising canoe. It was the only decked cruiser offered as a stock model in 1895. In 1903 another, the Wren, was offered. In a catalog published after Rushton's death, the Wren is replaced by the Nomad, and the Vesper still survives in the first decade of the new century. But the decked cruiser, the all-around canoe Rushton had slowly brought close to perfection, was no longer the mainstay of the Boat Shop.

In the twenty years after the founding of the ACA in 1880, the canoeing scene in America changed greatly. Many changes took place in Rushton's personal life during the same period. They were on his mind as he replied on April 11, 1900, to Commodore W. G. MacKendrick's urging to attend the twenty-first annual meet of the ACA in August:

I'd like to be there, you may be sure. I'm an old member of the A.C.A. in more ways than one. One August morn in 1880, as I walked over behind the boat house at Crosbyside, I found several men gathered around a bit of a fire. One was talking to the others. It was Bishop. He said: "We expect Mr. Rushton," and I answered, "Here." Then I was introduced to Longworth, Alden, Wulsin, and others. A committee was named to nominate first officers. I was on that committee twenty years ago. Many changes. Then I was a bachelor. Now I have a fourteen-year-old boy 4 in. and 18 lbs. bigger than I am. Longworth is over the great Divide. I haven't heard of

Alden, Wulsin nor Heighway for years. I had a letter just the other day from Bishop—from West Palm Beach, Fla. Mrs. Bishop is dead. She was a charming lady, and Bishop has sold his Lake George property. Well, well, I'm yarning it.

Oh, yes! One more I haven't heard from of late—Tyson. My regards to him if he is yet with you.

And "So long," as Nessmuk used to say.

Yours truly,

J. H. Rushton

P.S. — You will notice my A.C.A. number is 37. Also that I am a charter member, and that there are but twenty-two [other] charter members. I was No. 3, 4 or 5 to sign the constitution. How I got to 37 I never knew. Until years had gone by I did not think much of it. Now I wish I was numbered rightly.

R.

Since 1898 the Boat Shop had been back on an even keel. Seasonal loans for inventory building were held to manageable limits, and sales picked up again. The catalog of 1898 offered a houseboat and a line of powerboats. Present at the ACA meet of 1897 at Grindstone, Rushton had on exhibit there a canoe powered by a naphtha engine and capable of doing six to seven miles an hour. But his efforts to promote powered craft failed in the end. Will Kip hinted that his failure resulted from trying to use regular hull models for loads they were not designed to bear. At any rate, Rushton finally gave up this unprofitable line. In the introduction to his catalog of 1903 he put a good face on the matter by declaring in capitals: "I BUILD NO POWER BOATS OF ANY KIND."

He was much more successful with the open canoe, first the Canadian type and later his Indian models. The open canoe capable of carrying a crew of two or more and usually propelled by single-bladed paddles grew in popularity as the decked cruiser lost ground. "The ordinary open canoes are coming into greater use each year in the United States," said *Forest and Stream* in 1889, "and more are seen at the meets. For pleasure paddling and exercise, and especially for 'girling,' they are unequalled." It may have been girling that carried the day. The decked cruiser is ill adapted to this deservedly popular sport. The open canoe is more companionable. It is also cheaper. In 1903 Rushton offered the decked cruiser Vesper at $100 without fittings and $170 with; the Canadian models of the same sixteen-foot length but with short decks at the ends, at $85 for Grade AA and $59 for Grade A, including a pair of paddles.

The Canadian canoe, introduced in the United States at the first ACA meet in 1880, originated in the Peterborough region of Ontario. Because of a shortage of paper birch in that country, the Indian birchbark was little known, and the real progenitor of the Canadian model was the log dugout. About 1855 Ontario boatmakers began to replace the crude dugout with hulls made first of basswood, later of white cedar. The lines were sharp, the floor was broad and flat, and the topsides had a slight inward curve (tumble home)—a design perfected about the time MacGregor launched his first Rob Roy. This craft was widely used in the Peterborough country for hunting, fishing, and pleasure paddling before it was initiated to racing in a regatta held in 1857. With only a pretense of a deck at bow and stern, it was little used for sailing. The single-bladed paddle was standard. As a Canadian ACA member devoted to this craft said, "The virtues of the single paddle are, in fact, the virtues of the Canadian canoe, simplicity, strength and beauty."

Rushton followed the traditional lines in his Canadian models, the Ontario, the Ugo, the Igo, and the lighter and cheaper Arkansaw (in later catalogs, "Arkansas") Traveler. All were built with smooth hulls.

In addition to his Canadian models, Rushton offered several other open paddling canoes: a war canoe thirty feet long and accommodating a crew of seventeen, the lightweight Bucktail, the featherweight Nessmuk, the smoothskin Vaux, the clinker-built Huron and St. Regis, and finally, after the turn of the century, the Indian and Indian Girl models.

The Indian models were unique with Rushton and became

the mainstay of the Boat Shop in the last four years of his life. Their ancestor was not the dugout but the Indian birchbark with its greater sheer and rounded stems. Their lines were rakish and romantic, but the high ends made them more difficult to handle in a wind. Traditionally, the high ends were not for beauty but for utility, although they did provide the Indian birchbark builder large, well-placed areas for decoration. Indians and voyageurs alike were accustomed to use their upturned canoes for shelter; and the high ends made them more convenient for this purpose. Whereas Rushton's Canadian models Ugo and Igo had a depth of eleven inches amidship and eighteen at the ends, the Rushton Indian and Indian Girl were twelve inches amidship and twenty-four and twenty-one, respectively, at the ends.

Rushton may have built, as his son Harry recalled, a few all-cedar Indian models prior to 1900. But according to his own statement, he spent the two years 1900 and 1901 in designing and experimenting before he perfected what he called "the finest model canoe ever built" in a catalog statement. The Indian and the Indian Girl were offered in the catalog of 1902: the first either in all cedar or canvas covered, in one length only, fifteen feet; the second, with canvas-covered cedar hull, in three lengths—fifteen, sixteen, and seventeen feet. In 1903 an eighteen-foot Indian Girl was added to the line. Rushton declared that he was still a "staunch believer" in the cedar canoe without canvas covering, but that he was always willing to oblige his customers, many of whom were asking for canvas. He credited several builders in Maine with developing the canvas-covered canoe and believed that it resulted from the lack of high-grade cedar in the Maine woods. It is interesting to note that in the same year Rushton first offered canvas-covered canoes, 1902, the Old Town Canoe Company, of Old Town, Maine, was incorporated. Today it is the leading builder in the Northeast of this type of canoe.

It was to Maine that Rushton looked for a man experienced in constructing canvas-covered canoes. In 1902 he announced that he had hired "a skilled builder from Maine, a man with fourteen years' experience in this class of work, to superintend the construction." This was Melvin F. Roundy, who moved to Canton from Bangor, Maine, in 1902 or 1903, built a house in the village, and remained till 1908. Throughout this period he was under contract to build canvas-covered canoes for the Boat Shop. He brought his brother, Clarence, and his brother-in-law to work with him. He also employed some of Rushton's workmen and hired others locally to produce what rapidly became the most popular craft of the Boat Shop in the new century. Later two other Indian models, the American Beauty, designed by Harry Rushton, and the Navahoe, the cheapest of all, were added. The American Beauty resembled the Indian in sheer, with its twenty-four inch depth at the bows, but had a longer deck.

Simpler in construction than the all-wood canoe open or decked, the canvas-covered models could be sold for little more than half the price. The cedar planks of the hulls were not beveled but abutted straight edge to straight edge. The canvas sheathing made the craft watertight. The all-wood Indian model, weighing forty-seven pounds, was offered in 1903 at $65, including paddles. The same model in canvas, weighing fifty-nine to sixty-five pounds, was offered, without paddles, at $40 for Grade A and $32 for Grade B. Indian Girls were priced from $30 to $43 according to length and grade. Paddles were three dollars extra.

The beauty of these canvas-covered canoes, particularly the Indian Girl, combined with their steadiness, strength, and low cost, made them one of the outstanding values in the history of small-boat building. In the last year of Rushton's life the Boat Shop broke all unit production records. But Rushton's satisfaction must have been tempered by his continuing belief in the superiority of the all-wooden canoe, which he had devoted the knowledge of a lifetime to perfect.

The momentum of an industrial society at last outstripped the cunning, the craft, of the resourceful boatmaker of Canton.

The canoe he believed in was no longer wanted. A cheaper one had replaced it. So, after designing a beautiful hull for the new craft, he stepped aside and left construction in the hands of the man from Maine. Possibly this was a gesture of resignation rather than of scorn, for Rushton was now a sick man.

Chapter XIII

CLOSING OF THE BOAT SHOP

IN 1904 an exchange of letters between Rushton and his old friend Lucien Wulsin was resumed after a lapse of nearly twenty years. A partner in the Baldwin Company, Wulsin was now a prominent industrialist and philanthropist in his home city. He was a patron of the Cincinnati symphony orchestra, a trustee of the University of Cincinnati and of the State Historical Society, a much-loved citizen, and a world traveler.

Rushton wrote from Canton on February 9:

It is a very long time since I heard from you and I can only suppose that you too are doing business at the same old stand. When I saw you last I was a bachelor. My oldest boy graduates from St. Lawrence University next June at eighteen. Everything went to the bad with me in '96, but I am on my feet again, with a good trade. All these years my family have used an old rattle trap piano—a family relic. All these years we have *talked* about a new one. I wrote you once in this matter. Well, it seems as if I could stand for something of the sort the present season and I thought I would write you and see what you had that would hit the situation. An upright, medium price. If I could work in a canoe or two on a deal I would like to and I will mail you a copy of my '04 catalogue as soon as I get them from the printers....

Wulsin replied two days later:

I am delighted to have your letter of February 9th. I have never forgotten you and continue to cherish the dear memories of our former meeting at Lake George.

I, too, have a couple of boys who are growing up and who talk canoeing, though, as yet, none of them have had practical experience.

It afforded me a great deal of pleasure last year and the year before to recommend you to some parties who asked me about canoes. One of them was Mr. Perrin of Indianapolis. I hope you heard from him. [Wulsin then recommends either a style L Hamilton at $225 or a style 18 Ellington at $300, both at a discount from the quoted selling price.]

As to my taking a canoe on account, if I carry out my present plans, there is no doubt that I shall have to either repair my old canoes or buy at least one canoe or boat this summer. It is not our custom, however, to make trades. My boys are twelve and fourteen years of age and anything that they get now would be very simple and plain simply as a start. I would rather leave this matter open as you are sure to have my trade whenever the time comes. If you will write me more fully your wishes after reading the above, you may be sure we will serve you in the very best way and give you the fullest value for whatever amount you wish to invest.

On February 16 Rushton wrote two letters to Wulsin, one inquiring about the quality of Pacific Coast spruce. The other left to his friend the choice of a piano, in mahogany finish, to be delivered about the time of Leah's birthday on March 31 and paid for in full by early May. He also inquired about old friends of the Cincinnati Canoe Club. Three days later Wulsin replied:

I have your two letters of February 16th. The one about the spruce we will answer from the Factory.

On the subject of the piano, I am going to select for you a style 18 Ellington in mahogany and have it ready for shipment at any time you may instruct. I am sure that you and Mrs. Rushton, as well as your family, will be pleased in every way with the piano. Should it not prove what you want in every respect, we will change it without expense to you. The instrument is, of course, warranted in every respect as to quality and durability. As to the price—$300—you can pay it as you propose; we would count same as cash. Included in the price for you will be a stool and scarf and we will also prepay the freight so that the piano will be F.O.B. Canton.

Our old canoeing friends, Ellard, Crane, Steadman, and a number of the others are alive and well, though not as young as when we met in Lake George. Judge Longworth you know died some fifteen years ago. Greenwood has passed away also, as has my brother Clarence. Heighway is lost sight of. You doubtless know that our mutual friend, Bishop, died some two years ago.

I continue to cherish the memories of our old days and am hoping some time to take my boys to camp on the Islands in Lake George.

In a letter of February 22 Rushton asked that the piano be shipped to the Boat Shop, so that he could surprise his wife, and added:

I am pleased that you mention the old timers, even if some have gone on beyond. Yes, I knew that Longworth and Bishop had passed away. And I had lost sight of Heighway too, but I do not think I remember hearing of the death of your brother and Mr. Greenwood. I can look back along the road and see where many a friend or acquaintance has stepped from the trail and soon I too will be among them. At twenty it's a very long while to thirty. At sixty it's but a few days to seventy, and I am sixty.

Perhaps already he doubted that he would live to three score and ten. His health, never reliable, had taken a turn for the worse in recent months and continued to fail till his death twenty-six months after the above letter was written.

He no longer had the strength to supervise all the work at the Boat Shop. His initial contract with Melvin Roundy to build canvas-covered canoes using the facilities of the Boat Shop and some of its working force was probably for a term of a year or two. If so, Rushton must have been relieved at Roundy's willingness to renew the contract. Indian Girl canoes in canvas became the best-selling product of the shop, but Rushton doubtless preferred to devote his failing energies to the all-cedar craft, now in limited demand.

Harry Rushton took an increasing share of responsibility in the office work. For several years while attending school he had been "office boy" on Saturdays and during the summers. Taught at home by his mother till he was eight, he had had a head start in school, skipped several grades, and graduated from St. Lawrence University in Canton, at the age of eighteen, in 1904. After working in the Boat Shop that summer, he entered Albany Business College in the fall for what was to be a year's course. But he returned in February to recover from a severe attack of measles and stayed on to take more and more of the burden off his father. A few days after his return to Canton, his grandfather, Peter Rushton, died.

Business was now in an upsurge. In the fall of 1904 Rushton built a twenty-four by fifty-two foot addition to the shop and installed steam heat and electric lights. Early in 1905 he had a force of twenty-five men working ten hours a day. In February fifty canoes were shipped to Seattle to one dealer alone. In 1906 all production records were broken. A total of seven hundred and fifty Indian Girls were turned out and over one hundred and fifty all-wood craft.

In the summer of 1905 Harry took over full management. Late in July Rushton left Canton with his wife to spend the rest of the summer at Cranberry Lake, hoping that the climate would be beneficial to his health. No lasting benefit resulted, however, and his condition worsened in the winter months. He died at home on May 1, 1906, five months short of his sixty-third birthday. His death was attributed to Bright's disease, or inflammation of the kidneys.

The Universalist minister of Canton officiated at the funeral. Rushton's brothers, George, Judd, and Edward, and his brothers-in-law were bearers. Joe Ellsworth and Milton Packard, his early Canton friends, were among the mourners. According to tradition, in passing before the casket of their old protégé, they fell into dispute over whether he looked as natural as in life; and this was the only occasion on which grief, or anything else, silenced them before they had fully explored the possibilities of a quarrel. Perhaps it was to one of these old friends, now approaching eighty, that the death notice referred in *Forest and Stream* on May 12: "Of him it is written by one of his oldest friends, 'Worthy man, good friend, hail and farewell.'"

The principal asset at Rushton's death was a going business. The large house on Hodskin Street, evidently in Leah's name, did not figure in the estate. In Leah's final appraisal as administratrix the value of the shop was set at only $3,500 and of a new storehouse at $1,250. Six hundred boats and canoes in stock were valued at $12,000, a low figure even though most of them were low-priced canvas-covered Indian Girls. Total assets came to a little over $26,100 and debts to $13,400, including a bank loan of nearly $10,000. As Rushton left no will, the net estate of $12,700 was divided among Leah and her two sons.

The Boat Shop was immediately incorporated under the title of J. H. Rushton Inc., with a capital stock of $15,000 par value. The officers were Mrs. Rushton, president; W. N. Beard of the First National Bank, vice-president and treasurer; and George H. Bowers, secretary. Beard probably represented the bank's interest in the $10,000 loan. Bowers, as Leah's attorney, represented her interests. Harry Rushton, not yet turned twenty, and Sidney were minors ineligible for office. In spite of his youth, Harry became general manager of the Boat Shop.

Difficulties soon beset the new regime. The bank loan was paid out of assets and profits from operation. But in 1908 another depression descended on the country, and sales skidded downward as on such occasions in the past. The cost of materials meanwhile escalated. Quality white cedar became scarce. The price of Michigan cedar went into an upward spiral in the years of Harry's management and was hard to find at any figure. He also felt that his youth and inexperience had been handicaps. The older men in the shop did not like taking orders from so young a man. Roundy was intent only on fulfilling his current contract and getting out. After his departure in late 1907 or early 1908, canvas-covered canoes were dropped temporarily, though the Indian and Indian Girl models continued to be offered in all-cedar. Production of canvas canoes was resumed not later than 1910, probably because of sales resistance to the all-wood models, the prices of which climbed with the mounting cost of prime Michigan cedar.

Harry devoted his energies wholeheartedly to the business as long as his mother lived. But the rewards were slim, the frustrations many. When Leah died in December, 1911, at the age of forty-nine, Harry decided to relinquish the management. He was married by this time and wanted to provide a better future for his family than was in prospect at the Boat Shop. He retained his share of the capital stock until 1915, but left Canton and moved downstate with his bride.

Suffering from cancer, Leah had sold the house on Hodskin Street in 1910 and moved to the Boston area, where better medical attention was available. She was buried beside her husband in Fairview Cemetery, Canton.

After Harry's departure the business was managed by Judd W. Rushton, J. Henry's half-brother. Judd had worked in the Boat Shop till about 1894. Later he had operated a small wood-working shop of his own on Water Street. Now he returned as part owner and manager and issued a new catalog under the title of "Rushton Canoes and Boats" and his name, "J. W. Rushton." In this issue, canvas-covered canoes were featured as the leading line. Also offered were the all-wood open canoes Arkansas Traveler, Ugo, Huron, St. Regis, Vaux, and Nessmuk; the decked cruisers Nomad and Vesper; and several rowboats. Again difficulties arose in a business sensitive to the ups and downs of the economic cycle and changes in the leisure-time activities of the public. Judd was a good craftsman but a poor businessman, hesitant to make decisions and slow to execute them.

In 1916 two changes of ownership took place. In February Sidney Rushton bought out his uncle's share in the factory. But six weeks later he quitclaimed back to Judd. After leaving Canton briefly in the fall to marry a girl from Oakland, California, Sidney returned to work for his uncle. But the Boat Shop was in its last days. In April, 1917, the United States declared war on Germany, and again the market for pleasure boats collapsed. After taking other employment in Canton for a few months, Sidney moved to California with his bride. Examination of surviving records and of my own and fellow Cantonians' memories has failed to fix the date when the nails were clinched on the last canoe in the Boat Shop. The once flourishing enterprise came to an end late in 1916 or in the forepart of 1917. After the closing a former workman living near Canton made canoes from Rushton patterns for local people and repaired old craft. Then he too passed from the scene. In 1926 Judd sold the Boat Shop to a farmer, who tore it down and built a large dairy barn with the lumber.

Rushton's name, however, is still alive. If boats lasted as long as violins and were cherished as much, he might become the Stradivarius of the canoe. Now that a few of his craft are preserved in museums, the possibility cannot be ruled out.

APPENDIXES

Appendix A: Rushton's Methods of Construction*

Hull Construction of Rowboats and Canoes

Our method of construction is an improved lap streak or clinker. A keelson three-quarters to one inch thick and four inches wide is rabbeted to receive the garboard—or bottom—streak. To this keelson are attached the stem and stern posts. These are all fitted with plane, chisel, rasp and sandpaper until the garboard streak, when in place, will make a *perfect joint*. From six to ten streaks on each side are used, according to the size and model of the boat. Each pair— one for each side—are shaped for the places they are to fill, and the edges beveled more or less as may be necessary to make a perfect joint where the *streaks lap*. No two pair are alike either in shape or bevel. *That shape and bevel wholly determine the model of the boat;* the tightness of the joints depends upon the skill of the workman who bevels the edges and nails them together—*once every inch* when the ribs are in—with copper nails that are carefully clinched on an iron block. No lead is used to make tight joints; it is unnecessary. When the "shell" is up we take it from the forms. Right here is where the superiority of this system is seen. In the *old fashioned* lap streak built boats, a good deal of warping and twisting *was* necessary to bring the nearly straight streaks of planking into proper place. The natural tendency of the wood to return to its original position was aided by the working of the boat—when in use—and resulted soon or late in causing the seams to open. To obviate this and keep the boat in proper shape, knees, braces, seats and gunwales were made stout—and therefore heavy—and were quite indispensable. *By our improved system,* the boat, which at this stage of construction—when taken from the forms—consists of simply the keelson, stems and siding nailed together, retains its perfect shape and could even be used with a light load. Light gunwales are

* The quotations in this appendix are taken from Rushton's catalogs.

now put on, and the ribs—half-round ¼ x ½ inch and larger ones at the rowlocks—are put in, 1½ inches apart [from edge to edge]. The boat may now be used with perfect safety—as indeed our small, light canoes, 10½ to 20 lbs. are left in this manner as complete— and when the seats and decks are added, the *same weight of material* can be used in no other manner to give *equal strength. Why?* Because each and every piece of siding being cut and not warped to fit has the least possible strain put upon it. In case of accident, to which all boats are liable, no other kind can so easily be repaired, as, if necessary, a section of any streak, or a whole streak, can be cut out and a new piece inserted by any ordinary carpenter, without injury to any other streak, and with the addition of oil and varnish be as good as new again.

Another important improvement is the great number of streaks used. It enables us to get much finer lines, and last, but by no means least, it aids largely in keeping the boat tight and in proper shape. All wood is affected more or less by water or the absence of it. If a board contains water and is exposed to high temperature it shrinks. The amount of that shrinkage depending on the amount of water, the kind of wood, and width of the board. We may say that under certain conditions a board a foot wide will shrink ¼ inch. Then if a streak be three inches wide it will vary in width 1/12 in. [*sic*] from wet to dry. No injurious effect will be felt from this amount, which is given as a maximum for white cedar, under the most adverse circumstances. But suppose one whole side of the boat were in a single piece. Its width would vary from 18 to 40 inches, according to size of boat; and the variation in width caused by shrinking and swelling, would be from ⅜ to over ¾ of an inch. What is the result? When it shrinks beyond a certain point (being fastened at the edges) it must split. When it swells beyond a certain point it must bulge out or in, and a constant repetition of either soon ruins the boat; it either becomes leaky and soon goes to pieces, or warps and twists out of shape. When we take any other wood than oak, cedar, or mahogany the variation is a great deal more. Of course all boats are supposed to be protected by oil, paint or varnish, but no wood can be so protected that it will not be affected in some degree. As witness: all attempts to *cement* wood together so that the pieces would not separate have been entire or partial failures, as hundreds of disgusted sportsmen and canoeists can attest, while glass which is not affected by water, is readily cemented and made to hold even hot water. This also proves that a copper nail well clinched, or a brass screw where a nail can not be clinched, is the best, strongest, most durable and really the only suitable fastening used in the construction of boats. Boats defective in the principles of their construction may be made to last a short time by using them with care. Now we advise anyone to take good care of his boat whatever the kind or whoever the maker; the better care he will take of it the longer it will last him, but it is not always convenient to spend as much time on it at the end of a day's cruise as is required to groom a trotting horse at the end of a race. A smooth, level place for it to rest upon can not always be found, and any boat should be of such construction and material as to stand a reasonable amount of hardship with a like amount of care. *From the catalog of 1886.*

Construction of the Cruising Canoe

Since the organization of the A.C.A., canoe clubs have been formed in many places, canoes classified and everything pertaining to them greatly improved. These improvements are due to the efforts of builders to fully meet the demands made upon them for fine work. The material used in all first-class canoes varies but little. Oak keelson, oak or hackmatack stem and stern-posts, white cedar siding with top-streak of Spanish cedar; timbers of white cedar, deck and hatches of mahogany, ribs of red elm, coaming, battens and gunwales of black walnut and all fastenings of copper and brass. All canoes are finished in oil and varnish and the decks highly polished.

In weight of material and mode of construction the hull of a canoe is the same as an open boat. After the shell is up it is oiled inside and shellacked and the ribs put in. Then the deck timbers, about $3/4$ x $7/8$ inch in size (small knees supporting them throughout the center of the boat), bulkhead, coaming, mast steps and air-tanks are put in; after this the inside is shellacked again and varnished, and then the deck and hatches go on. The after air-tank goes aft of the dandy mast, which is stepped about 30 to 32 inches from tip of stern post. The forward mast tube is stepped close up in the bow. In class A canoes it is about two feet from point of stem (these canoes have not sufficient width or thickness of stem to step closer) and the air-tank goes forward of the tube.

In class B we put two for'd mast tubes. The first about 15 inches from point of stem. The second 30 inches, with the air-tank between. The size of these air-tanks varies in the different sized canoes. The smallest pair support 70 lbs. dead weight, and the largest about 100 lbs., or will float from three to five persons weighing from 150 to 160 lbs. each, in the water, keeping their heads above the surface. With these you *always* have an *Air-Chamber* that will float the crew and cargo, even if the canoe itself be crushed or broken up. Of course you cannot use them for storage. You do not need them. They only occupy space in the canoe where very little could be stored.

The dry stowage compartment in a canoe should be forward. . . . It is formed by the hull and deck of the canoe, the forward air-tank and permanent bulkhead placed just forward of the cockpit.

The "fathers of canoeing" told us to build the cockpit 3 ft. long. This length has been gradually increased until 5 to 7 ft. is the standard. Hereafter we will build 5 ft. in 14 ft.; 5 ft. 6 inches in 14 ft. 6 inches; 6 ft. in 15 ft. and 7 ft. in 16 ft. canoes, unless otherwise ordered. The cockpit will be covered by a hatch in four pieces, made to lock up without the aid of the old fashioned bar and lock-up. *From the catalog of 1886.*

The Clinker-Built Hull

Take two thin pieces of wood, lap the edges ½ to ¾ inch and thoroughly nail and clinch, and you have a very much stronger job than to simply put them edge to edge and dowell or calk. *From the catalog of 1892.*

The Smoothskin Hull

Smoothskins we make by beveling each streak to an edge inside and out, and at the curve or bilge working the streak hollow and round from thicker material. [Rushton began offering this type of hull in 1887.] *From the catalog of 1892.*

APPENDIX B: Further Notes on Construction

Times have changed since the Rushton boat business came to the end of its road. Our economy, our educational process, and our way of life have all changed in basic ways. Among these changes has come a practical end to hand craftsmanship as a way to earn a living. The economic pattern of this country has driven the cost of craftsmanship to such heights that only a few men catering to highly specialized markets are still fine workmen in the sense in which J. Henry Rushton undoubtedly understood those words. Thus today there are fewer and fewer people who know the painstaking process by which selected woods were transformed with hand tools into Rushton's superb canoes.

Fortunately, a partial description of Rushton's methods and processes has survived. In the late 1950's, when this book was first taking shape, the late J. H. (Harry) Rushton was still living. He had worked in his father's shop and succeeded to the leadership of the business, and he called upon his memory of the days and ways there to write down in two separate letters to the author the details of the processes and methods he knew. These statements follow in this appendix.

They were written by a man who was not a professional writer; who was, however, a very literate man and a gentleman. He was remembering the endless detail of an obsolete trade—trying to make clear to the unskilled the combination of knowledge, dexterity, and careful attention to detail which he had learned years before. Some matters which seemed clear to him, which were to him self-explanatory, may not be as clear to our generation, skilled in other ways. His letters do not always follow a single train of thought to its logical end; memories crowded upon him; he compared one method with another; he shared tricks of his trade with us; he saw it all as a consistent coherent whole. But, where it is hard to understand today, make no mistake: Harry Rushton understood it. He knew what he was talking about—he had designed and developed the boats himself.

His statements are printed in this appendix with a minimum of editing. In some cases, his spelling or style has been slightly altered to conform more smoothly to modern practice. A few personal asides have been dropped without remark. A few words have been added, always in square brackets, for clarity. But no continuity or new material has been added, for fear that the result would be farther from his meaning instead of nearer to it. This appendix is simply what Harry Rushton said about how Rushton boats were built.

From Harry Rushton to the author, written in 1959:

I think that I will build (on paper) a few of the RUSHTON boats and canoes. Will try to get in all of the details, most of which will be of no use to you although possibly of interest.

To start with, the design—different, of course with all models, yet basically the same. As I recall, we started with a scale (1½" to 1') and when all lines seemed to be O.K., enlarged to full scale.

The essential lines of a drawing are the profile, cross sections (vertical, perpendicular to keel) and waterlines, on these drawings spaced 2" to 3" apart.

From here on, for a while, the Indian Girl (canvas covered and all-cedar) and the Saranac Laker are to be forgotten—construction is different.

Full size "moulds" were made from drawings of cross sections (mentioned above) with proper allowance for thickness of planking. These moulds were notched to take the keel, and fastened to a bed piece. All boats were planked bottom side up. Keels were tapered at each end and a notch cut out to allow for the planking to be nailed on and to leave a slight projection to protect the planking when the boat was dragged up onto a dock, etc. Keels generally of red oak. Red oak stems were steam bent over forms to shape the curves; one 1" board over another, to get a "pair" of inside and outside stems. The inside stem was bevelled to conform to the shape of the boat and screwed to keel. Outside stem, also bevelled, was attached with screws from inside of hull after all planking was nailed up. Keels were (temporarily) fastened to end moulds by hooks (like the ones on your barn door) to hold keel down tight to forms and hold the necessary curve.

With moulds and keel attached to "bed piece," next came the planking. The number of boards depended on the size of the boat. Suppose we take nine for the number. A ¼" basswood board was "scribed" against the keel. Laid upon the moulds, a divider was set and equal distances marked off on this board from points along the keel. A thin, narrow straight-grained strip was nailed to this board, touching all of the marks as above, a line drawn connecting the points, and the board then cut out on this line. It was then placed against the keel and the edge planed off to a perfect fit. [It was] tacked into place, measurements of length of the moulds (around the curve) were made at several points; each measurement divided by nine (the number of boards to be used), and these measurements laid off on that ¼″ basswood at proper points (where it laid on each mould). These marks were connected as above, the line "trued up" so it would not be wavy, board cut out—there was the pattern for the garboard (plank next to keel). This process was repeated until patterns were made for all of the planking and the patterns were, of course, saved for the next boats of the same design. When this was done we had the *shell*.

The garboard streak was fastened to the keel with copper nails, as I recall, and to the stems with small brass screws. Copper nails were used to fasten together the planks on a lap-streak boat, and copper tacks on the smooth skin jobs. Those nails were spaced to be about 1″ apart with space left for the rib nails.

After the shell was planked up, it was taken off the moulds, turned right side up and, as I recall, given a coat of boiled linseed oil on the inside only. Then we marked a center line for each rib and punched a hole on this line at each joint of the planking. Sometimes on very wide boards there might be a hole in the center of the plank, but not often. Then the shell was turned over and nails put in each one of the holes. Next, the shell was turned right side up, placed on a bed piece curved to fit the curve (rocker) of the keel, and shored down from the ceiling. Ribs were next put in. They were of red (slippery) elm, steamed until soft, put into shell and nailed in. There was no loafing on this part of the job, because after about 120 seconds (by the watch) the rib got so hard that a nail could not be driven.

The next step was the trim, about one day's work for one man. Rib ends were cut off, gunwales and inwales put on, decks put in, seat cleats attached and seats cut and put in. Most rowboats and many canoes had what we called a "bottom board," sort of a loose floor of ¼″ basswood that could be kept in place with buttons. After this the outside was sponged off with hot water to remove hammer marks, sanded, oiled and varnished.

Tacks were sharp-pointed nails shaped like the old wrought-iron nails you have seen. Smooth-skin boats and canoes were nailed up from inside as well as out, the heads of tacks being next to the thin edge of the wood. Joints or laps [were] 1½ to 2 times thickness of planking. With the cedar planking it was not necessary to bore holes for either nails or tacks, except for the ribs. These holes were made with a brad-awl, not a drill.

Decks were of three types: For dinghies, small canoes and the Indian Girl, just a corner brace; larger canoes and rowboats, narrow strips about ¾" parallel to gunwales, blind nailed, center joints covered with a thin strip; and sailing canoes (except Nomad model), ¼" mahogany put on in quarters.

There were quite a number of sailing models built at one time and another—the Princess, etc.—but my personal recollection is of only two, Vesper and Nomad. The Vesper was an older model, curved bow stem and straight sternpost, smooth skin, solid (¼") mahogany deck, folding centerboard, two sails, sliding seat, rudder blade hinged to lift when hitting an obstruction. The other, Nomad, was a 16' by 30" open paddling model Ugo, decked with cedar strips running parallel to gunwales, folding centerboard, two sails, and designed for use with a double-bladed paddle on the lower Hudson, as well as for sailing. Both models had watertight bulkheads fore and aft, for stowage of duffle and also for [the] purpose of floating the canoe in case of upset. Each compartment had a circular hatch, made watertight with an endless [circular?] rubber tube about ½" diameter.

The Adirondack Guide Boat, our Saranac Laker, was built differently, except that the planking was smooth-skin nailed up in the standard manner. In this model, the ribs were cut to shape from tamarack knees. These ribs really were half-ribs doubled over the keel. [Although] I do not remember what wood was used for keels, [it was] likely a soft wood. Full ribs were screwed to keel, spaced about 4" centers, and then brought to exact shape and fitted by hand. This was done so that planking when laid on would touch at all spots. I believe planking was screwed to the ribs, and nailed at joints as with all other smooth-skin jobs. This model had a gunwale (outwale) but no inwale, and was equipped with hardwood oars and oarlocks pinned to the oars (no feathering).

All planking joints were hand fitted. I can recall Nelson Brown putting a board into place, bending over to check the fit, and then scratching with the nail of his index finger any spots where a little more wood should be removed. All joints were laid up with a special heavy varnish, the only waterproof glue available at the time. Eventually this would harden so that the joints were stronger than the planking itself.

The canvas-covered canoes were built in an entirely different manner. The mould over which they were built was made—forms (cross sections) were put in place and covered with strips about 1″ thick, edge nailed to make a reasonably solid form. Galvanized iron strips were fastened around this mould, used for clinching the nails when the shell was planked up. Inwales and stems were put in place in the mould, then 5/16″ cedar ribs steamed, bent, put in place and nailed to inwales. Planking was nailed to the ribs, beginning at a center line. Most of the boards were strips 2½″ or 3″ wide, but not cut to pattern. Ash or cherry was used for inwales, white (water) elm for stems. After shell was finished, it was sponged off with hot water (to remove hammer marks, if any), dried, sanded and given a coat of boiled linseed oil. Then the canvas was put on. Next, canvas received two coats of filler, sanded between; then returned to builder for finish trim—gunwales, decks, seats, bang irons. First stem ["first step"? (in finishing)] was to tighten the canvas. Then the finished job went to the paint room for paint and varnish.

The first canvas-covered model was the Indian, built around 1900. The newer model, Indian Girl, was a modification with finer lines, and caught on for several years. We also tried a De-luxe model, American Beauty [which Harry Rushton designed], but for some reason, probably price, this never did take.

We also built a few all-cedar canoes of the Indian Girl model. This canoe was built over cedar ribs like the canvas-covered model, but the planking was cut to pattern, smooth joints laid up in varnish and nailed like all other all-wood canoes.

Note: I followed up Harry Rushton's first reply with inquiries concerning several photographs which had accompanied my letter. His subsequent reply was a much more detailed exposition, illustrated with sketches of various aspects of the canoes under construction. This second communication is quoted verbatim except for the minor changes mentioned earlier. Please note that the photographs to which Rushton refers have been included in this volume. They may be found on the ninth through eleventh pages of the illustration section following page 60 (note caption references).

Saranac Laker (Guide-Boat) Construction

I think the keel was cedar and protected against wear with two or three thin brass strips screwed on. It was tapered at both ends. The stems were natural crook tamarack, notched to receive ends of keel; shaped to conform to the lines of the model. Each rib was made

½ LENGTH
SIDE PROFILE OF
GUIDE BOAT

¼ TOPSIDE
PROFILE

SKETCH 1 (adapted by author)

in two parts, and joined at the keel. Ribs were also of tamarack, natural crook. Each was cut to pattern. As these crooks were (probably) at least 1¼″ thick, each pattern was laid on and after the rib was cut out, this piece was resawed to make the pair of ribs. Lines were drawn on the keel—I think 4″ apart—and each pair of ribs, which had been fastened together, was fastened in place on the keel [see Sketches 2 and 3]. The patterns for the ribs were drawn from drawings along the lines which my sketches B, C, & D [Sketch 1] will suggest. Each rib was an inch or so longer than in the finished boat.

The next step was to fasten keel to bed piece as shown in Photo #1 [see note above concerning photographs]. The strip to which you refer as an "inwall" (we called it inwale) is a temporary strip of thin hard wood, screwed to ends (which will be cut off) of each rib. This was used to line up and square up each rib to be sure spacing was even and correct.

Corners of the keel were planed off to line up with each rib [see Sketch 2, portion "X" is planed off]. Then each rib was bevelled off so that the planking, when laid on, would be tight against it. [See detail of Sketch 3.] This was done with a small hand plane, a thin

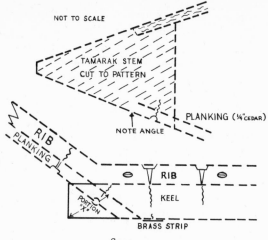

NOT TO SCALE

TAMARAK STEM
CUT TO PATTERN

PLANKING (¼"CEDAR)

NOTE ANGLE

RIB

PLANKING

RIB

PLANKING

KEEL

PORTION "X"

BRASS STRIP

SKETCH 2

strip of wood being laid on lengthwise like the planking, and each rib fitted.

As you can see from the photo [#1], planking was fastened to keel, stems and each rib, with brass screws, probably about #4 by ½". The model was our smooth-skin, planking with bevelled seams laid in a heavy varnish, and nailed up from the outside with 5/16 inch copper tacks. Each board was cut to pattern; bevel about ½", this done by hand.

After the hull was all planked up, it was removed from the bed piece. Planking nailed up from the inside, 5/16" tacks. Ends of ribs cut off even with edge of planking and ends rounded over. An outwale (we called it gunwale) of hard wood was screwed on from inside

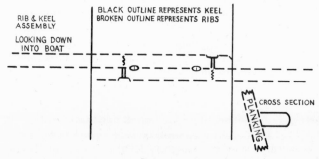

RIB & KEEL
ASSEMBLY

LOOKING DOWN
INTO BOAT

BLACK OUTLINE REPRESENTS KEEL
BROKEN OUTLINE REPRESENTS RIBS

CROSS SECTION

PLANKING

SKETCH 3

even with top of planking. Think this was about ⅞ by 1¼″ deep with corners taken off but not made half-round. Ends of stems were cut off and shaped, cleats put in for seats and seats fitted.

Boat finished with one [coat] boiled linseed oil, two coats of varnish. We furnished as oars, square shanks, with rowlocks that had a pin through them so oars did not feather.

For making holes for screws, I expect for the small ones, size #4, they used a "brad-awl." This is a round piece of wood, barrel shape, with a sharp piece of steel wire in one end. I think the point was wedge shape, not a sharp point, and it was adequate for use through soft wood and much faster than a drill. A drill was never used for making holes for nails, anywhere, anytime.

Those nice straight lines of nails were pure artistry and nothing else. The first row of nails on each boat were in the keel and spaced about 1″ apart. The others simply followed down. It was only necessary to keep each nail squarely under the one on the plank previously nailed on.

[From this point on, Mr. Rushton is discussing the construction of other types, essentially canoes, rather than the Saranac Laker or guide-boat.]

Photo #1. Our term for what you see in the lower left is a "form" or "set of forms." Again please refer to B, C & D [Sketch 1]—it is from these drawings that the forms are made. You will note the construction, and how they are wedged in place on the bed piece. Bed piece, in turn, was wedged into standards, one near each end, as shown in lower right-hand corner of Photo #1. Lower end of standard fitted into grooves in boards fastened to floor, as you will note in Photo #2. Also at farther end of the set of forms you will note a standard to which stem of boat was fastened during building of the hull. All of our all-wood boats and canoes (except the all-cedar Indian Girl and Saranac Laker) were built over such forms.

What we termed a "mould" was of rather solid construction, like the one (Photo #3) over which the Indian Girl model was built. We used them for shaping the stems of the boats and canoes, also for the inwales and gunwales of the canvas-covered Indian Girl canoes.

The form was made of 1″ basswood, notched except end form, to receive the keel. Stems were red oak, steam bent one piece over the other, on form as shown in Sketch 4, detail C. 1″ oak used, about 2″ wide, and resawed (split) after bending so that each bend made the stems for both ends of the boat. (I am going to use the word "boat"

Smoothskin construction:

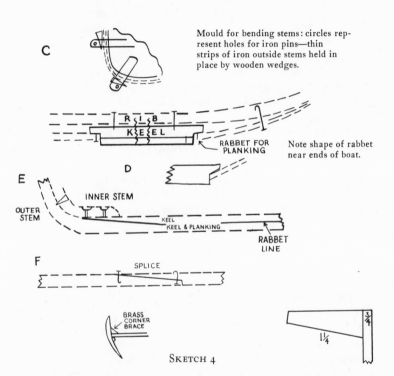

A — Smoothskin construction: planking joint nailed with "tacks" both inside and outside during building of shell, inside after shell is removed from forms.

PLANKING · PLANKING
RIB — NAILED AT JOINTS

LAP-STREAK CONSTRUCTION

B — PLANKING · PLANKING
RIB — NAIL AT PLANKING JOINTS ONLY

C — Mould for bending stems: circles represent holes for iron pins—thin strips of iron outside stems held in place by wooden wedges.

R I B
K E E L
RABBET FOR PLANKING

D — Note shape of rabbet near ends of boat.

E —
OUTER STEM
INNER STEM
KEEL
KEEL & PLANKING
RABBET LINE

F —
SPLICE

BRASS CORNER BRACE

$\frac{3}{4}$
$1\frac{1}{4}$

SKETCH 4

for both boats and canoes.) The keel was also of 1″ red oak, tapered at both ends, and a rabbet cut out for the planking. About ¼″ was left to extend below the planking to protect the cedar against rubbing.

Inside stems were screwed to the keel and this assembly put onto the forms. Keel fastened in two places to forms with screw hooks and stems plumbed and fastened to standards. Towards the ends of the boat the planking met the keel at quite a sharp angle, so the keel had to be shaped so the planking would lay tight.

165

When I use the *noun* nails, I mean a nail similar to the old-fashioned hand-made cut iron nails with a wedge-shaped point. The *noun* tacks means a sharp-pointed tack like the ones, probably iron, that you can buy anywhere today. When I use the *verb* nail, it will refer to either one. Nails were used to fasten the garboard plank to the keel of all jobs and to fasten in the ribs, also the planking of lap-streak jobs. Tacks were used both inside and out on all smooth-skin jobs, [both] boats and canoes.

Each board was cut to pattern. I think that at one time my father bought ¼" cedar, but when I was around we bought the commercial inch stuff. This was air dried before using. Board (planking) was sawed out about ¼" wide of the pattern on both edges, resawed (split), planed to thickness. Full length boards were not practical for two reasons—lumber wide enough to cut the necessary curves and long enough was hard if not impossible to get and at the ends the planking cut out of such boards would have the grain of the wood running nearly across the finished plank. For this reason all planking was spliced with the joints staggered lengthwise of the boat. We had a special saw for cutting the splices, after which these joints were nailed up, with tacks. [See Sketch 4, detail F.]

All joints between planking were beveled by hand to fit, both on smooth-skin and lap-streak boats. Joints were laid in a heavy varnish in lieu of a waterproof glue, which was not on the market at that time. Eventually these joints became stronger than the wood. I have had boats out a few years returned for new pieces of planking. The joints would not come apart, being stronger than the solid wood, and it was necessary to use a chisel to get down to the joint itself.

The planking was nailed on beginning at the keel, and when this was done we called it a "shell." This was removed from the forms and is shown in back of the forms, in front of the doors (Photo #2) before the outside stem is put on. Photo next to right shows the outside stem. The cross brace shown in this view is to hold the shell in place for the ribs. (Shell next to left of this one, #2, has only inside stem in place.)

Next step was to mark for ribs which were spaced 2½" to 3" depending on size of the boat. The keel was marked off at these intervals, commencing at the center, and then lines were drawn inside the boat, from each such mark, and to top of planking square to the keel.

A pliable strip of wood was used. One end had a small piece of hardwood attached, maybe ¼ x ½, into which had been driven two small iron brads with the ends pointed to stick into the keel so one end would not slip. Next small holes were punched (with a brad awl) at each joint and sometimes, where exceptionally wide planking had been used, in the center of such wide boards. The shell was then turned over and nails stuck into each hole. The holes were small enough to hold the nails without having them stick out into the shell. If they did, the rib would force them out, and that was not good at all. The shell was taken to another room and placed right side up on a bed piece which was about 2' above the floor. There was a small steam boiler, wood fired, and a long box to which it was piped. The ribs were placed in this box, a pail or two of hot water thrown on them, and the boiler fired up. Ribs were of red (slippery) elm, half round and from ½" to ¾" wide on the flat, according to size of the boat.

It took two men, one on each side, to "rib" a boat. Actual time of nailing one rib was one minute for a small boat, and that was about as long as a rib would stay soft. The ribs when hard and dry were very brittle and would split; and if a nail or two had fallen out it was an even bet whether the rib could be used, or whether it had to be taken out and replaced. One man fired, pulled ribs from steam box, held in place while the other nailed it to the keel, and then both finished nailing it into place. Ends were left sticking up two or three inches, to be cut off later.

Next step was to attach the trim—gunwales, inwales, decks, coamings, seat cleats and seats, floor boards (loose) and brass strips on stems, with a mooring bolt through the bow stem. Gunwales on rowboats were "D" shape [in cross section], inwales nearly square cross section cut out to take ends of ribs. Decks were strips about ¾" wide, blind nailed to follow the gunwale line, joints grooved with an instrument of steel about pencil size and sharpened to make a "V" shaped shallow groove. Coaming was a piece of thin hardwood bent to shape and fastened in. Forgot the deck timbers—see them in the end of boat in the background Photo #2. Seats were solid wood, on cleats screwed in from outside of hull, and had corner braces to stiffen the job.

Gunwales were left square on top at two or three points to take rowlocks. Outside of shell was sponged off with hot water to remove hammer marks, sanded when dry. Boat finished with coat of boiled linseed oil, one coat of undercoat varnish and one coat spar varnish.

The Nesmuk model canoe was lap streak. Gunwale was "D" shape, no inwale. Rib ends were fastened to gunwales with small brass "brads" and ends of ribs rounded off to give a finish.

The all-wood canoes had gunwales shaped as shown above. Otherwise finish was about the same as other boats. Nessmuk had only corner braces, solid wood, in place of decks.

In nailing up a boat, we used what we called a "clinching iron." [See below]. This was a smooth piece of cast iron, about 1″ x

CLINCHING   IRON

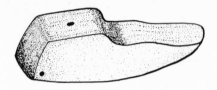

2″ x 4″ slightly curved on one face, and very smooth. When nailing, this was held inside the shell to cover the spot where the point of the nail or tack should come through. If held properly, the nail just touched it and curled back into the wood. You look at that job you have [Rushton speaks here to the author and refers to the Arkansas Traveler, the Burger canoe now in the Adirondack Museum], and you will see that you need to look close to see points of the tacks. The "iron" used for clinching nails through ribs was heavier, about 2 x 2 x 4, one face with considerable curve and a groove of about ½″ radius to go over the rib. Ends of planking were fastened to stems with small brass screws.

At one time and another we had several models of sailing canoes. All of them [such as the Princess design] except the Vesper and Nomad were before my time. Vesper is the earlier of the two models I have named. It had a straight sternpost, which was made from a knee, probably tamarack, as was the stem; and both would be shaped and rabbeted in manner similar to the Saranac Laker. Otherwise it was built, smooth skin, like our other boats up to point where ribs were installed. Decks were different, being of ¼″ mahogany screwed to (curved) deck timbers. Decks were put on in quarters; joints amidships being beveled on a timber and fastened with small screws. Lengthwise joint, fore and aft, was covered with a thin strip perhaps 3″ wide. There was a coaming some 3″ high, pointed forward and curved aft. Canoe was equipped with a Radix folding centerboard (there is one in that sail boat at Blue Mountain Lake), sails fore and aft, sliding seat and rudder with blade that would swing up if the canoe hit a rock etc., both for buoyancy and storage.

Each hatch cover was circular, had a rubber tube for packing, and could, of course, be screwed down tight.

At one time, all sailing canoes with mahogany decks were finished with several coats of varnish, each coat being rubbed down with pumice stone. A room over the office had a zinc floor with edges raised some six or eight inches, so the water from this process would not soak down into the office.

The Nomad was a 16′ decked U-G-O (paddling) model, and built like most other canoes with curved stems, smooth skin and otherwise as described, until shell was ribbed. The decking was of cedar strips about ¾″ wide, following line of gunwale, blind nailed, and with center joints covered with battens as described under Vesper. It had a similar coaming, watertight bulkheads and hatches. Equipment, optional, usually included a double paddle. This model was designed especially for use of canoeists on the lower Hudson River, out of upper New York City.

Photo #3 is of the mould used for the Indian Girl. This was made of 1″ basswood, as I recall. Forms were made solid, like the one shown in Photo #2, allowance being made for planking of the mould itself, galvanized iron strips, and ribs and planking of the canoe. On these forms the mould was planked up, using strips about 1″ square, blind nailed. At the upper edge (lower in photo) the mould was recessed to admit the inwale; also rabbeted out to take inboard ends of stems. As shown plainly in photo, galvanized iron strips some 2½″ wide were put on, one for each rib. These strips took the place of the clinching iron used on the all-wood boats. The mould was cut off square at each end, which was a solid piece, in a way replacing the stems on the other boats.

Stems and inwales were first put on the mould. The stems were steam-bent white (water) elm, over a mould similar to the one I show on Sketch 4C. The inwales were about 1″ x 1″, ash or oak for the Grade "B" canoes, and cherry for the Grade "A." The ends, back maybe 36″, were steamed and bent over a mould to get the right curve; this was not necessary through the center of the canoe. Note inwales fastened (temporarily) to mould with thumbscrews (clamps) [see Photo #4].

In background [of Photo #4] is a shell planked up ready to come off the mould. The vertical board along [where] the keel [should be] is a piece curved at the bottom to conform to shape of finished canoe and shored down from ceiling of work room. Steamed soft wood has a tendency to straighten out when drying, not holding its shape as does a hard wood, and this board was required to keep the ribs in place, and also to hold them tight against the galvanized strips on the mould.

Ribs were of 5/16 inch cedar and I think 2½″ wide in the center, tapered at both ends above the waterline.

The planking was 3/16 inch cedar, planed one side, that side to go inside the canoe next to the ribs. Two 3″ strips were used in the center (bottom), and the rest of the planking, so much as was nailed on while the hull was on the mould, was 2½″. Most of the pieces are of uniform width. However, the girth was less at what we called the "quarters" and, as you will note on shell in foreground, some boards were narrower at the ends. Shell was removed from mould at this point before attaching inwales to stems because finished canoe is narrower at gunwale line than at water line and the inwales could not have been separated from the mould otherwise. Another reason was that a second shell could be built on the mould while a different gang was finishing planking the first one.

Inwales were notched, fastened to stems, decks put in and balance of planking nailed on. Shell at right background shows this complete except for a strip at each end. If you refer to Photo #5, you will note three black squares in bottom of shell. These are holes. When shell was to be planked up after being removed from mould, it was put on a bedpiece with proper curve of keel line, a wide board put into the shell, heavy staples through bedpiece came up through these holes and this board, and the inside board was wedged in to hold the shell in shape. The last job in building was to replace these three squares which had been cut out while the shell was on the mould.

Shell was sponged off with hot water to remove hammer marks and swell grain of the wood, sanded smooth and given a coat of boiled linseed oil.

Canvas was folded lengthwise and held at ends by clamps. Shell was put into this canvas, a wide board put into bottom of canoe and shored from ceiling. Canvas was nailed, both sides, to three or four ribs in center of shell, and then canvas drawn up tight with a small windlass attached to clamp at one end. Two men, one on each side, tightened the canvas. One man had a pair of curved nose pliers with which to pull on the canvas, while the other nailed through each rib. Where the canvas was too wide, near the bows, it was slit to approximate gunwale line. Ends of canvas were turned around the stem, laid in white lead and nailed, one side lapping over the other.

The covered shell then went to the paint room, where the canvas received a coat of heavy filler, then a light coat of filler and was sanded smooth; and the inside got a coat of oil.

Returned to the building floor, the nails were drawn from the canvas, a thin wide strip of metal (I think it was a hand saw with the teeth filed off) was run between the canvas and the shell, and the canvas renailed. Then the gunwales and thwarts were put on and seats fitted; also bang irons attached. Canoe was then ready for inside varnish and outside paint and varnish.

At the suggestion of Howard I. Chapelle, curator of transportation, the Smithsonian Institution, the following line drawings have been prepared for this book. Unfortunately, no specific data on the design and construction of Rushton boats was available directly from the builder's hand, and no such original information appears to exist. Not a single form, pattern, "mold," or set of drawings and "takes" used during the entire life of the Rushton Boat Shop has been found. The line drawings and specifications included in Rushton's sales catalogs are not sufficiently complete to warrant reproduction.

With the assistance and cooperation of the director of the Adirondack Museum, a professional draftsman was secured to inspect a number of Rushton boats held by the Museum and reconstruct plans and specifications for them. Orvo Markkula, professor of mechanical drawing and draftsmanship at the University of the State of New York Agricultural and Technical College at Canton, New York, accepted the assignment. Luckily, Professor Markkula is an avid canoeist and outdoorist, and already had two canoes of his own making to his credit.

Five canoes, one pleasure boat (a rowboat), and one Adirondack guide-boat, all by Rushton, were selected. Two of the canoes are of historical interest and importance, and these plus the other three canoes provide sufficient diversity of design and type to give some indication of the scope of Rushton's design and craftsmanship. The two canoes of historic record are Nessmuk's celebrated *Sairy Gamp,* now on loan to the Adirondack Museum from the Smithsonian Institution, and the *Diana,* which was entered in the 1882 race meet of the American Canoe Association by Lucien Wulsin and his brother, Clarence Wulsin. The *Diana* was donated to the Adirondack Museum in 1964 by the Wulsin family of Cincinnati, Ohio. The *Sairy Gamp,* built by Rushton on Nessmuk's order in 1883, was one of the five famous featherweight canoes Rushton turned out for the old cobbler between 1880 and 1885. In design the *Diana* is a Princess-type canoe, a decked sailing canoe. The Honorable Nicholas Longworth, member of the old Cincinnati Canoe Club and commodore of the American Canoe Association, 1881–82, is credited with designing the Princess canoe. A prototype was shipped to Rushton, who became the official builder for the Cincinnati club. Rushton added this model to his catalog listings, and it became one of his most popular models during the 1880's, the golden decade of the ACA.

The other three canoes from which measurements and drawings were taken are: a Rushton Ugo-type canoe, the *Vayu*, now owned and used by the author. The Ugo design was developed from Rushton's first open Canadian canoes of 1887 and also his celebrated Arkansas Traveler. The *Vayu* is definitely a cruising model for general use, a family-type craft, staunch and exceptionally seaworthy even in stiff winds. Next is one of Rushton's Nessmuk types, laid up on the original forms used for Nessmuk's canoes. This is the *Wee Lassie,* authenticated as having been built by Rushton in 1893 for the Durant family's use at their famous Pine Knot Camp in the Adirondacks. The demand for this type of canoe continued as long as the Boat Shop was in business. The third canoe is one of the very best and last of Rushton's decked sailing canoes, a smoothskin and a beautiful example of skilled craftsmanship. This is one of the Nomad models and coincidentally bears the name *Nomad* on its plate. It originally came from the Whitney Preserve. In effect, the Nomad design is practically identical with the Ugo design in hull construction.

The other two sets of drawings and "takes" give barely a suggestion of Rushton's diversification of craft, his many types of boats propelled by oars, each type produced in various sizes or models. The rowboat *Wanderer* is of lapstreak construction and is equipped with two pairs of oars and mast holes for two sails. This particular boat was given to the Adirondack Museum by the Ogden Reid family and came from their fleet of fine old craft at the Reid camp on Upper St. Regis Lake. Rushton built many rowboats, dinghies, livery boats, sloops, and other craft of varied types and designs. Only a few Rushton rowboats have survived.

Much interest, of course, centers in the Adirondack guide-boat turned out over many years by Rushton. Rushton listed the guide-boat in his catalogs as the Saranac Laker. The item from which drawings and specification measurements were made came to the Adirondack Museum during the summer of 1966 from its original owners and their summer place on Twitchell Lake.

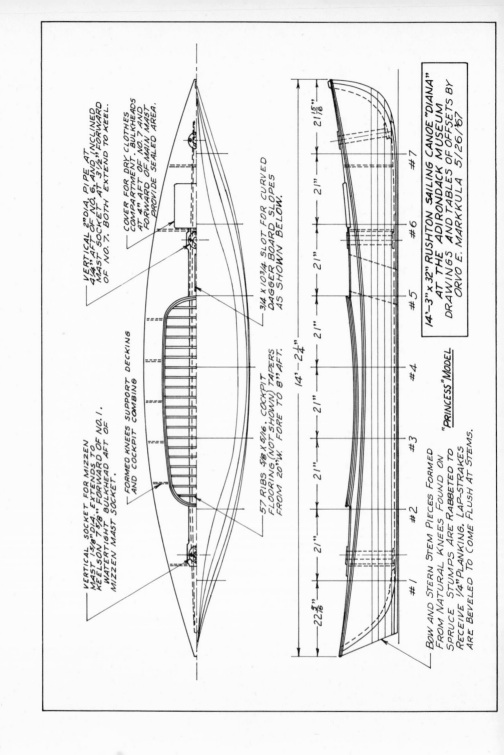

VERTICAL SOCKET FOR MIZZEN MAST 1⅝"DIA. EXTENDS TO KEELSON 7⅝" FORWARD OF NO.1. WATERTIGHT BULKHEAD AFT OF MIZZEN MAST SOCKET.

VERTICAL 2"DIA. PIPE AT 4½" AFT OF NO. 6, AND INCLINED MAST SOCKET AT 3½" FORWARD OF NO.7. BOTH EXTEND TO KEEL.

COVER FOR DRY CLOTHES COMPARTMENT. BULKHEADS AT 4" AFT OF NO.7 AND FORWARD OF MAIN MAST PROVIDE SEALED AREA.

FORMED KNEES SUPPORT DECKING AND COCKPIT COMBING

¾ x 10¾ SLOT FOR CURVED DAGGER BOARD SLOPES AS SHOWN BELOW.

57 RIBS ⅝ X ⁵/₁₆. COCKPIT FLOORING (NOT SHOWN) TAPERS FROM 20"W. FORE TO 8"AFT.

14'- 2¼"

22⅝" | 21" | 21" | 21" | 21" | 21" | 21" | 2 1⁵/₁₆"

#1 | #2 | #3 | #4 | #5 | #6 | #7

14'-3" x 32" RUSHTON SAILING CANOE "DIANA" AT THE ADIRONDACK MUSEUM DRAWINGS AND TABLES OF OFFSETS BY ORVO E. MARKKULA 5/26/'67

"PRINCESS" MODEL

BOW AND STERN STEM PIECES FORMED FROM NATURAL KNEES FOUND ON SPRUCE STUMPS ARE RABBETED TO RECEIVE ¼"PLANKING. LAP-STRAKES ARE BEVELED TO COME FLUSH AT STEMS.

OUTSIDE CENTER-LINE ELEVATIONS ABOVE BASE — KEEL AND STEMS
14'-3"X32" RUSHTON SAILING CANOE "DIANA"

MEASUREMENTS AND DRAWINGS BY O.E.MARKKULA

O.S.℄ — KEEL		STERN & BOW STEMS			
FORM NO.	ELEV. ABOVE BASE	STERN IN. FROM #1 O.S.℄	RABBET	ELEV. ABOVE BASE	BOW STEM IN. FROM #7 TO O.S.℄
a)#1-15 3/8	1/2			1 1/4	a) #7+9 5/8
#1	5/16	-6	-5 3/4	2	+13
#2	5/16	-6 3/4	-10	4	+16 1/16
#3	5/16	-7 5/8	-12 3/4	6	+18 1/2
#4	5/16	-8 1/2	-14 5/8	8	+19 5/8
#5	5/16	-9 1/4	-16 3/8	10	+20 1/4
#6	3/8		-17 3/4	12	+20 1/2
#7	3/4		-18 5/8	14	+21
a)#7+9 5/8	1 1/4	-20 3/8	-20	16	+21 3/8
				18	+21 11/16
				20	+21 7/8
		b)-22 5/8		20 5/8	b) +21 15/16

a) KEEL END
b) END GUNWALE TOP

OFFSETS for 7-STATION FORM
14'-3"x32" RUSHTON CANOE "DIANA" AT THE ADIRONDACK MUSEUM

TABLES OF OFFSETS AND DRAWINGS BY ORVO E.MARKKULA   8/21/'67

HALF-WIDTHS
OUTSIDE SURFACE OF PLANKING   FORMS SPACED 21" ℄ TO ℄

ELEV. ABOVE BASE	#1	#2	#3	#4	#5	#6	#7
2	1 7/16	5 9/16	11 1/2	13 3/8	11 1/2	5 7/16	1 1/2
4	2 7/8	9 3/8	13 5/8	15 3/16	13 11/16	9 7/16	3 1/4
6	4 1/4	11	14 5/8	15 1/16	14 1/16	11 3/16	4 13/16
8	5 9/16	11 3/4	15 1/8	16	15	12 1/4	6 3/16
10	6 5/16	12 1/8	14 7/8	15 1/2	14 3/4	12 1/2	6 5/16
*11				*16 1/16			
*11 1/4			*15 3/16				
*11 5/8					15 1/8		
12	6 3/4	12 1/2				12 5/16	7 3/8
*13 1/2						*12 7/16	
14							7 5/8
*14 7/8	*7 3/8						
*16 1/2							*7 7/8

* OUTSIDE EDGE GUNWALE TOP.
  PINE DECKING COVERS ROUNDED
  GUN'L STRIP WHICH IS 1/2 X 3/4.
b) ALSO GUNWALE WIDTH AT 12 3/4 ELEV.
  COCKPIT COMBING 2 1/2 x 3/8 WITH 1/2 x 3/8
  REINFORCING AROUND OUTSIDE TOP.

KEEL WIDTHS AT STATIONS SHOWN
(RABBETED KEEL–KEELSON PROJECTS 3/8")

STATION#	1-15 3/8	1	2	3	4	5	6	7	7+9 5/8
KEEL WIDTH	5/8	1/4	2	2 1/2	2 5/8	2 1/2	2	1 1/8	5/8

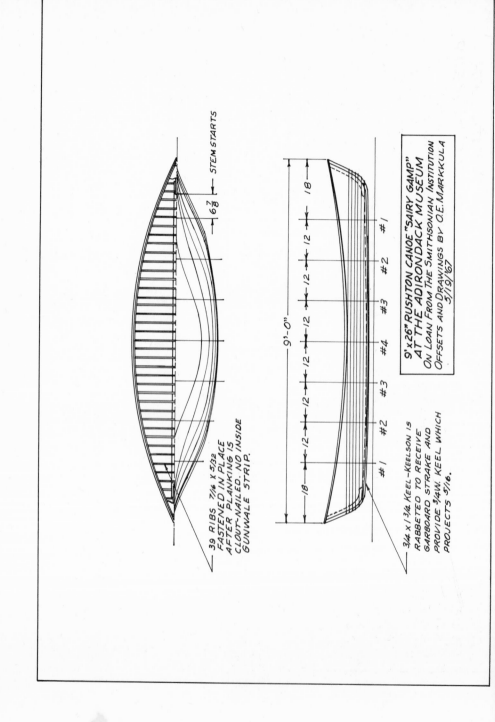

STEM STARTS

6 7/8

39 RIBS 7/16 X 5/32
FASTENED IN PLACE
AFTER PLANKING IS
CLOUT-NAILED. NO INSIDE
GUNWALE STRIP.

9'-0"

18 | 12 | 12 | 12 | 12 | 12 | 12 | 12 | 18

#1 | #2 | #3 | #4 | #3 | #2 | #1

3/4 X 1 3/4 KEEL-KEELSON IS
RABBETED TO RECEIVE
GARBOARD STRAKE AND
PROVIDE 3/4W. KEEL WHICH
PROJECTS 5/16.

9'x26" RUSHTON CANOE "SAIRY GAMP"
AT THE ADIRONDACK MUSEUM
ON LOAN FROM THE SMITHSONIAN INSTITUTION
OFFSETS AND DRAWINGS BY O.E.MARKKULA
5/19/'67

OUTSIDE CENTER-LINE ELEVATIONS ABOVE BASE — KEEL AND STEM
9'X26" RUSHTON CANOE "SAIRY GAMP"

MEASUREMENTS AND DRAWINGS BY O.E. MARKKULA

O.S. ℄ — KEEL

STATION NO. OR INCHES FROM NO. 1	ELEV. ABOVE BASE
NO. 4	1 3/8
NO. 3	1 7/16
NO. 2	1 3/4
NO. 1	2 —
NO. 1 + 10 1/2 ①	2 1/2

① END OF RABBETED KEEL-KEELSON. 1 3/4 X 3/4 X 7'–9". O.S. KEEL 3/4 WIDE—EXTENDS 5/16"

O.S. ℄ — STEM

STATION (INCHES FROM STATION 1)	ELEV. ABOVE BASE
NO. 1 + 10 1/2	2 1/2
" + 11 7/8	3
" + 12 3/4	4
" + 13 3/8	5
" + 14 1/16	6
" + 14 9/16	7
" + 15 1/8	8
" + 15 5/8	9
" + 18 —	14 1/2

NOTE: RABBETED STEM 1 1/8" WIDE STARTS AT 1 + 6 7/8

GENERAL NOTE:
STEAMED RIBS 7/16 X 5/32 SPACED 2 5/8 ON CENTERS, FASTENED IN PLACE AFTER PLANKING AND AFTER REMOVAL FROM FORM.

OFFSETS FOR 7-STATION FORM
9'x26" RUSHTON CANOE "SAIRY GAMP" AT THE ADIRONDACK MUSEUM

ON LOAN FROM THE SMITHSONIAN INSTITUTION

OFFSETS AND DRAWINGS BY O.E. MARKKULA

	FORM 4 MIDSHIP 1 REQ'D.	FORM 3 12" TO 4 2 REQ'D	FORM 2 12" TO 3 2 REQ'D.	FORM 1 12" TO 2 2 REQ'D.
ELEVATIONS ABOVE BASE	HALF-WIDTHS a) OUTSIDE SURFACE OF PLANKING			
2	8	6 1/4	1 1/2	
3	10 1/4	8 3/8	5 —	1 7/16
4	11 1/4	10 11/16	7 11/16	2 1/2
5	11 7/8	11 5/16	9 1/4	4 7/16
6	12 3/8	11 7/8	10 1/8	5 13/16
7	12 9/16	12 1/8	10 7/16	6 7/16
8	12 3/4	12 1/4	10 7/8	6 11/16
8 3/4	* 13 3/16			
9		* 12 5/8	11 —	7 1/16
9 7/8			* 10 1/2	
11 1/4				* 7 3/8

* AT GUNWALE HEIGHT.

a) PLANKING IS LAPSTRAKE 5/32" THICK WITH 6 STRAKES ON EACH SIDE BECOMING BEVELED-LAP AT STEMS.

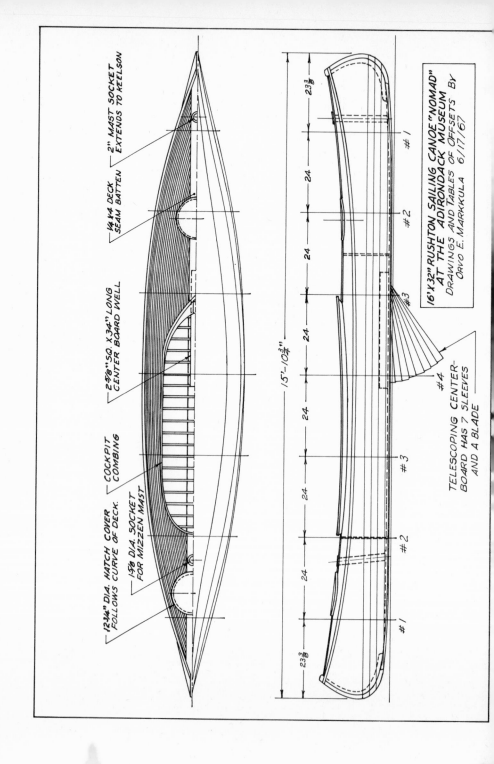

16' X 32" RUSHTON SAILING CANOE "NOMAD"
AT THE ADIRONDACK MUSEUM
DRAWINGS AND TABLES OF OFFSETS BY
ORVO E. MARKKULA 6/17/67

TELESCOPING CENTER-
BOARD HAS 7 SLEEVES
AND A BLADE

2" MAST SOCKET EXTENDS TO KEELSON

¼ X ¼ DECK SEAM BATTEN

2⅝" SQ. X 34" LONG CENTER BOARD WELL

COCKPIT COMBING

12¾" DIA. HATCH COVER FOLLOWS CURVE OF DECK.

1⅝ DIA. SOCKET FOR MIZZEN MAST

15'-10¾"

23⅜

24

24

24

24

24

24

23⅜

#1

#2

#3

#4

OUTSIDE CENTER-LINE ELEVATIONS ABOVE BASE — KEEL AND STEMS

16'X32" RUSHTON SAILING CANOE "NOMAD"

MEASUREMENTS AND DRAWINGS BY O.E. MARKKULA

O.S. ℄ — KEEL ①

STATION OR FORM NO.	ELEV. ABOVE BASE
NO.4 (MIDSHIP)	1/2
NO.3	1/2
NO.2	1/2
NO.1	1 1/8
* NO.1 + 14 1/4"	2 —

* END OF KEEL AND START OF STEM.

① KEEL-KEELSON IS 2 5/8" WIDE OUTSIDE AND PROJECTS 3/16". WIDTH INSIDE 4". RABBETED TO RECEIVE PLANKING.

O.S. ℄ — STEMS

INCHES FROM FORM NO. 1	ELEV. ABOVE BASE
NO. 1 + 14 1/4	2
" + 20 3/4	4
" + 22 1/2	6
" + 23 1/4	8
" + 23 3/8	10
" + 23 1/8	12
" + 22 1/2	14
" + 21 7/8	16
" + 20 1/2	18
" + 19 —	20
" + 18 —	21 1/4

STEMS ARE RABBETED TO RECEIVE 1/4" PLANKS AND EXTEND 1 1/2" BEYOND.

DECK PLANKED WITH 3/8" W x 1/2" DEEP TONGUE AND GROOVE CEDAR WHICH PARALLELS CONTOUR OF GUNWALE. DECK SUPPORTED BY BULKHEADS, FRAMES AND KNEES.

OFFSETS FOR 7-STATION FORM

16'x32" RUSHTON SAIL CANOE "NOMAD" AT THE ADIRONDACK MUSEUM

TABLES OF OFFSETS AND DRAWINGS

BY ORVO E. MARKKULA 6/17/'67

ELEVATIONS ABOVE BASE	HALF-WIDTHS OUTSIDE SURFACE PLANKING ① FORMS SPACED 24" ℄-℄			
	NO. 4	NO. 3	NO. 2	NO. 1
2 INCHES	9 7/8	8 1/4	4 7/8	1 1/8
4 "	13 7/8	12 3/8	8 3/4	3
6 "	14 3/4	13 5/8	10 1/2	4 3/4
8 "	14 13/16	14 —	11 5/16	5 3/4
10 "	14 3/4	14 1/16	11 9/16	6 1/8
12 "	*15 3/4	14 1/8	11 5/8	6 7/16
* 12 1/4 "		*15 1/4		
* 13 "			*12 5/8	
14 "				6 3/8
16 "				*7 1/16

* O.S. TOP OF GUNWALE

NOTES:

① PLANKING 1/4" CEDAR AND WITH 7 STRAKES ON A SIDE—BEVELED SEAM DOUBLE ROW CLOUT-NAILED WITH HEADS ALTERNATING IN & OUT.

② 51 RIBS 5/8 W. X 5/16 THICK, HALF-ROUND INSTALLED AFTER PLANKING.

③ HULL IS SYMMETRICAL ABOUT NO. 4.

④ GUNWALE STRIP MEASURES 7/8 x 3/4 TAPERING TO A 3/16" RADIUS ON O.S.

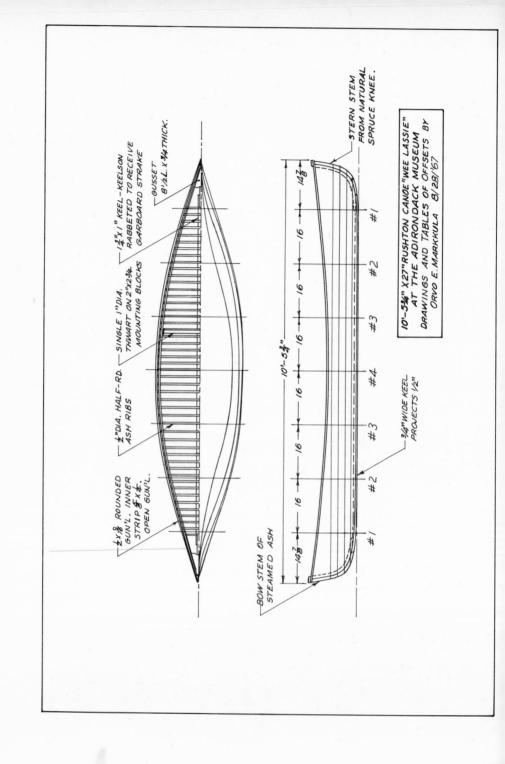

½"x⅞" ROUNDED GUN'L. INNER STRIP ⅝"x¼. OPEN GUN'L.

¼"DIA. HALF-RD. ASH RIBS

SINGLE 1"DIA. THWART ON 2"x2¾ MOUNTING BLOCKS

1¾"x1" KEEL-KEELSON RABBETED TO RECEIVE GARBOARD STRAKE

GUSSET 8½"L.x¾"THICK.

STERN STEM FROM NATURAL SPRUCE KNEE.

BOW STEM OF STEAMED ASH

¾" WIDE KEEL PROJECTS ½"

10'-5¾"

14⅞
16
16
16
16
16
16
14⅞

#1   #2   #3   #4   #3   #2   #1

10'-5¾" X 27" RUSHTON CANOE "WEE LASSIE" AT THE ADIRONDACK MUSEUM DRAWINGS AND TABLES OF OFFSETS BY ORVO E. MARKKULA 8/28/67

OUTSIDE CENTER-LINE ELEVATIONS ABOVE BASE — KEEL AND STEMS 10'–6" x 27" RUSHTON CANOE "WEE LASSIE"

MEASUREMENTS AND DRAWINGS BY O.E. MARKKULA

O.S. ℄ – KEEL Ⓑ

STATION NO. OR DISTANCE BEYOND NO. 1	ELEV. ABOVE BASE
NO. 4 (MIDSHIP)	0
NO. 3	0
NO. 2	1/8
NO. 1	1/4
NO. 1 + 5 1/4" Ⓐ	7/16

O.S. ℄ – STEMS

STATION (DISTANCE FROM NO. 1)	ELEV. ABOVE BASE
NO. 1 + 5 1/4 Ⓐ	7/16
" + 10 1/8	2
" + 12 1/8	4
" + 13 1/4	6
" + 13 11/16	8
" + 14	10
" + 14 7/16	12
" + 14 3/4	* 14 1/4

Ⓐ BOW END OF KEEL AND START OF STEM PIECE. NOTE THAT STERN END OF KEEL IS AT NO. 1 + 4 3/4". THIS FACT WITH THE DIFFERENT PROCESS USED FOR BOW AND STERN STEMS SHOWS THE CUSTOM METHOD OF BUILDING.

* TOP OF GUNWALE AT STEMS.

Ⓑ KEEL – KEELSON 1 3/4" X 1" OAK, ALSO BOTH STEMS RABBETED TO RECEIVE 3/16" PLANKING.

NOTE: HALF-RD. RIBS (47) FROM 2" AFT OF NO. 1 TO 2" FORWARD OF NO. 1.

DOUBLE-ENDED 8' LONG PADDLE HAVING 18" X 6 1/4" BLADES AND 1 1/4" D. FERRULE JOINT IS NOT SHOWN.

OFFSETS FOR 7-STATION FORM 10'- 6" x 27" RUSHTON CANOE "WEE LASSIE"

TABLES OF OFFSETS & DRAWINGS

BY ORVO E. MARKKULA 8/28/'67

ELEVATIONS ABOVE BASE	HALF-WIDTHS (TO OUTSIDE SURFACE OF PLANKING) HULL SYMMETRICAL ABOUT #4			
	NO. 4	NO. 3	NO. 2	NO. 1
2 INCHES	9 3/4	8 7/8	4 3/8	7/8
4 "	11 7/8	11 1/16	7 13/16	2
6 "	12 3/4	12 1/8	9 1/8	3 5/16
8 "	12 7/8	12 1/4	9 1/2	4 3/16
9 5/8 "	* 13 5/16			
9 7/8 "		* 12 1/2		
10 "			9 7/16	4 3/4
10 3/4 "			* 9 7/8	
12 3/8 "				* 5 1/4

* AT ELEVATIONS SHOWN, O.S. EDGE OF GUNWALE. OPEN TYPE GUNWALE BETWEEN NO.'s 1 AND 1.

NOTE: PLANKING 3/16" CEDAR, 6 STRAKES ON EACH SIDE. FIRST 2 STRAKES FROM KEEL ARE LAP-STRAKE TO NO. 1 — THEN BECOME BEVELED-LAP TO COME FLUSH AT STEMS. REMAINING 4 STRAKES HAVE APPEARANCE OF LAP-STRAKE ON THE OUTSIDE BUT ON THE INSIDE APPROACH THE BEVELED-SEAM OF THE SMOOTH-SKIN CANOES.

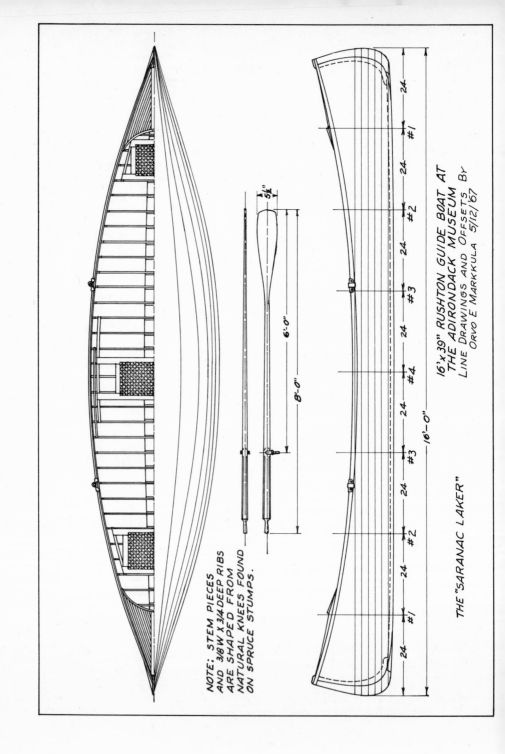

NOTE: STEM PIECES
AND 3/8 W X 3/4 DEEP RIBS
ARE SHAPED FROM
NATURAL KNEES FOUND
ON SPRUCE STUMPS.

16'x39" RUSHTON GUIDE BOAT AT
THE ADIRONDACK MUSEUM
LINE DRAWINGS AND OFFSETS BY
ORVO E MARKKULA 5/12/'67

THE "SARANAC LAKER"

OFFSETS FOR 7-STATION FORM 16'x39" RUSHTON GUIDE BOAT AT THE ADIRONDACK MUSEUM

OFFSETS AND LINE DRAWINGS BY ORVO E. MARKKULA 5/12/67

ELEVATIONS ABOVE BASE	STA. 4 MIDSHIP 1 REQ'D	STA. 3 24"TO 4 2 REQ'D	STA. 2 24"TO 3 2 REQ'D	STA. 1 24"TO 2 2 REQ'D
	HALF-WIDTHS OUTSIDE SURFACE OF PLANKING			
2	8	7 7/8	4 3/16	
4	13 1/8	11 7/8	7 3/8	3 1/8
6	16	14 13/16	10 3/8	4 5/16
8	17 5/8	16 7/16	12 7/16	5 7/16
10	18 5/8	17 3/8	13 11/16	6 3/8
12	(A) 19 3/4	18 3/16	14 1/2	7 5/16
13	* 19 1/2			
13 3/4		18 3/8		
14				7 13/16
15 1/8			* 15 1/8	
16				8 3/16
18				(B) 8 3/16
19 3/8				* 8 3/16

(A) O.S. EDGE GUNWALE TOP
(B) LOWER EDGE GUNWALE
* O.S. EDGE PLANKING AT GUNWALE TOP

OUTSIDE CENTER-LINE ELEVATIONS ABOVE BASE — KEEL AND STEM 16'x39" RUSHTON GUIDE BOAT

MEASUREMENTS AND DRAWINGS BY O.E. MARKKULA

O.S. ℄ — KEEL		O.S. ℄ — STEM	
STATION NO. OR INCHES FROM NO.1	ELEV. ABOVE BASE	STATION (INCHES FROM NUMBER 1)	ELEV. ABOVE BASE
NO.4 (MIDSHIP)	3/8	1+16 7/8	1 1/16
NO.3 (FORE ℄ AFT)	3/8	1+20 1/16	2
NO.2 (FORE ℄ AFT)	1/2	1+22 5/8	4
NO.1 (FORE ℄ AFT)	15/16	1+23 3/4	6
NO.1+16 7/8 (END)	1 1/16	1+23 3/4	8
		1+23 5/8	10
		1+23 1/2	12
		1+23	14
		1+23	16
		1+22 1/2	16
		1+22 1/8	18
		1+21 5/8	20
		1+21	22
		*1+20 3/8	24 3/8
		1+20 1/8	(A) 25 1/8

(A) PEAK OF STEM
* END GUNWALE TOP

HALF-WIDTHS OF RABBETED KEEL AT INDICATED LOCATIONS

STATION #	4	3	2	1	1+16 7/8
HALF-WIDTH	3	2 3/4	2 1/8	1 3/8	11/16

NOTE: PLANKING IS 5/16" CEDAR, 7 STRAKES ON A SIDE, BEVELED-LAP SEAMS, SMOOTH.

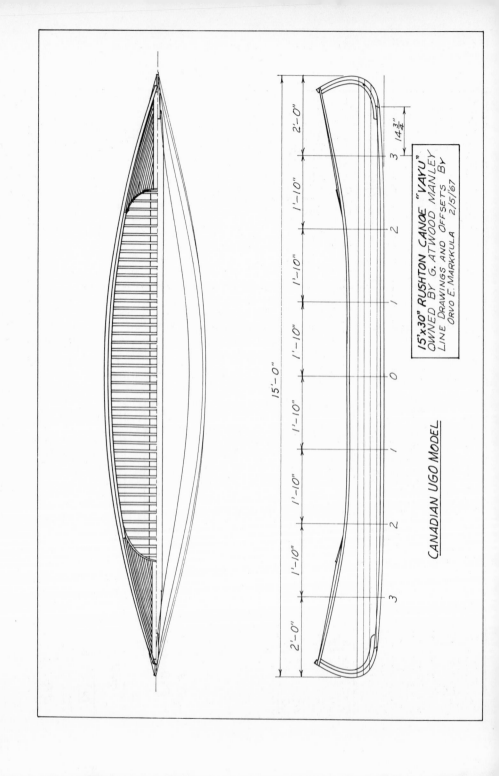

15"x30" RUSHTON CANOE "VAYU"
OWNED BY G. ATWOOD MANLEY
LINE DRAWINGS AND OFFSETS BY
ORVO E. MARKKULA   2/5/67

CANADIAN UGO MODEL

15'-0"

2'-0"   1'-10"   1'-10"   1'-10"   1'-10"   1'-10"   1'-10"   1'-10"   2'-0"

3   2   1   0   1   2   3

14 3/4"

OUTSIDE CENTER-LINE ELEVATIONS ABOVE BASE — KEEL AND STEM
15'x30" RUSHTON CANOE "VAYU"

MEASUREMENTS AND DRAWINGS BY O.E. MARKKULA

O.S. ℄ — KEEL		O.S. ℄ — STEM	
STATION OR INCHES FROM NO.3	ELEV. ABOVE BASE	STATION (INCHES FROM STATION 3)	ELEV. ABOVE BASE
NO. 0	0	NO.3 + 14 3/4	1 5/16
NO. 1	0	" + 18	1 13/16
NO. 2	0	" + 20 1/4	2 13/16
NO. 3	0 3/8	" + 21 13/16	3 13/16
NO.3 + 8 IN.	0 13/16	" + 23 1/8	5 13/16
NO.3 + 14 3/4	1 5/16	" + 23 5/8	7 13/16
		" + 23 3/4	9 13/16
		" + 23 1/16	11 13/16
		" + 23 1/16	13 13/16
		" + 22 7/16	15 13/16
		" + 21 1/2	17 13/16
		" + 20 7/8	18 13/16
		" + 20 1/4	19 13/16
		" + 19 3/4	20 9/16

*ALSO GUNWALE TOP BOTH ENDS →

SECTION AT STATION "O"
SHOWING 1"x4" RABBETED KEEL,
1/2 X 7/8 INNER AND 1/8 X 3/4 OUTER
GUNWALE, AND BEVELED-LAP
SEAM CONSTRUCTION.

OFFSETS FOR 7-STATION FORM 15'x30" RUSHTON CANOE "VAYU"

OWNED BY G. ATWOOD MANLEY

OFFSETS AND LINE DRAWINGS BY ORVO E. MARKKULA   2/5/67

ELEVATIONS ABOVE BASE	FORM "O" MIDDLE 22"to 0" 1 REQ'D.	FORM "1" 22"to 0" 2 REQ'D.	FORM "2" 22"to 1" 2 REQ'D.	FORM "3" 22"to 2" 2 REQ'D.
	HALF – WIDTHS			
	OUTSIDE SURFACE OF PLANKING			
13/16				
1 13/16	4 5/8	4 9/16	2 7/8	1 —
2 13/16	10 1/16	8 13/16	5 5/8	2 —
3 13/16	12 11/16	11 1/4	7 5/8	3 3/16
4 13/16	14 —	12 1/16	9 1/16	4 —
5 13/16	14 5/8	13 3/8	10 —	4 3/4
6 13/16	14 13/16	13 7/8	10 5/8	5 1/2
7 13/16	14 7/8	14 —	11 1/16	5 7/8
8 13/16	14 15/16	14 1/8	11 7/16	6 3/8
9 13/16	15 —	14 3/16	11 1/2	6 1/2
10 13/16	15 —	14 1/4	11 1/2	6 5/8
11 1/4	15 —	14 1/4	11 9/16	6 3/4
11 5/16	*15 —			
11 13/16		*14 1/4	11 5/16	
11 15/16			*11 3/16	
12 13/16				6 7/16
14 13/16				6 3/8
15 9/16				*6 3/8

* (AT GUNWALE HEIGHT)

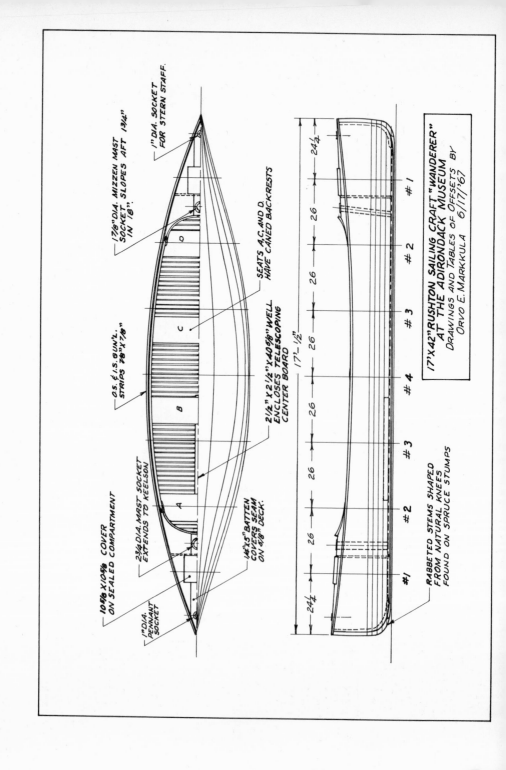

17" X 42" RUSHTON SAILING CRAFT "WANDERER" AT THE ADIRONDACK MUSEUM
Drawings and Tables of Offsets by
ORVO E. MARKKULA 6/17/'67

1" DIA. SOCKET FOR STERN STAFF.

1⅞" DIA. MIZZEN MAST SOCKET SLOPES AFT 1¾" IN 18".

SEATS A,C, AND D. HAVE CANED BACKRESTS

2½" X 2½" X 40⅝" WELL ENCLOSES TELESCOPING CENTER BOARD

O.S. ⅛" S. GUN'L. STRIPS ⅞"X⅞"

2¾" DIA. MAST SOCKET EXTENDS TO KEELSON

10⅜" X 10⅜" COVER ON SEALED COMPARTMENT

¼"X⅝" BATTEN COVERS SEAM ON ⅝" DECK.

1" DIA. PENNANT SOCKET

RABBETED STEMS SHAPED FROM NATURAL KNEES FOUND ON SPRUCE STUMPS

17'- ½"

24¼   26   26   26   26   26   26   24¼

#1   #2   #3   #4   #3   #2   #1

OUTSIDE CENTER-LINE ELEVATIONS ABOVE BASE — KEEL AND STEMS

17' X 42 1/2" RUSHTON SAIL CRAFT "WANDERER"

MEASUREMENTS AND DRAWINGS BY O.E. MARKKULA

O.S. ℄ — KEEL		O.S. ℄ — STEMS	
STATION OR FORM NO.	ELEV. ABOVE BASE	INCHES FROM FORM NO. 1	ELEV. ABOVE BASE
NO. 4 (MIDSHIP)	1/2	*NO. 1 + 17 1/4	3/4
NO. 3	1/2	" + 21 3/16	2
NO. 2	1/2	" + 23 1/8	4
NO. 1	1/2	" + 23 3/4	6
*NO. 1 + 17 1/4"	3/4	" + 24 —	8
		" + 24 —	10
		" + 24 —	12
		" + 24 1/16	14
		" + 24 1/8	16
		" + 24 3/16	18
		" + 24 1/4	20
		" + 24 1/4	24

* END OF KEEL AND START OF STEM

NOTE: 2 FLOOR BOARDS 3/8 X 7 3/4 CLEATED TOGETHER EXTEND FROM MAST TO MAST

WIDTH OF RABBETED KEEL AT STATIONS (KEEL PROTECTED BY 1/16" THICK STEEL)

STATION #	4	3	2	1	1+17 1/4
WIDTH	1 7/16	1 7/16	1 1/8	3/4	3/8

OPENING FOR CENTER-BOARD IS 1" WIDE AND EXTENDS FROM #4+10 1/4" TO #3+21"

OFFSETS FOR 7-STATION FORM

17' x 42 1/2" RUSHTON SAIL CRAFT "WANDERER"

AT THE ADIRONDACK MUSEUM

TABLES OF OFFSETS AND DRAWINGS

BY ORVO E. MARKKULA 6/17/'67

ELEVATIONS ABOVE BASE	HALF-WIDTHS (OUTSIDE SURFACE PLANKING)① FORMS SPACED 26" ℄-℄			
	NO. 4	NO. 3	NO. 2	NO. 1
2 INCHES	5 3/4	5 1/2	3 1/4	1 1/4
4 "	15 5/8	13 3/4	8 1/4	2 7/8
6 "	18 7/8	17 3/16	11 5/8	4 3/16
8 "	19 15/16	18 1/16	13 3/4	5 1/2
10 "	20 7/16	19 3/16	14 13/16	6 11/16
12 "	20 1/2	19 3/16	15 3/16	7 9/16
14 "	20 9/16	19 5/16	15 5/16	8 1/4
16 "	20 1/4	19 3/16	15 3/8	8 5/8
17 7/8 "	* 21 1/8	*19 7/8		
18 "				8 11/16
18 7/8 "			*16 1/4	
20 "				8 3/4
21 "				*9 1/2

* OUTSIDE EDGE GUN'L TOP.

① PLANKING 1/4" LAPSTRAKE WITH NINE STRAKES ON A SIDE, BEVELED AT STEMS. HULL IS SYMMETRICAL ABOUT NO. 4

81 RIBS — HALF-ROUND 5/8 DIA. ASH.

The following is the eighth of nine articles entitled The Bucktail in Florida, *by George W. Sears (Nessmuk), in* Forest and Stream. *It appeared in the issue for July 16, 1885.*

Monday, May 18, was a good day for canoes. It was barely sunrise, and I was monkeying around the fire with a condensed milk can by way of coffee pot, when Jake, the darkey carter, passed within ten rods of camp with an oblong box on his cart, heading straight for Kendall's ranch. He hailed me with, "I'se got a little boat here fer de cap'n; come ober an' see her."

"All right, Jake, you've got a little boat there for me, too, I reckon?"

"No sah. Box ain' big enough for two boats," and he drove on.

Now, the Captain's ranch is just about seventy rods from my camp, and before the leaves grew so dense on the black-jacks the camps were in sight of each other. Even now I catch glimpses of light from his windows at night, while he can always see my blazing camp-fires of a dark evening. And as I leisurely drank a cup of black coffee (which is the proper thing to do of a morning in this climate) I heard a hammering and rending clatter over at the Captain's house, as of one who opens a dry goods box with a store hatchet, and there came a clear ringing hail, which I answered, and then walked over to the ranch. I found the Captain contemplating the contents of the open box with a smile of grim satisfaction, while Mrs. K. was actually dancing with delight like an excited school girl. Her little canoe, the long looked for, clinker-built cedar, had come at last, and was nestling snugly and safely in its packing without scratch or crack. Well, she was a beauty, and light as a cork, turning the scales at sixteen and a half pounds barely. Finished in oil and varnish, and of a different model from any of the light open canoes I have seen, though the difference is slight. On the whole I prefer her model to that of the *Bucktail,* though the latter was built strictly on the dimensions given by myself. Her length is 10½ feet, beam 26 inches, with 9 inches rise at center, twelve inches at stems.

But what interested me most was another and lighter canoe nested neatly and safely inside the first. This was the little *Rushton* ordered nearly a year ago, with no directions save as to name and weight. She must in any case weigh less than ten pounds. And the name to be painted neatly on each side of one stem in gold and scarlet letters. This was meant as a slight compliment to the man who has done more and better canoe work for me than any man living. Other makers might have done just as well, but they all, I believe, use white lead or some other waterproof material to make close joints. Other things being equal, I prefer naked wood to wood; close joints by close work. When I have rattled my canoes until they leak, I can do the daubing myself. The *Rushton Fairbanks* at just 9 pounds, 15 ounces, is 8½ feet long, and has 23 inches beam, with 8 inches rise at center, and 10¼ inches rise at stems. I thought she had rather a tubby look when first placed on the water. Her very flat bearings, with the way she carried her width out toward the stems, made her look like the model of a Dutch galliot; but, turning her keel up, she showed lines and curves that looked like gliding over water very fairly. Balancing her on the end of a finger, she really did seem too frail—too trifling for real work. But I remembered the handsome behavior of the *Sairy Gamp* (only nine ounces heavier) and decided to test her fairly.

We formed a procession of three down to the landing, Mrs. K. leading, and jubilant at the thought that she could make her own carries without help from the male element, whereat the M. E. gave me a side wink and grinned sardonically.

I do not like Kendall's landing—not for an open canoe. The water is too deep and the bank too steep. I prefer a gentle slope of soft sand where the canoe can glide up to a stop easily, and I may walk out or in on the keelson. It was agreed that Mrs. K. should launch out first; and with some trepidation and a little help from the Captain, she got safely off and began to ply the double blade. Gingerly at the start, but finding the canoe steady and easy under paddle she grew confident and put on muscle, paddling up and down the river, in and out of bayous, and handling the light craft skillfully as a squaw. Finally she landed and lifted the canoe out of water, saying, "Oh, she is just lovely; worth half a dozen spring bonnets." Then the Captain hinted he would like to see the *Rushton* "go," and I dropped her into the water with a spat, dropped a folded blanket into her for a seat, and crept in, rather carefully it must be owned.

But once in and fairly seated I found her, to my surprise, steadier than the *Bucktail* of more than twice her size; i.e., she did not tip or rock so easily, and she required less propelling to the mile than any boat or canoe I had ever handled. I saw that she would trim with fifteen or twenty pounds in addition to my own weight, and I had not paddled her half an hour before deciding that, if she would stay in a lumpy sea, I would adopt her as my cruising canoe.

We went down to the Springs, the Captain, Mrs. K. and I. It is only a mile as the crow flies. By the tortuous channel of river and bayou it is nearly three, and a pleasant trip we made of it. Of course, the light canoes attracted a crowd; they always do that, even in towns where canoes are common, but the crowd was not a large one. The Northern tourists had flitted, and the permanent population of the Springs is less than one hundred. We paddled back in the cool of the evening and agreed that it was good to be there.

"It's the first time three double-bladers ever hauled in at one landing on this coast," said the Captain. And I think he was right.

This was more than a month ago, and I have kept the *Rushton* pretty well in use since.

Every well built canoe, yacht or ship has some individuality, some peculiar trait of its own. The peculiar trait of the *Rushton* is to take in spray heavily when going to windward, say four points off. This is owing to her sharp, short curved lines. We went outside, Tarpon and I, to test her against a brisk sea breeze—he to lie off, watch her closely, and give his opinion as canoeist, builder and sailor. For he is all these. I put her straight in the wind's eye with a choppy lump of sea against her, and she rode it like a duck. I turned and ran before it, and she got away from the seas like a whale boat. Then I laid her beam on, and—well, it took some balancing, but she kept dry. Lastly I tried her with the wind about four points abaft the stem, and she slashed the spray in, a few spoonsful at a time, until I was obliged to creep under Tarpon's lee and sponge out.

Then he gave his opinion, "Let me deck her and you can stay out as long as the seas don't break under you. That will swamp any canoe." So she is to have a light cloth decking and a cockpit withal, like the able-bodied canoes of the A.C.A....

APPENDIX E: Rushton Canoes Today

Acting on a friend's suggestion, I have kept a check list of existing Rushton rowboats and canoes since the summer of 1959. I knew then of two all-cedar canoes and three or four Indian Girls whose canvas was badly worn. Boats suffer from rough usage and neglect. Wood rots. No one was more aware of this than Rushton himself. In 1904, in reply to an inquiry from Lucien Wulsin, Rushton wrote: "I could not tell, without seeing them, what could be done in way of repairs on your canoes. A boat twenty-four years old stands quite a chance of being decayed in some parts, even if not used at all for many years, and once we begin to cut, no knowing what we will find." An undated catalog issued after Rushton's death (probably 1908) states that the Boat Shop occasionally received for repairs Rushton boats as old as twenty years. A check list made today means a life of fifty to ninety years.

I expected to find few authentic Rushton craft and therefore made no systematic search. The list has grown in a haphazard way. Yet at this writing (summer of 1966) it numbers more than fifty, five of which have turned up during the last two months. Almost all are well authenticated. Most have the Rushton nameplate, imprint on the wood, or engraving in the metal bang strip of the stem. Some with no such identification—nameplates can easily be lost or imprints obliterated—have well-documented histories supported by a study of methods of construction and specifications.

The canoes located represent every decade of Rushton construction except the first—the 1870's. These discoveries have been most helpful. It is one thing to study Rushton's catalogs; it is quite another to examine and use surviving Rushton craft. One comes to understand the force of the remark made to me in 1959 by A. Fred Saunders, commodore of the ACA from 1917 to 1919 and for forty years its historian: "When I joined the ACA in 1910, four years after Rushton's death, his name was still magic." A half century later the magic survives for viewers of Rushton canoes in museums and elsewhere, for the lucky owners, and most of all for users.

Here I should like to tell how some of the fifty-odd Rushton craft have been found. To me their chance appearance has in it a touch of the Rushton magic. Readers impatient with authorial self-indulgence are at liberty to stop here.

The first discovery came as a response to an article of mine on Rushton in the April, 1958, issue of the St. Lawrence County Historical Association *Quarterly*. Mr. Chelson Sayer, of Rochester, formerly a native of St. Lawrence County, wrote to say that he had a Rushton guide-boat in good condition and was willing to sell it. A year later when Professor Edward J. Blankman, of St. Lawrence University, inquired whether the *Quarterly* article had brought to light any old Rushton boats, I gave him Mr. Sayer's address. Thus this lover of North Country antiques added a new department to his collection. The smoothskin Saranac Laker he bought from its Rochester owner was the only Rushton guide-boat I had thus far located. In the summer of 1966, however, the Adirondack Museum acquired one in mint condition; its black-painted hull recalls Rushton's catalog description of his guide-boat as "the black snake of the wilderness." A third possibility, not yet authenticated, is a guide-boat in the great hall of the castle in Litchfield Park.

Professor Blankman has since added three other Rushtons to his collection: a clinker-built row-and-sail boat (St. Lawrence skiff), a remade Indian Girl canvas-covered canoe, and an all-cedar Canadian model dating from the early 1890's. He and his family are using these craft at his camp on the Raquette River.

The Canadian canoe, named *Punkie,* is one of three all-cedar Rushton smoothskins found by Professor Blankman's brother Lloyd, of Clinton, New York. While visiting Brantingham Lake in the western Adirondacks, Lloyd Blankman inquired about Rushton canoes of an old guide and woodsman, Earl Taylor, who acknowledged that he had three stored in a barn. Lloyd bought the one in best condition, the *Vayu,* on the spot, carted it home, and in 1964 sold it to me. In the *Vayu,* a Canadian model Ugo, Dr. Paul F. Jamieson and I have explored many lakes and streams in the forever-wild areas of the Adirondacks. It needed no repairs. After two days' soaking it is tight. It is a graceful, steady, and responsive craft. Lloyd Blankman later bought the second of Taylor's canoes, the *Marymac,* and it is now the property of Franklin Brandreth of Akron, Ohio, and Brandreth Lake in the Adirondacks. All three have been traced to two previous generations of owners in a single family. The *Punkie* was purchased from Rushton about 1891 and the two others between 1911 and 1914 by the same individual as gifts for her two daughters. The *Punkie* needed repairs and has since been given an outer coating of fiber glass.

Earlier I owned a 1910 Arkansas Traveler, also a smoothskin. When I acquired it in 1961, the stern section of a garboard plank was bruised and split. In replacing the twenty-four-inch section with a new piece of cedar planking, I had an opportunity to study the methods of beveling and nailing used by Rushton workmen. This canoe is now in the Adirondack Museum.

Last summer on Cranberry Lake I located an older Arkansas Traveler with a type of deck Rushton offered as an option—a three-inch inwale deck along the sides with a two-and-a-half-inch coaming encircling the cockpit. James Gardner found it in nearly perfect condition in a summer cottage formerly owned by the Abbott family of Gouverneur. Worth Abbott had purchased it while spending the summers on Cranberry a few years before his death in 1906.

The most beautiful of all my finds is the smoothskin *Nomad*, a late-model cruising-sailing canoe with graceful lines and decking in alternate strips of dark and light woods. A birthday reunion led to the discovery of this craft. When David Short came to Canton to attend the seventieth birthday reunion of his uncle, Everett Brown, I asked him whether he knew of any Rushton canoes on the large Whitney Park in the Adirondacks, where he was caretaker. He replied that all canoes on the preserve are now of aluminum for ease of maintenance, but that a Rushton sailing canoe had been sold four years earlier to Stanley Johnson, a Tupper Lake contractor. I conveyed this word to Robert Bruce Inverarity, then director of the Adirondack Museum, and two weeks later the lovely *Nomad* became part of the permanent boat exhibit. It is in an excellent state of preservation and original in every detail. Its woodwork and finish warm the heart of a cabinetmaker. The *Nomad* was developed from a Ugo hull, like my *Vayu*, with decking, centerboard, cockpit, and sail rigging added.

In 1887 Rushton began offering some of his craft in smoothskin hulls. The oldest example of his smoothskins I know of today dates to 1889. It is the *Cheemaun*, a canoe I have known since my earliest memories. It is still in use, still staunch in every seam and joint. It is the property of Mrs. Dorothy Cleaveland (Elon G.) Salisbury, of Takoma Park, Maryland, the daughter of Frank Nash Cleaveland, who with Ledyard P. Hale ordered it from Rushton in 1889. Members of the St. Lawrence Canoe Club, the Cleavelands and the Hales shared ownership and use of the *Cheemaun* for many years. According to their instructions, Rushton inserted between the beveled edges of the planks layers of linen soaked in white lead. This added weight to the canoe but gave it strength and durability proved by time. Eventually it passed to the ownership of the Cleavelands. From 1924 to 1948 it was in storage in Canton. In the latter year Dr. and

Mrs. Salisbury had it recalked and varnished and took it to their Takoma Park home. In 1949 Mrs. Salisbury's mother, four days before her ninety-ninth birthday, enjoyed a good paddle in the *Cheemaun,* as a photograph and a feature article in the *Washington Post* testify. The Salisburys have used the canoe on the Chesapeake and Ohio Canal, the upper Potomac, streams in Virginia's Dismal Swamp, and other canoeing waters in the vicinity.

The survival of the *Cheemaun* for nearly eighty years is perhaps not so remarkable as that of the lightweight Bucktails and the featherweight Nessmuks. In the latter class is the *Sairy Gamp,* cruised in the Adirondacks by Nessmuk himself in the summer of 1883, now the property of the Smithsonian Institution and on loan to the Adirondack Museum. The museum has another canoe of the Nessmuk type, formerly owned by Clifford Judd, whose father and uncle bought it secondhand in 1888. These Nessmuks with their planks planed to a thickness of three-sixteenths of an inch support Rushton's view that the clinker-built hull has greater strength than the smooth one. Captain Kendall once testified to the sinewy strength of Rushton's featherweights in a letter to *Forest and Stream* (August 23, 1900) : "Sixteen years ago a drayman drove up to Tarpon Ranch with two canoes packed in one box—the *Smarty,* weighing sixteen pounds, and the *Rushton,* weighing nine pounds fifteen ounces." Both were put to heavy use in ensuing years, by Nessmuk himself while he was a guest of the Captain, by a young woman, and by Kendall and his wife. "And the two canoes, barring a few scratches, are as ready for the water as the day they were taken out of the box sixteen years ago."

It is possible now to add a postscript to the Captain's testimony. His Nessmuks survived at least sixteen years of fairly steady use. The *Sairy* for most of her career has had tender care in museums. A recent discovery throws a new light, however, on the durability of these craft. In 1959 an item in a little mimeographed publication of Old Forge in the Adirondacks, *Log Cabin News,* led to correspondence with Charles Larkin II, of Buffalo, New York. In 1910 his father, still living in 1966, purchased a Nessmuk and a Bucktail from the Rushton shop. As described by Mr. Larkin, the canoes are about ten feet, six inches in length and weigh twenty-one and twenty-five pounds. For many years the family also owned an Indian Girl but finally sold it. The Nessmuk and the Bucktail have been in use for fifty-five years. In 1965 Charles Larkin I celebrated his ninetieth birthday by taking a paddle in the Nessmuk model.

Today, wherever Charles Larkin II goes with these two canoes racked side by side on the top of his car, he soon has an admiring audience asking questions about them.

A letter of inquiry addressed to the Old Town Canoe Company in 1962 brought to light two Rushton all-cedar Indian canoes. Dean Gray, vice-president of the Old Town factory, informed me that in the same mail with my letter had come another asking how to refinish an old Rushton canoe. I wrote to the address he gave. Yes, Woodward Burkhart, of Baltimore, had two Indian model canoes. His father had purchased *Shawondasee I* secondhand about the turn of the century. *Shawondasee II* was found in the 1920's embedded in sand and silt offshore on Lake Hopatcong, New Jersey. It was raised and repaired. Photographs of these two canoes later seen in my album by a young couple, Ned and Nancy Merrill, led to the discovery of a duplicate. The Merrills soon reported from their summer place at St. George's Cove on the Maine coast that they too had an all-cedar Indian bearing the Rushton trademark. Ned's father had brought it to the coast from his family's camp on Upper St. Regis Lake in the Adirondacks. Today, refinished, it is once more in use.

On an August afternoon in 1965 I located two more all-cedar Indians while paddling the *Vayu* with Paul Jamieson around the shores of Upper St. Regis Lake. Some of the forty-odd summer camps on this and Spitfire Lake have been in the same families for three or four generations. Craft of many kinds have accumulated in boathouses, some dating to the last century and all scrupulously cared for. The familiar lines of two canoes in a boathouse with an open front caught my eye. The owner, just then reefing and mooring an Idem model sailboat near his dock, noticed our interest and offered to show us the contents of the boathouse. The two canoes, freshly varnished, were indeed all-cedar Indians with the Rushton imprint. Both were acquired by the owner's father and are now in use by the third generation.

Probably the oldest items on the check list are sister canoes of the Princess model. Both have an interesting history. In 1928 a young attorney (now surrogate judge) of Canton, New York, Lott H. Wells, heard that an old cedar canoe had been stored for many years in the Ellsworth family barn. Inspection showed that one side of the hull had been pierced by a .22-caliber bullet but that otherwise the craft was in good condition. J. Stanley Ellsworth had inherited the canoe from his father, Joseph, Rushton's early employer in Canton and his lifelong friend. According to family tradition, the canoe came from the Boat Shop in the early 1880's, about the time Rushton began listing Princess models in 1882.

Mr. Wells acquired the canoe and repaired the damaged clinker-built hull. Ever since, it has been at the Wells's island camp in the St. Lawrence River. It was seriously damaged some years ago when it broke from its moorings in a gale and was dashed on a rocky shore. Judge Wells restored the hull in conformity to original lines. The canoe matches the specifications of the Princess model in Rushton's catalog of 1882. Today it is sailed as well as paddled on the St. Lawrence.

The story of the second surviving Princess involves one of those accidental discoveries which biographers must rely on and learn to wait for more or less patiently. My glance happened to stray from the editorial page of the *New York Times* of January 15, 1964, to a headline on the opposite page: "Lucien Wulsin, Piano Maker, 74 —Baldwin's Board Chairman Is Dead in Cincinnati." This could only be a descendant of the Lucien Wulsin who in 1879 accompanied Siegfried and Barnes on a canoe voyage to the Mississippi headwaters and who was one of the charter members of the American Canoe Association. The deceased was in fact the son of the canoeist and cofounder of the D. H. Baldwin Company and is survived by today's Lucien Wulsin, the president of the corporation.

A cordial reply to my inquiry brought the richest single reward of eight years of research. Mrs. Ann Shepherd, head of the Historical Records Department of the Baldwin Company, to whom my letter had been referred, wrote that their files contained a large amount of material concerning Lucien Wulsin I and his association with early canoeing in America. There were many letters from J. H. Rushton, copies of letters to him, letters from other canoeists such as Stephens, Bishop, and Woodman; material concerning the 1879 Itasca trip, including Wulsin's diary; material too about the early days of the Cincinnati Canoe Club and of the American Canoe Association. In due time the entire file was boxed and shipped to the Owen D. Young Library of St. Lawrence University to be made available for my use in preparing this study of Rushton and his times. Evidence of my indebtedness to this material appears throughout these pages. Mr. Wulsin kindly permitted the Adirondack Museum to microfilm large portions of the file. The originals have since been turned over to the museum of the Cincinnati Historical Society.

In the course of the correspondence over the Wulsin files, another surviving Rushton canoe was located. At a summer home in Ontario at the eastern end of Lake Superior, Mr. Wulsin had an old canoe which by family tradition was a sister of the *Kleiner Fritz-Betsy D*. He offered to donate this to the Adirondack Museum. Thus in the fall of 1964 the cedar paddling-sailing canoe *Diana* made the journey to Blue Mountain Lake and is now part of the Rushton exhibit there. Study of this canoe indicates that it is not a duplicate of the *Kleiner Fritz* but matches in every specification the first Princess model, designed by Judge Longworth, built in the Boat Shop, and first listed by Rushton in 1882. During the early part of that year several of these canoes were made for members of the Cincinnati club. The *American Canoeist* for September, 1882, confirms that Lucien Wulsin entered the *Diana* in one of the ACA races at Lake George that August. Though the evidence does not amount to certain identification, it seems probable that the *Diana* Wulsin had at Lake George was one of the Princess models Rushton built the same year for the Cincinnati club and is the same boat Lucien Wulsin, the grandson, recently donated to the Adirondack Museum. If so, it is the earliest built of the surviving Rushton canoes as yet located.

These and other Rushton canoes have long outlived the modest claims made for them by their builder, who, as Nessmuk once said, "builded better than he knew."

INDEX

Abbott, Worth: 193
Adirondack Club: 11
Adirondack guide-boat: viii, 10, 158, 160, 164, 172, 173, 192
Adirondack Museum: 21, 54, 172, 192, 193, 194, 196, 197
Adirondack poet. *See* Carter, Cornelius
Alden, William L.: 26, 27, 60, 67, 83, 139, 140
Alice: 39, 40
Alnumbra: 29
American Canoe Association: First Call, 57, 58; founding, 57–68 *passim;* charter members, 58, 59; officers, 59; regatta committee, 62–65 *passim;* constitution, 63; meet of 1881, 70; meet of 1882, 81, 172, 197; meet of 1883, 70; meet of 1885, 90, 99, 100; meet of 1884, 95–97; meet of 1886, 101, 102, 104, 105–13; meet of 1900, 139; meet of 1897, 140; mentioned, ix, 2, 70, 76, 80, 90, 94, 98, 99, 100, 101, 103, 135, 191
American Canoeist: 15, 27, 60, 77
American House: 7
Ampersand Pond: 11
Annie Dell: 72, 74, 75
Aquatic Monthly: 28, 29
Atlantis: 108
Aurora: viii, 2, 80, 82, 98, 106

Baden-Powell, Warington: 17, 27, 28, 101, 106, 109
Baldwin Co.: 31, 32, 145, 196
Barnegat Sneak Boat: 83
Barnes, J. M.: 26, 32, 37, 41, 58
Barney, E. H.: 108–11 *passim,* 127
Battle Ground, The: 118
Beard, Wriley N.: 130
Belmont, August, Jr.: 73
Betsy D.: 32, 34, 58, 77
Biffen, William: 106
Big Deer Pond: 119
Bishop, Nathaniel Holmes: 29, 30, 57, 61, 66, 96, 98, 114, 139, 140, 147

Blanche: 106
Blankman, Edward J.: 192
Blankman, Lloyd: 192
Blue Mountain Lake: 168
Bowdish and Son: 127
Bowsfield, C. J.: 109
Brantingham Lake: 192
Brenan, Dan: 49
Brentano, Arthur: 60, 67
Brower, J. V.: 42
Brown, Nelson: 47, 160
Bucktail: 54, 188, 189
Bucktail in Florida, The: 55, 188
Bulwagga Club: 126
Burgess, W. Starling: 53
Burkhart, Woodward: 195
Butler, Paul: 106

Canoes: descriptions of Rushton's first, 15, 18
—types: paper, viii, 29, 30; Indian birch-barks, viii, 37, 39; aluminum, viii, ix, 139; open, viii, 138, 140–42; double-masted, 33; decked cruisers, 35, 138, 141, 150; tandem, 83; canvas covered, 142, 143, 149, 150
—models: Canadian, viii, 141, 173, 192; Baden-Powell, 17; Rob Roy, 17, 23, 24, 26, 28, 31, 34, 39, 46, 65, 67, 68, 77, 83; Nautilus, 26, 28, 77, 101; Shadow, 27, 65, 68, 75, 82, 83, 102; Nessmuk, 51, 83, 97, 141, 150, 167, 194; Princess, 65, 80–84 *passim,* 90, 98, 102, 160, 168, 172, 195; American Traveling, 67, 68, 75, 76, 77, 83, 97; Jersey Blues, 68; Stella Maris, 75, 76, 83, 98, 102; St. Lawrence, 83, 102; Ellard, 84, 98, 102; Grayling, 84, 98, 102, 103, 109; Daisy, 97; Mohican, 97, 99, 100, 102, 138; Springfield, 97, 102; Bucktail, 97, 122, 194; Tandem Princess, 102; Diamond, 109; Vesper, 122, 125, 138, 139, 141, 150, 160, 168; Peterboro, 138; Wren, 139; Nomad, 139, 150, 160, 168, 169, 173; Ontario,